101

Baseball Places to See
Before You Strike Out

Baseball Places to See Before You Strike Out

SECOND EDITION

Josh Pahigian

Guilford, Connecticut

An imprint of Rowman & Littlefield

Distributed by NATIONAL BOOK NETWORK

British Library Cataloguing-in-Publication Information Available

Library of Congress Cataloging-in-Publication Data

Pahigian, Josh.
  [101 baseball places to visit before you strike out]
  101 baseball places to see before you strike out / Josh Pahigian. — Second Edition.
     pages cm
  "Distributed by NATIONAL BOOK NETWORK"—T.p. verso.
  Includes bibliographical references and index.
  ISBN 978-1-4930-0478-2 (paperback : alk. paper) 1. Baseball—United States—History—Guidebooks. 2. Baseball—Museums—United States—Guidebooks. 3. Baseball fields—United States—History—Guidebooks. 4. United States—Guidebooks. I. Title. II. Title: One hundred one baseball places to see before you strike out.
  GV863.A1P34 2015
  796.3570973—dc23

                          2014031666

Contents

Introduction

It is with good reason that baseball is often called "America's Game." The sport has transcended generations, social classes, and regional primacy to bring together Americans from all walks of life to play, watch, and celebrate. The culture of the game—too rich and vibrant to be called a subculture—is as diverse and varied as the fabric of America itself and extends

to all reaches of the North American continent. Yes, other sports have made inroads into our sporting consciousness through the years and at times have laid claim to being the country's preeminent sport. And other nations have adopted baseball as their favorite game. But make no mistake, baseball is and will continue to be the American "National Pastime."

This book will remind you of all those qualities that make the game we play and watch at so many levels such a uniquely American delight. It will recall how baseball has stood the test of time as our nation has grown in previously unimaginable ways. It will explain how the story of baseball's evolution is intertwined with the story of America's growth and change. It will explain how baseball, above all other sports and forms of entertainment, has brought us together, acting as a great unifier. It will highlight the many different ways there are to enjoy the game. It will make you smile, and laugh, and maybe even cry. And it will do all this within the framework of 101 chapters dedicated to 101 special baseball landmarks spread across this great land of ours.

If you are a frequent traveler, whose leisure or business excursions take you far from home, the book will be your guide, leading you to your own magical baseball experiences. If you're more the homebody type, the book will convey the spirit of each location so that you may live

vicariously through it from the comfort of your easy chair.

In writing this second edition of *101 Baseball Places to See Before You Strike Out*, my goal was largely to stay out of the way and let these amazing baseball places tell their own stories, which together tell baseball's story. The book is meant to be a celebration of the game as it is played, watched, and revered at so many levels. I have striven to highlight the traditions the game has established through the years in small towns, big cities, and all the communities in between. I have taken the liberty of ranking the sites from 1 to 101, but please keep in mind that this ranking is just one man's opinion. I acknowledge that the site I consider my forty-third favorite might just turn out to be your favorite one of all. My hope is that you will arrive at your own conclusions regarding the baseball places profiled in the book; I'd even encourage you to re-rank the sites according to your own preferences as you wander baseball's blue highways.

This new edition includes twenty-five brand-new chapters that were not in the original edition of *101 Baseball Places to See Before You Strike Out.* The baseball landscape is ever-changing, and as baseball destinations have closed, relocated, or fallen into disrepair, I have replaced them with new sites that have since opened or further evolved to the point where they merit inclusion. I have also re-ranked the entire list from 1 to 101.

Within this new edition, you will find more than twenty baseball museums—ranging from well-known haunts like the National Baseball Hall of Fame and the Negro Leagues Baseball Museum to lesser-known repositories like the ones dedicated to Ty Cobb, Joe Jackson, Cy Young, Nolan Ryan, and Roger Maris. There are also entries devoted to the gravesites, statues, and monuments spread across the country that memorialize some of the game's most revered and influential figures. These need not be players—a monument in Anaheim, California, for example, honors the contributions of songsmith Jack Norworth, who penned the lyrics to "Take Me Out to the Ballgame." Sites related to more recent baseball pop culture also receive their due, as the *Field of Dreams* and *Bull Durham* movie sites are represented, as are two of the historic ballparks used in the filming of the Jackie Robinson biopic *42*. Places that figure prominently in baseball lore, like the Chicago Cubs' "Curse of the Billy Goat," and "Mudville" from Ernest L. Thayer's poem "Casey at the Bat," are also included. The book also shines a light on special baseball neighborhoods, watering holes, and restaurants, and even features a chapter on an amusement park owned by former Boston Red Sox slugger Mike Greenwell.

And what would a book like this be worth if it didn't afford proper page space to the fields where players of all ages and skill levels play the game? The book includes entries devoted to select major-league, minor-league, spring training, amateur, and youth ballparks that are a cut above the rest, and there's even a chapter dedicated to one very special Wiffle Ball field. Other chapters take you to some of the classic ballpark sites where you can explore the remnants of famous hardball cathedrals of yesteryear. It's pretty mind-blowing to stand in the exact spot from which more than a century ago the great Cy Young delivered the first pitch of the very first World Series game, or to dig in beside a home plate that still lies where it was when Joe Jackson first kicked off his shoes and batted barefoot to earn his famous moniker, "Shoeless Joe." I dare say it's impossible not to get goose bumps as you rub elbows (or toes) up against baseball history in places like these. And in the end, that's what this book is about: goose bumps. It brings you to the places across America (and that includes Alaska, Hawaii, and Canada) that are sure to make your heart beat a little faster for the game. Some are fun, like the relocated New York Mets' Home Run Apple that used to rise from beyond the outfield fence at Shea Stadium; some are solemn, like the Chicago courthouse where eight members of the Chicago White Sox were tried on the charge of purposely losing the 1919 World Series; some are inspiring, like Pasadena's trail of Jackie Robinson landmarks; some are mysterious, like the spot where every glob of mud that's been rubbed on big-league balls since the 1950s has been dredged from the Delaware River; and some are just plain silly, like the minor-league ballpark that features "life size" statues of Homer, Marge, Bart, and Lisa Simpson on its concourse in homage to one of the popular cartoon's all-time favorite episodes. As author, my hope is that by reading about or visiting these places, you will come to know the most magical game of all a bit more fully. And I hope you'll fall in love with baseball even more deeply.

Enjoy the ride!

We know now that Cooperstown, New York, was not the place where the game of baseball magically emerged from the primordial soup of other bat-and-ball games that had preceded it. Cooperstown was neither the place where the game's field dimensions nor its rules were formalized. But nonetheless, the bucolic village in Upstate New York plays the part of baseball's Garden of Eden just perfectly. Its small-town atmosphere reminds us of the many pastoral communities spread across America where baseball was played in various forms and continued to evolve throughout the 1800s. But that's just one of the reasons why the more than 300,000 baseball pilgrims who visit Cooperstown each year will tell you it is the undisputed king of baseball attractions. The other reasons—and there are many—reside within the National Baseball Hall of Fame and Museum.

The story of how baseball's grandest shrine came to reside in Cooperstown is one that involves some biased research, fortunate timing, and visionary thinking on the part of Cooperstown's forefathers. The story goes something like this: Three decades after former big-league pitcher and sports equipment magnate Albert Spalding's Mills Commission erroneously concluded, "The

1. The National Baseball Hall of Fame and Museum

⬦⬦⬦⬦⬦⬦⬦⬦⬦⬦⬦⬦⬦⬦⬦⬦⬦⬦⬦⬦⬦⬦⬦⬦⬦⬦⬦⬦⬦⬦⬦⬦⬦⬦⬦⬦

25 Main Street
Cooperstown, New York 13326
(888) HALL-OF-FAME
http://baseballhall.org

first scheme for playing baseball, according to the best evidence available to date, was devised by Abner Doubleday at Cooperstown, New York, in 1839," the game found itself approaching its one hundredth birthday. It seemed only natural that a centennial party should take place in the town where Spalding's investigation—which had been intent from the start on proving baseball was an *American* game and not derivative of British sports—claimed it had originated. And so, Major League Baseball commissioner Kenesaw Mountain Landis, National League president Ford Frick, and American League president William Harridge all agreed to celebrate the game's birthday with a ceremony in Cooperstown in the summer of 1939.

The National Baseball Hall of Fame and Museum opened in 1939.

The Hall of Fame's plaque gallery honors more than 300 inductees.

As the preparations were being made, an ancient cloth-stuffed baseball was conveniently discovered in the attic of a farmhouse just outside Cooperstown. The withered sphere, dubbed "the Doubleday Baseball," lent further evidence, so the locals said, to the claim that America's Game had been invented in Cooperstown. Recognizing the potential significance of the find, local philanthropist Stephen C. Clark purchased the ball for five dollars and began displaying it in the Cooperstown municipal offices. Soon other locals came forward with mementos from their families' baseball past, helping Clark build a one-room shrine in the village's central office. Inspired by the pride that his fellow villagers took in celebrating Cooperstown's role in the invention of baseball, Clark and his friend Alexander Cleland began exploring the idea of

establishing a national baseball museum. The idea was blossoming at the same time Frick was campaigning for the establishment of a baseball hall of fame. And before long, the two parties merged forces to conceive the National Baseball Hall of Fame and Museum.

The facility opened in time for the game's birthday party on June 12, 1939. Twenty-six baseball legends were formally inducted into the Hall that day, including the five players—Ty Cobb, Babe Ruth, Honus Wagner, Christy Mathewson, and Walter Johnson—who had been elected on the very first ballot of baseball writers in 1936. Amazingly, the scribes had snubbed several men whom we now think of as baseball immortals, refusing to make first ballot Hall of Famers out of Nap Lajoie (64 percent), Tris Speaker (59 percent), Cy Young (49 percent), and Rogers

Hornsby (46 percent), all of whom fell far short of the 75 percent threshold. Fortunately, subsequent elections in 1937, 1938, and 1939 added an additional twenty-one names to the Hall's roster by the time its doors officially opened.

Through the years, more than 200 players have been inducted, but never has there been a unanimous selection. From Ted Williams who was named on just 93 percent of the ballots to Mickey Mantle and Joe DiMaggio who both earned just 88 percent of the vote, to Bob Gibson who was named on only 84 percent of the ballots cast by voting members of the Baseball Writers Association of America, the scribes always fall short of complete agreement. Heck, even Greg Maddux (97 percent) was left off sixteen ballots when he was elected in 2014. As for the highest percentage of votes any player has received? That's the 98.2 percent Tom Seaver earned in 1992.

Through the decades this awe-inspiring baseball repository has undergone several expansions to accommodate the thousands of donations it has received from private collectors, players, teams, fans, and generous others who have contributed to its collection. Visiting Cooperstown today, you find more than 300 bronzes in the Hall's trademark plaque gallery, honoring the players, coaches, executives, umpires, journalists, and other individuals who made profound impacts on the game. In addition, you find an artifact-laden timeline of the game's history that begins in the 1800s and continues all the way to the present. There are also exhibits dedicated to Babe Ruth; Hank Aaron; Jackie Robinson; the no-hitters and perfect games; every World Series since 1903; baseball cards; baseball records; US presidents and their involvement in the game; youth baseball; the minor leagues; the Negro Leagues; women in baseball; old-time ballparks; the current

major-league teams; the Cy Young, MVP, and Gold Glove awards; baseball in the Caribbean; baseball art; baseball in cinema; baseball writers and broadcasters; and much more.

There are nearly 40,000 three-dimensional artifacts in the Hall's collection, and more than 135,000 baseball cards, including the famous T206 Honus Wagner. There are also countless photos, scorecards, newspaper clips, team publications and other two-dimensional items. Next door, meanwhile, the Hall of Fame Library, which opened in 1968, meets the research needs of baseball historians, writers, filmmakers, and trivia buffs.

The Hall's signature event is its annual Hall of Fame Weekend and Induction Ceremony, which takes place over four days in July. During this special time, throngs of baseball lovers flood Cooperstown, including many of the Hall's nearly seventy living members. Although Cooperstown is the most crowded and festive during this time of year, it attracts a steady stream of baseball pilgrims year-round. Just as every child dreams of going to Disneyland, every true seam-head dreams of going to Cooperstown. But unlike the Land of Mickey and Goofy, which may leave you feeling as if the whole experience was over-hyped and over-commercialized, the museum in Cooperstown delivers a thoroughly satisfying, enriching, and altogether mesmerizing experience.

The Hall of Fame is open every day of the year except for Thanksgiving, Christmas, and New Year's Day. From Memorial Day through Labor Day, its hours are 9:00 a.m. to 9:00 p.m. The rest of the year it's open from 9:00 a.m. to 5:00 p.m. Admission costs $19.50 for adults, $12.00 for senior citizens, $7.00 for children age seven through twelve, and admission is free for children under the age of seven and for active duty and retired US military members.

2. The Negro Leagues Baseball Museum

1616 East 18th Street
Kansas City, Missouri 64108
(816) 221-1920
www.nlbm.com/s/index.cfm

After Moses Fleetwood Walker played his last game for the Toledo Blue Stockings in 1884, a long era of segregated baseball began in Major League Baseball that would not be challenged until Jackie Robinson took the field with the Brooklyn Dodgers in 1947. Spanning the decades in between, regional teams of black stars formed across the United States and barnstormed around the country playing one another. In the early 1900s several efforts were made to unite these teams under the umbrella of a central league, but none of these efforts succeeded. Finally, in 1920, Rube Foster—a former player, manager, and owner of the Chicago American Giants—brought together representatives from several prominent Midwest teams and formed the Negro National League. The highly successful league inspired the formation of other "black" circuits like the Negro Southern League, Eastern Colored League, and Negro American League.

Over the next three decades, the leagues were constantly in flux, competing for one another's players, expanding and contracting their ranks, and relocating teams to accommodate new cities eager to field clubs. But one thing remained constant—the passion that African Americans had for America's Game. Try as the racist guardians of the major leagues might, they failed mightily in their nefarious effort to sanctify baseball as a "white" game. Out of the abomination that was baseball's color barrier, something beautiful grew: a rich network of Negro Leagues teams that offered African Americans of the time period a black institution in which they could take pride. The teams were run by blacks, populated by black players, and followed by mostly black fans. The presence of the Negro Leagues and their many talented players made the major leagues something of a farce. Sure, the National League and American League had some great players, but the claim that they were composed of the *best* players in the land rang hollow. Baseball's eventual integration, of course, signaled the bittersweet end of the Negro Leagues; as African Americans permeated the big leagues, no longer was a separate version of the game necessary. By the early 1960s, the last of the black teams had vanished.

Today the pioneering spirit, immense talent, and unfailing love for the game of baseball that helped the Negro Leagues flourish are remembered at the Negro Leagues Baseball Museum. This important baseball attraction was born in the early 1990s, when a group of Kansas City businesspeople, historians, and former Negro Leagues players opened a small museum in the city's Lincoln Building. The museum quickly outgrew its one-room gallery, buoyed by the interest in the Negro Leagues brought about by Ken Burns's excellent documentary *Baseball*. Perhaps most importantly, the PBS miniseries introduced the nation to Buck O'Neil, a former Kansas City Monarch, who captivated viewers with his vivid memories of black baseball's Golden Age. Over the next few years, Kansas City contributed more than $20 million to build a 50,000-square-foot home for the Negro Leagues Baseball Museum and the adjoining American Jazz Museum. The

The Field of Legends is populated by statues of Negro Leagues greats.

two museums opened in 1997 in Kansas City's Historic 18th and Vine Jazz District.

The Negro Leagues Baseball Museum offers a self-guided tour that traces the history of black baseball and of American race relations. The photograph- and artifact-laden chronology begins with an exhibit devoted to baseball's earliest days, following the Civil War. Then it examines the experiences of a largely unknown cast of African-American pioneers who integrated baseball at the semi-pro, college, and professional levels in the 1880s and 1890s. Next there appears an exhibit on the "gentlemen's agreement" that banned blacks from the major leagues at the turn of the century and on the barnstorming teams of black stars that formed as a result.

The next section of the museum, devoted to the founding and four-decade history of the Negro Leagues, is the largest. It tells the stories of how the Negro National League was born; how

night baseball debuted in the Negro Leagues in the 1930s; how the Negro Leagues experienced a renaissance during the Great Depression; how Satchel Paige became the most famous black star of all; and how black baseball spread to Mexico. Next there appear exhibits related to the integration of the major leagues and to the eventual dissolution of the Negro Leagues.

After learning about the founders and great stars of the Negro Leagues, your tour ends when you step onto a replica baseball diamond in the center of the museum. This "Field of Legends" is home to twelve life-size statues that portray some of the best Negro Leaguers ever to play the game. The bronze likenesses include Foster, O'Neil, Paige, Josh Gibson, Buck Leonard, Pop Lloyd, Judy Johnson, Ray Dandridge, Cool Papa Bell, Oscar Charleston, Leon Day, and Martin Dihigo. Among this group, O'Neil is the only player not also honored with a plaque at the National Baseball Hall of Fame. Many within the baseball establishment consider this oversight a travesty, but O'Neil, who passed away in 2006, never shed any tears on his own behalf. He was happy to keep telling stories about the great Negro Leagues players and teams, and he turned out at the Negro Leagues Baseball Museum regularly to share his love of the game with others. In 2008, the Hall of Fame posthumously honored O'Neil's eight decades of contributions to the game with the creation of the Buck O'Neil Lifetime Achievement Award, which is presented periodically to "individual[s] whose extraordinary efforts enhanced baseball's positive impact on society, broadened the game's appeal, and whose character, integrity and dignity are comparable to the qualities exhibited by O'Neil." A statue of O'Neil was installed at the Hall of Fame at the time of the award's creation.

Aside from Cooperstown, you'll find no finer a baseball shrine than the Negro Leagues Museum. Through the years it has been visited by Bill Clinton, George W. Bush, Colin Powell, Jesse Jackson, Maya Angelou, Walter Cronkite, Kareem Abdul-Jabbar, Barry Bonds, Tony La Russa, Bobby Valentine, and countless other celebrities and fans. It is open Tuesday through Saturday from 9:00 a.m. to 6:00 p.m., and Sunday from noon to 6:00 p.m. Admission costs $10.00 for adults and $6.00 for children age five through twelve.

3. The *Field of Dreams* Movie Site

28995 Lansing Road
Dyersville, Iowa 52040
(888) 875-8404
www.fodmoviesite.com

Fans of the classic baseball movie *Field of Dreams* will remember that throughout the film a voice implores main character Ray Kinsella to turn his unprofitable Iowa cornfield into a baseball diamond. "If you build it, he will come," the voice echoes, and "Go the distance." Ray gets to work, turning under his crop, laying sod, and spreading infield clay. He accepts the idea that some beneficent force is guiding him. He knows the mystery he's unraveling doesn't yet make sense, but he's willing to believe it eventually will. In the end, his magical field affords him the chance to play one last game of catch with the ghost of his father. And as the movie ends the field is on the fast-track to becoming a tourist site that will help Ray pay his many overdue bills. As the credits roll, a stream of cars wends its way up the dirt road leading to the field.

In a case of life imitating art, the Iowa field created for and used in the filming of the movie has drawn more than a million visitors since Universal Studios released *Field of Dreams* in 1989. And, in a second case of life imitating art, in recent years financial uncertainty has threatened the long-term sanctity of the field as a place where you can pull up in your road-trip car and play a game of catch or take a few batting practice cuts in as magical and pastoral a baseball setting as you can imagine.

For years two local families owned the field. The Lansings held the deed to the infield and right field parcel and lived in the white farmhouse you likely recall from the movie. The Ameskamps owned the left field and center field

The Field of Dreams with its familiar white farmhouse

portion of the field. Don Lansing, the elderly gentleman who had lived in the farmhouse since his birth, made sure to tend the lawn, sculpt the infield, and maintain the small set of bleachers so all would appear exactly as in the movie. Both families kept small souvenir stands on their property, and for years people made the pilgrimage to Dyersville to rekindle a little bit of the magic from the beloved movie. As time passed, the site drew visitors from such faraway places as Australia, Chile, England, France, Germany, Holland, Japan, Norway, Spain, Scotland, and Switzerland, as well as from across North America.

The field was ensconced in innocence in the eyes of fans. Though it had been created in a commercial endeavor—the production of a Hollywood blockbuster—for years it had been open to the public at no cost, and when fans visited, they harkened back to the movie, which had portrayed a vision of the game that existed in a heavenly realm. Away from the bright lights and commercialism of a big-league stadium, the ghosts of big leaguers played the game they loved. At a time when real-life players were signing nine-figure

contracts and the cost of bringing a family of four to a big-league park had approached the equivalent of a mortgage payment for many families, the "field of dreams" came to symbolize a more innocent vision of the game.

But as the early 2000s played out, the winds of change came rustling through the Iowa cornstalks. The Lansings acquired the Ameskamps' portion of the field in 2007, then they put the entire property—the field, white farmhouse, and accompanying 193 acres—on the market in 2010. In December of 2012, a group called Go the Distance Baseball, LLC, purchased the plot for $3.4 million. Within days of closing on the deal, the Chicago-based president and CEO of the group, Denise Stillman, announced the group's intent to build a twenty-four-field youth baseball and softball complex beside the Field of Dreams. "All-Star Ballpark Heaven," as the envisioned facility was dubbed, would host a rotating crop of youth teams for tournament play all summer. Soon Hall of Famer Wade Boggs and former *Friends* actor Matthew Perry attached their names and checkbooks to the project as investors. And the dormant independent Northern League announced that it hoped to resume play in 2015 and that it would locate a team at a stadium to be built within All-Star Ballpark Heaven.

Almost immediately, many of the citizens in Dubuque County recoiled. Local opposition to the proposed development revolved chiefly around two concerns: first, that the sprawling youth complex and Northern League stadium would rob the movie field of its pastoral charm; second, that the complex would adversely affect the quality of life of local residents. With regard to the latter concern, locals cited their worries about the extra visitor traffic. They wondered how they would safely operate their agricultural equipment on area roads if children were present; how they would dust and spray their crops with pesticides with so many children in the area; whether the fetid manure they laid would draw complaints from the baseball campers; and whether the complex would create water runoff issues that would impact their irrigation systems.

Committees were formed, petitions signed, and lawsuits filed. Construction on the complex was delayed and then delayed again.

As of June 2014, All-Star Ballpark Heaven was moving forward with a plan to build an initial six youth fields but had not yet begun construction on the site. Meanwhile, the Field of Dreams' new owners were maintaining that they did not intend to change the original field. They even hosted a twenty-fifth anniversary party for the movie over Father's Day weekend of 2014, hosting Kevin Costner, several of his costars, Bob Costas, Matt Lauer, and former major leaguers Bret Saberhagen, Glendon Rusch, and Ryan Dempster for a nighttime screening of the movie in center field and other festivities.

Whether a full-blown youth camp will eventually spring up beside the Field of Dreams is still an open question. In the meantime, Ray Kinsella's magical field continues to sit where it has since 1988—in the shadows of the white farmhouse, surrounded by swaying cornstalks—attracting visitors. The field is open April through October between the hours of 9:00 a.m. and 8:00 p.m., and in November between 10:00 a.m. and 4:30 p.m. So bring a ball, bring a mitt, and bring your imagination. Have a catch on the Field of Dreams. The experience may just be magical.

● ●

4. Rickwood Field

◇◇◇

1137 Second Avenue West
Birmingham, Alabama 35204
(205) 458-8161
www.rickwood.com

Part museum and part working ballpark, Rickwood Field offers you the chance to step back in time and experience the oldest standing professional baseball park in the United States. Built at the dawn of the Classic Ballpark Era in 1910, Rickwood opened two years before Fenway Park and six years before Wrigley Field. To put that in further perspective, Rickwood hosted its first game the year after Forbes Field and Shibe Park opened. Forbes was torn down

Rickwood Field still hosts an annual throwback game between the Birmingham Barons and one of their Southern League foes.

in 1971 and Shibe in 1976. Four decades after those venerable yards ceased to exist anywhere but in the baseball history books and in our collective memory, Birmingham's old yard is still welcoming fans for games at a variety of levels, including the professional level, and is still drawing oohs and aahs from those who visit.

Rickwood served as the home of Birmingham's minor-league team for nearly eight decades, hosting the club known as the "Barons" for most of that time. The team played in the Southern Association from 1910 until 1961, before joining the Double-A Southern League, to which it still belongs today. In addition to hosting the Barons, Rickwood was also the hub of Birmingham's Negro Leagues teams for many years, providing a home to the Birmingham Black Barons, who played at various times in the Negro National League, Negro American

League, and Negro Southern League between 1920 and 1960. As if that weren't enough use for the little ballpark on Second Avenue, Rickwood housed the spring training Philadelphia Phillies in 1911 and 1920 and Pittsburgh Pirates in 1919.

Although the park was semiretired in 1988 when the Barons moved to a stadium in nearby Hoover, a group of local volunteers has worked to ensure the park is preserved. These "Friends of Rickwood" have raised more than $2 million toward the restoration of the park, which was awarded National Historic Landmark status in 1993, and have helped organize the annual Rickwood Classic, a regular season throwback game played each spring between the Barons and one of their Southern League foes. The game has attracted national media attention since its inception in 1996 and has even been televised by ESPN.

Rickwood Field opened in 1910.

Rickwood is also used for a variety of amateur purposes. It is home to the Miles College Golden Bears, who begin play in the NCAA Division II Southern Intercollegiate Athletic Conference in February each year. It also hosts local middle school and high school games throughout the spring, and youth and men's adult league games throughout the summer. Rickwood also sees occasional use as a film site, having provided the backdrop for scenes of classic baseball movies like *Cobb*, *Soul of the Game*, and the Jackie Robinson biopic *42*. In one memorable scene in *42*, the actor portraying Robinson smashes a home run over the distinctive Rickwood scoreboard.

While attending the Rickwood Classic should rate high on your baseball bucket list, right there with attending a World Series game, attending an All-Star Game, and watching nine innings from atop the Green Monster at Fenway Park, don't despair if you're unable to find

your way to Birmingham on the one special day each year when the Southern Leaguers grace the field in old-time uniforms. Even when one of the aforementioned amateur games is not taking place, Rickwood is well worth a visit. The ballpark gates are open Monday through Friday from 8:00 a.m. to 4:30 p.m., allowing you to take the self-guided tour that wends through the stands, into the dugouts, onto the field, and behind the outfield fences. Markers provide plenty of historic information along the way.

Rickwood Field was designed to look like its contemporary, Forbes Field. It was the first minor-league park to be constructed of concrete and steel, instead of wood, and cost a then-astronomical sum of $75,000 to build. The construction was funded by Barons owner and eventual stadium namesake A. H. "Rick" Woodward. The park opened on August 18, 1910, when the first of many sellout crowds to pass through its gates watched the home team down the Montgomery Climbers 3–2 on a walk-off hit in the ninth inning. During the 1920s the Barons drew more than 160,000 fans in eight different seasons, including a high-water mark of 299,000 in 1927. After the lean baseball years brought on by the economic tumult of the Great Depression and World War II, attendance spiked in Birmingham again in the 1940s, when the Barons and Black Barons often played before sellout crowds. In 1948 the Barons, who were then a Boston Red Sox affiliate, set a franchise record, drawing 445,926 fans. That same year, the Black Barons won the National Negro League pennant, sparked by a seventeen-year-old center fielder named Willie Mays.

Rickwood was also home at various times to other baseball immortals, like Satchel Paige, Burleigh Grimes, Pie Traynor, Rube Marquard, Reggie Jackson, Rollie Fingers, Catfish Hunter, and Vida Blue. Future Hall of Famers Ty Cobb, Christy Mathewson, Honus Wagner, Dizzy Dean, and Rogers Hornsby played at Rickwood as well, as did Shoeless Joe Jackson. Babe Ruth and Stan Musial also played here as visiting players.

Visiting Rickwood today, you find it looking much as it did in the 1930s and 1940s, save for some metal bleachers and plastic seats that were added in the early 1980s to replace the old wooden ones. From the street outside, the upper level offers a pale green facade, while the lower level takes on a light cream hue. You pass through several square "arches" to enter the park, then spill into a grandstand, the back two-thirds of which is covered by a low roof that extends from the right field foul pole to the home plate area and then out to third base. The advertisements on the outfield fences and manually operated scoreboard in left are period-specific replicas that were added by Hollywood set designers during the filming of *Cobb*.

The distinctive light towers protrude out over the field.

The unique tiled-roof gazebo that sits atop the grandstand behind home plate once provided a place for the public-address announcer to sit and watch the game. The light banks project forward off the grandstand roof on metal staging, making the lights appear to hang right out over the foul territory along the baselines. The locker rooms, which are adorned by black-and-white photos of the many baseball legends that played at Rickwood, offer open-style wooden lockers. After spending a few minutes poking around this enchanting old yard, it seems possible, even probable, that Willie Mays and some of his contemporaries might emerge from the home dugout at any moment to trot out to their positions on the field.

While you're in Birmingham, you might also catch a game at the new $64 million stadium that opened for the Barons in 2013. **Regions Field** (1401 1st Avenue South), which sits just 3 miles east of Rickwood, lured the Barons back to Birmingham from Hoover. It incorporates many design elements that pay homage to Birmingham's longtime hardball hub, including its brick-and-steel exterior.

The new park abuts a plot of ground that will reportedly be transformed eventually into a local **Negro Southern League Museum** (16th Street). The museum will be staffed in part by elderly gentlemen who once played in the Negro Southern League and will include one exhibit that uses a hologram of Satchel Paige to provide you with the sensation of batting against the legendary hurler. Given Birmingham's role in the Civil Rights Movement, and the city's rich Negro Leagues history, such a museum would be a perfect fit in the city.

5. The Little League World Series

The Little League International Complex
539 US Route 15
South Williamsport, Pennsylvania 17701
(570) 326-1921, www.littleleague.org

The headquarters of the multinational non-profit Little League International offers a wealth of ways for you to connect with the game's past, present, and future, highlighted by the Little League World Series each August. No matter the time of year you visit, though, a trip to Williamsport allows you to check out two top-notch youth fields, a classy museum, a nearby minor-league park, and a historic marker commemorating the place where Little League was invented in 1939.

The centerpiece of this baseball extravaganza is Howard J. Lamade Stadium, which you'll no doubt recognize if you've watched Little League World Series games on TV. The park and surrounding 66-acre complex actually lie in *South* Williamsport. This has been the home of Little League since 1959. Prior to that, from 1939 through 1958, the organization had been based across the Susquehanna River in Williamsport.

The visionary who created a downscaled version of America's Game was a Williamsport clerk named Carl E. Stotz. Although he didn't have any children, Stotz enjoyed throwing batting practice and hitting grounders to his young nephews. Eager to provide his young friends the chance to experience the thrill of organized competition, Stotz began experimenting with different-sized fields and various rule and equipment modifications that would make the game more accessible to them. By 1939 he had enlisted the participation of two other coaches, thirty players, and three local sponsors. They called their small circuit "Little League." On June 6, 1939, the first Little League game was played, as Lundy Lumber beat Lycoming Dairy 23–8, at a town park on Williamsport's West Fourth Street. Later that summer, Lycoming Dairy redeemed itself, downing Lundy Lumber in a best-of-three-games championship series.

Fans fill the Lamade Stadium stands and sit on the hillside beyond the outfield fence during the Little League World Series.

By 1947 Little League had expanded to communities outside Pennsylvania, and had spawned an annual World Series that would evolve into the one we know today. In 1950 Little League spread outside the United States, establishing a league in Panama. After the first twelve Little League World Series were played on West Fourth Street, the league built the bigger complex across the Susquehanna, where its headquarters still resides. In 1974, Little League began including females, offering Little League softball.

Today, Little League is the largest youth sports organization in the world, engaging upwards of 2.4 million boys and girls per year. There are leagues in all fifty US states and in more than eighty countries. The organization includes teams from such diverse places as Australia, Belgium, Brazil, Bulgaria, China, Greece, Jamaica, Jordan, Kenya, Kuwait, Nigeria, Poland, Russia, Saudi Arabia, Sweden, Ukraine, and Venezuela. Each August, the very best of these teams convene in South Williamsport for the World Series.

The World Series actually begins on July 1 at sites around the world, involving more than 7,000 entrants. By early August the field has been winnowed to just sixteen teams that report to South Williamsport for the thirty-two-game finale of the tournament. In recent years future major leaguers like Gary Sheffield (1980), Jason Varitek (1984), Jason Bay (1990), and Jason Marquis (1991) received their first taste of national competition in South Williamsport. Varitek went on to play in the College Baseball World Series for Georgia Tech, and then in the Major League Baseball World Series for the Red Sox.

The most recognizable landmark in youth sports, Lamade Stadium has undergone many renovations since first opening in 1959. And yet, it retains its old-time charm. The grandstand runs along both foul lines and is covered by a low roof. The trademark tiered outfield hill hovers above the 225-foot-deep home-run fences. The stands seat 15,000, but Lamade can accommodate an additional 25,000 on its outfield hillside; it hosted its largest crowd in 2011, when 41,848 fans turned out for a first-round game between La Grange, Kentucky, and Clinton County, Pennsylvania. Fans of the Clinton County team, who had traveled just 30 miles to the game, went home disappointed when La Grange posted a 1–0 victory.

Except when overflow crowds are anticipated, early-round and consolation games are typically played at nearby Volunteer Stadium. The facility was added in 2001. It is a bit cozier than Lamade, offering just 5,000 fixed seats and limited lawn seating in the outfield. Only the grandstand immediately behind home plate is covered by a roof. Admission to both parks is absolutely free during the annual tournament.

Another popular attraction at the Little League complex is the Peter J. McGovern Little League Museum, which offers artifacts from the league's earliest games and from Mr. Stotz. It also provides interactive exhibits like batting and pitching cages and trivia games, and features an expansive collection of autographed balls and baseball cards. The highlight, though, is the Hall of Excellence, which honors people like Wade Boggs, George W. Bush, Kevin Costner, Tom Selleck, George Will, Kareem Abdul-Jabbar, Bruce Springsteen, Mike Schmidt, Cal Ripken Jr., Dale Murphy, Jim Palmer, Nolan Ryan, Tom Seaver, and Carl Yastrzemski, all of whom played Little League baseball when they were kids. The museum is open daily from 9:00 a.m. to 5:00 p.m. Admission costs $5.00 for adults and $2.00 for children ages five through twelve.

Two miles north of the complex, a historic marker honors "the founder of Little League Baseball," Mr. Stotz, at **Brown Memorial Park** (West Fourth Street). Across the street, you find **Bowman Field** (1700 West Fourth Street), a full-size professional diamond that dates back to 1923. One of the oldest working minor-league parks in the country, Bowman serves as home of the New York–Penn League Williamsport Crosscutters.

6. The Cape Cod Baseball League

Barnstable County
Cape Cod, Massachusetts
www.capecodbaseball.org

A haven for top-tier college players and baseball's weather-beaten scouts, the Cape Cod Baseball League also attracts a wide range of fans to its ten ballparks on the peninsula that serves as eastern New England's summer vacation mecca. The players who visit "the Cape" to take part in the invitation-only summer league play a forty-four-game schedule that begins in mid-June and concludes in mid-August. They live with local families who welcome them into their homes. They work part-time jobs during the day, often in support of the Cape's

The Cotuit Kettleers' Lowell Park sits near the shores of Nantucket Sound.

beach-tourism industry. They swim in the Cape's warm waters, and sun themselves on its sandy beaches. But first and foremost, they test their developing skills each night against the best amateur competition in the land.

For many players, this is the first time they are required to use wooden bats in a game setting, instead of the lighter metal models permitted in the college game. And it shows. Hard-throwing pitchers typically dominate on the Cape. And when a hitter does demonstrate that he can get around on a 95-mile-per-hour fastball using a heavier than usual wooden bat, base-ball's bird dogs take notice. With a good show-ing on the Cape, a college player whose skills might previously have been under-appreciated can dramatically improve his standing in the eyes of the baseball establishment.

The Cape's cozy fields have served as important proving grounds for up-and-comers like Dustin Ackley, Jackie Bradley Jr., Jeff Bag-well, Lance Berkman, Will Clark, Aaron Crow,

Jacoby Ellsbury, Kevin Gausman, Matt Harvey, Chase Headley, Todd Helton, Jason Kipnis, Tim Lincecum, Evan Longoria, Chris Sale, Kyle Sea-ger, Nick Swisher, Frank Thomas, Chase Utley, and Barry Zito. But that's just a short list of the scores and scores of Cape Cod Leaguers who have gone on to reach the big leagues.

The Cape Cod League actually dates back to 1885. It was a "town league" in those early days and wouldn't become a "college league" until 1963. As early as 1919, though, future Hall of Famer Pie Traynor was lacing up his spikes for the club in Falmouth. And in 1967 Thurman Munson batted .420 for Chatham, a record that would stand until 1976, when a youngster named Buck Showalter batted .434 for Barnstable.

In the 2000s the league experienced new levels of mainstream popularity. First, the 2001 film *Summer Catch*—starring Freddie Prinze Jr. as a baseball prospect playing on the Cape and Jessica Biel as his love interest—made the Cape Cod League a nationally known entity, even if the baseball scenes were filmed in North Carolina. Then in 2004, writer Jim Collins's excellent book *The Last Best League* told the story of his one season on the Cape following the summer storylines of several Chatham A's, including future big leaguer Tim Stauffer.

Today, during a typical major-league season about 250 Cape alumni appear in big-league uniforms, or to put it another way, one in every seven big leaguers today spends a summer on the Cape. As you might expect, the games are highly competitive. Not only do they showcase some of the heaviest hitters and hardest throwers from the college ranks, but they do so against the backdrop of incredibly intimate little ballparks, most of which double as high school fields in the spring.

The games usually begin between 5:00 p.m. and 7:00 p.m. Admission is free, but you're encouraged to make a small donation at the gate before finding a place to sit on the bleachers, standing along the fence, or setting up your lawn chair. Even at tiny ballparks like Cotuit's seventy-year-old Lowell Park, which has an official seating capacity of only 600, gatherings of 1,500 to 2,000 are common. At the games, you'll find yourself sitting among parents and friends of the players, who have come to the Cape for a few days' vacation and to check in on their budding baseball star, as well as local families, who root especially hard for whichever players have been sleeping in their spare rooms and mowing their lawns for the past few weeks, and lots and lots of scouts. You'll also encounter Major League Baseball front office staffers, local retirees, youth coaches who have brought their Little League teams to the games, summer vacationers, and other fans like you who appreciate the crack of the bat and thud of a heavy fastball smacking into the catcher's leather on a glorious summer night.

The league's ten fields are all located within 50 miles of one another. Ask ten locals which is their favorite, and you're apt to get ten different answers, although most will agree that three of the finest fields are the Cotuit Kettleers' pine-enveloped **Lowell Park,** the Orleans Firebirds' **Eldredge Park,** which provides seating on a

Fans fill the stands of Lowell Park during a Cape Cod League game.

Here is a complete list of the league's teams and parks, to set you on your way to many summer nights of baseball bliss:

Bourne Braves	Doran Park	220 Sandwich Road, Bourne
Brewster Whitecaps	Stoney Brook School	384 Underpass Road, Brewster
Chatham Anglers	Veterans Field	702 Main Street, Chatham
Cotuit Kettleers	Lowell Field	10 Lowell Avenue, Cotuit
Falmouth Commodores	Guv Fuller Field	790 Main Street, Falmouth
Harwich Mariners	Whitehouse Field	75 Oak Street, Harwich
Hyannis Harbor Hawks	McKeon Field	120 High School Road, Hyannis
Orleans Firebirds	Eldredge Park	78 Eldredge Park Way, Orleans
Wareham Gatemen	Spillane Field	Route 6 East, Wareham
Yarmouth-Dennis Red Sox	Red Wilson Field	210 Station Avenue, South Yarmouth

grassy hill, and the Chatham A's **Veterans Field,** which showcases stunning pink sunsets all summer long. Every one of the Cape Cod League parks is special, though, and well worth visiting.

You may also find it worthwhile to visit the **Cape Cod Baseball League Hall of Fame,** which is located on the basement level of the **John F. Kennedy Hyannis Museum** (397 Main Street, Hyannis). The museum is open Monday through Saturday; admission costs $8.00 for adults and $3.00 for children between the ages of ten and seventeen. In addition to the plaques honoring past players and organizers and administrators of the league, you'll find plenty of old photos and other mementos.

Finally, you might like to visit the **Barnstable Bat Company** (40 Pleasant Pines Avenue, Centerville), which has been making wooden baseball bats since 1992. The factory showroom displays more than 500 different models. The company store is open Monday through Friday from 10:00 a.m. to 4:00 p.m.

7. The Green Monster

Fenway Park
4 Yawkey Way
Boston, Massachusetts 02215
(617) 226-6666
http://boston.redsox.mlb.com/bos/
ballpark/index.jsp

The most famous wall in American sports stands at Boston's Fenway Park, where the towering Green Monster begins its ascent just 309 feet and 2 inches from home plate down the left field line and rises 37 feet, 2 inches into the Boston sky. "The Wall," as it is often also called, continues for 231 feet—228 of which are in fair territory—before dropping to "just" 17 feet in height in center field. It is one of the chief attractions that draw fans to Boston's "little lyrical bandbox of a ballpark," as John Updike once characterized Fenway.

If you've followed the game for a while, you have surely observed that the Wall is an ever-evolving edifice. While some aspects of it have remained the same, others have changed rather drastically with time. When Fenway Park originally opened in 1912, a hill rose at the back of Fenway's left field lawn, and atop the hill stood a 25-foot-high fence that separated the field from the city beyond. In these early days, Red Sox left fielder Duffy Lewis became a master at scaling the hill while pursuing fly balls, and thus the rise of land came to be known as "Duffy's Cliff." And you probably thought the center field knoll known as "Tal's Hill" at Minute Maid Park in Houston was the most treacherous ankle-breaker the game's owners have ever dreamt up!

With the advent of the lively ball, the Red Sox leveled the hill in 1934 and constructed the towering Wall you find at Fenway today, using more than 15 tons of iron. The Wall's trademark slate scoreboard also debuted in 1934, but the green paint did not appear until 1947, at which time the two familiar light towers were also added above the Wall to facilitate night games. Originally, the Wall was plastered with advertisements for products like soap, shaving cream, razors, shoes, cigarettes, and clothes. In 1936, a 23-foot-high screen was added up top to protect pedestrians and motorists on Lansdowne Street from outgoing balls. The screen stood above Lansdowne collecting homers and the occasional foul ball until 2003, when the Red Sox added 294 Green Monster Seats in its place.

For old time's sake, even after they removed the screen, the Red Sox left on the face of the Wall the ladder that members of the grounds crew had used for generations to climb to the top and retrieve home-run balls. Today, batted balls that hit the ladder are in play. Should a ball hit the ladder and bounce over the Wall, the batter is awarded a ground-rule double. Likewise, balls that disappear through one of the slots on the scoreboard are automatic doubles.

In addition to adding the Green Monster Seats and adding massive green billboards above the wall-top seats, current Red Sox management has stamped giant ads on the green portion of the Wall and has also elongated the scoreboard so that it too can offer ad space. But few in Boston have quibbled with this intrusion of words and images onto the face of the Wall. The coveted Green Monster Seats and the team's recent world championships have bought management a lot of goodwill.

The Wall definitely affects the game. As Boston fans are fond of saying, "The Wall giveth

Fans atop the Green Monster wait for home-run balls during batting practice.

and the Wall taketh away," meaning that sometimes a batter hits a rising liner that would be a home run in any other park that winds up being just a line-drive single off the Wall, while other times, a batter lofts a lazy fly to left that would be a flyout to the left fielder anywhere else that goes for a Fenway-fly homer. For generations the popular wisdom was that right-handed hitters flourished at Fenway, and left-handed pitchers struggled as a result. But if you think about it, many of the Red Sox' best hitters through the years have batted from the left side of the plate: e.g., Ted Williams, Carl Yastrzemski, Wade Boggs, Mo Vaughn, and David Ortiz. Many of these savvy sluggers cited their ability to "get beaten" by the pitcher on an offering on the outside of the plate and still go the other way for a double off the Wall as one of their reasons for thriving at Fenway. Boggs, especially, was a master at lofting 320-foot fly balls off the Wall.

Not surprisingly, the Wall has played a role in some of Fenway Park's most memorable moments. In Game Six of the 1975 World Series, Carlton Fisk swatted a twelfth-inning homer that clanked off the foul pole above the Monster to give the Red Sox a 7–6 win against the Reds. The classic image of Fisk waving the ball fair along the first base line was captured on film thanks to a rat inside the scoreboard. According to legend, a massive rodent startled an NBC cameraman stationed inside the Wall; instead of following the flight of the ball, the frightened cameraman left his lens fixed on the first base line, where Fisk did his impromptu dance.

The Wall made its presence known before a national television audience again in 1978, when the Yankees traveled to Boston for a one-game playoff to decide the American League East title. With the Red Sox leading 2–0 in the seventh inning, light-hitting Yankees infielder Bucky Dent blooped a fly ball to left field that settled into the net for a three-run homer. The dinger propelled the Yankees to victory.

More recently, in Game Six of the 2013 American League Championship Series, Boston's Shane Victorino lofted a high fly down the left field line against the Tigers that eventually plopped into the Monster Seats for a grand slam that turned a 2–1 deficit into a 5–2 Red Sox lead. The "Olde Towne Team" held on for the series-clinching win, and then won its third World Series in ten years.

If you visit Fenway Park on game day, you'll find scores of fans lingering on Lansdowne Street behind the Wall before the gates open. Here, you can wait for batting practice homers to fly into the street while you eat a scrumptious grilled sausage prepared by one of the vendors on the sidewalk. Once the ballpark opens, you can make your way to Section 33 of the Outfield Grandstand to pose for a picture or two in front of the Wall and to rap your knuckles on it. Once the game begins, the 294 lucky fans holding tickets for the Green Monster Seats watch the game from the most remarkable vantage point

in baseball, perched high above left field. The K-Men are a fixture in this part of the park too, holding up big red K signs whenever a Red Sox hurler records a strikeout.

If your trip to Boston occurs on a day when the Red Sox don't have a game, you should still visit Lansdowne Street to pay homage to the Wall's exterior and to have a Fenway Sausage. One vendor, the Sausage Guy, often sets up on off-days, especially when the Fenway District clubs are hopping. You can also access Fenway via the Red Sox Tour, which takes you up to the Green Monster Seats. Tours run from 9:00 a.m. until 5:00 p.m. daily year-round, departing on the hour. The cost is $17.00 for adults, $14.00 for seniors, and $12.00 for children. You may purchase tour tickets at Gate D on the corner of Yawkey Way and Van Ness Street.

8. The College World Series

TD Ameritrade Park Omaha
1200 Mike Fahey Street
Omaha, Nebraska 68102
(402) 554-4422
www.cwsomaha.com

Ranking right up there with the Little League World Series, the NCAA Men's College World Series (CWS) is one of the most intense and compelling amateur tournaments you'll witness in your baseball travels. The eight-team double-elimination culmination of the NCAA Division I baseball tournament takes place in June, just as spring is turning to summer. The

mood is festive, the crowds are raucous, and the games are almost always nail-biters. Afterward, you leave Omaha feeling pretty certain you'll be seeing some of the tournament's brightest stars again sometime soon . . . in the big leagues!

The CWS has been taking place since 1947, when the University of California beat future US president George H. W. Bush's Yale team 8–7 in a one-game championship played in Kalamazoo, Michigan. Team captain Bush led his Bulldogs back to the finale the next season, but they lost again, this time to the University of Southern California by a score of 9–2. The next year, the tournament moved to Wichita, Kansas, and Texas downed Wake Forest in the championship. Finally, in 1950 the tournament landed in Omaha, taking place at Johnny Rosenblatt Stadium. After more than six decades at

Fireworks set the sky aglow over TD Ameritrade Park Omaha.

"The Blatt," gorgeous new TD Ameritrade Park Omaha opened in 2011.

In building the $130 million facility, Omaha ensured it would host the CWS through at least 2036. With its wide-open first-level concourse that encircles the entire field, its low second deck that extends nearly from foul pole to foul pole, and its striking outfield views of the city skyline, the 24,000-seat stadium seems more like a downscaled major-league park than an oversized college or minor-league one. Actually, it was built according to specs designed to make it easily expandable to 35,000 seats, just in case Omaha should ever be considered for a big-league expansion team, but it's really the perfect size just as it is now. It's small enough to be cozy, but big enough to accommodate the college baseball crazies who flock to it each June.

In 2013, the fourteen different sessions of the CWS drew 341,483 fans, or an average of 24,392 per opening. As always, the competition included the final eight teams remaining in the NCAA Division I baseball tournament. As the college season begins each year, there are nearly three hundred Division I teams dreaming of making a postseason run. The best sixty-four of them make the tournament and play opening-round games at sites across the country. Then, after the field is culled to the final eight Super-Regional winners, those teams advance to Omaha for the double-elimination World Series, which takes place over ten days in the latter half of June. All games are broadcast on ESPN.

Many of the fans who make the trip to Omaha are baseball-happy collegians, who bring a fanaticism to the stands more commonly observed at college basketball games. You also find plenty of scouts and player agents in attendance at the CWS, as well as alumni of the participating schools and baseball junkies who have no direct connections to the competing teams but want to watch some great baseball and see the next wave of big-league stars before they report for their Rookie League assignments.

The story of how the College World Series arrived in Omaha is the story of Johnny Rosenblatt, a local semi-pro player who entered politics after his playing days. As the mayor of Omaha,

TD Ameritrade Park Omaha during batting practice.

Rosenblatt championed the cause of building a stadium. The ballpark was originally called Municipal Stadium until it was renamed in honor of Rosenblatt in 1964. It opened as the home of the Western League Omaha Cardinals in 1949 and attracted the College World Series a year later.

Rosenblatt Stadium was where future big leaguers like Sal Bando (1965), Dave Winfield (1973), Bob Horner (1977), Terry Francona (1980), Barry Bonds (1983 and 1984), Roger Clemens (1983), Mike Mussina (1988 and 1990), Nomar Garciaparra (1994), Todd Helton (1995), Tim Hudson (1997), Huston Street (2002, 2003, and 2004), and Jackie Bradley Jr. (2010) first stepped into the national spotlight. In its later years, The Blatt showcased an impressive historic display on its concourse that celebrated Nebraska baseball history, offering you the chance to learn about the five Nebraskans—Grover Cleveland Alexander, Richie Ashburn, Wade Boggs, Sam Crawford, and Bob Gibson—enshrined at the National Baseball Hall of Fame, as well as about the playing and political careers of Rosenblatt, whose

old mitt and bat were on display in a locker that also included a team photo of Rosenblatt posing beside Babe Ruth and Lou Gehrig.

After the construction of TD Ameritrade Park Omaha, however, The Blatt, or "Diamond on the Hill" as some locals called it, was demolished in 2012 to allow for an expansion of the Omaha Zoo. In a classy move, the zoo transformed part of the new space into an **Infield at the Zoo** exhibit that includes a bronze home plate marking the location of home plate at Rosenblatt Stadium, as well as manicured base paths that allow you to follow in the footsteps of the many college stars who circled the bases in CWS competition. The Blatt's original foul poles still stand in their original locations too, and many of the old ballpark's seats are installed for zoogoers to enjoy.

Although Rosenblatt Stadium hosted minor-league baseball for years, the local Pacific Coast League team—the Omaha Storm Chasers—today plays at **Werner Park** in nearby Papillion, Nebraska. College baseball's Creighton Blue Jays, meanwhile, utilize TD Ameritrade Park Omaha during the NCAA's regular season. Creighton and its Big East Conference foes begin play in February each year but don't usually begin playing games as far north as Omaha until mid-March.

● ●

Each year brings with it the departure of several retired baseball heroes to that "big ball field in the sky." Whether the deceased was a perennial All-Star who went on to assume his rightful place in the National Baseball Hall of Fame or a mere mortal who played alongside the gods of his era, if his career held special meaning to our team or our city, we mourn his passing and recall his exploits during the halcyon days of his youth. As the decades fly past, these losses become all the more meaningful to us, perhaps because we realize our own glory days are fading further and further into memory. When such weighty thoughts besiege us, we turn perhaps to the game for comfort, losing ourselves in the rhythms and routines of its marathon season. After a nine-inning, three-hour diversion, those thoughts of our own mortality don't seem so close or menacing. And when death revisits the game, taking with it another of our heroes, we pretend, maybe in jest or maybe in wistful acknowledgment of our own ignorance of the great beyond, that he really might be up there in heaven, toeing the rubber, or crouching into a fielding stance, or kicking up some dirt in the batter's box. He's young again, playing the game he loved to play.

But where do fans fit into this afterlife fantasy camp? Does the big ball field in the sky come complete with field boxes and a roving hot dog vendor or two? We rarely extend the metaphor that far, though many more of us shuffle off our mortal coil each year than former players. And that brings us to Beyond the Vines, which was constructed thanks to the tireless work of a Chicago Cubs diehard before his passing. The

9. Beyond the Vines Columbarium

Bohemian National Cemetery
5255 North Pulaski Road
Chicago, Illinois 60630
(773) 539-8442
www.bohemiannational
cemeterychicago.org

24-foot-long facsimile of Wrigley Field's famous outfield wall was erected and opened for "visitors" at this cemetery on Chicago's North Side in 2009. The columbarium was the brainchild of Dennis Mascari, a Cubs rooter who borrowed money from friends and family to fund the design and construction of some unique luxury boxes. Then Mascari became one of the columbarium's first lifetime ticket holders in 2011, when he lost his battle with cancer at age sixty-three. Prior to his death, Mascari explained in various newspaper accounts of his project that when he visited the final resting places of his relatives, he was always left feeling depressed. He built Beyond the Vines in the hope that his loved ones and those of other Cubs fans might have a less somber cemetery experience.

Visiting Beyond the Vines, you find a wall covered in ivy, joined by four box seats that once resided within Wrigley Field, a bench that once sat in the Cubs' bullpen, a home plate set in infield dirt, and a patch of sod that once grew at

The Beyond the Vines Columbarium offers Cubs fans an ivy-covered resting place.

Wrigley. The unique resting place has 288 niches to house the cremated remains of Cubs fans. These spots can be purchased for about $2,000. A stained-glass window in the center of the wall replicates the famous Wrigley bleachers, complete with the scoreboard and rooftop viewing decks in the background, and reads "Cubs Fans Forever: Beyond the Vines." Beneath the stained glass, visible through a veil of ivy and written in yellow paint, is the number "400." This looks just like the outfield marker at Wrigley, where—you guessed it—the distance from home plate to center field measures 400 feet. The clock on the top of this unusual monument is set to 1:20, which is the traditional starting time for Cubs' afternoon games.

Although the Cubs have no affiliation with this cemetery, a licensing partnership between the Cubs and a funeral products manufacturer makes it possible for loved ones to honor their deceased relatives with oversized placards that look a lot like baseball cards, bearing the Cubs' iconic blue, white, and red "C" logo. The placard belonging to one gentleman, whose birth year is listed as 1911 and year of death as 2009, reads: "I saw Ruth and Gehrig play." As for Mr. Mascari, his placard showcases a photo of him smiling contentedly at Wrigley, alongside the words: "Please tap here after they win."

You may visit this impressive monument to the lives of one team's most ardent rooters within Section V of Chicago's National Bohemian Cemetery, which is bounded by Pulaski Road on the West, Foster Avenue on the South, Bryn Mawr Avenue on the North, and Central Park Avenue on the East. The cemetery is open daily from 7:30 a.m. to 4:00 p.m.

If you like old ballpark sites, you'll be delighted to explore the corner of Lexington Avenue and East 66th Street in Cleveland. Here you find the recently restored remnants of League Park. You can walk out onto the field that hosted the National League's Cleveland Spiders from 1891 until 1899, and then later served the Indians from 1901 until 1946. You can also peruse the old brick ticket house and brick wall that ran along the right field line; both look much as they did when the park was built in 1910. As an added attraction, you can wonder at a restored version of the long-absent 60-foot-high right field fence that stands just 290 feet from home plate.

The long-term viability of this baseball landmark was very much in doubt when the first edition of this book was published in 2008. In fact, parts of the structure were literally crumbling, but thanks to a major restoration conducted between 2012 and 2014, the park has been preserved. The $6.5 million project was funded by general-obligation bond proceeds, ward allocation funds, and support from the Ohio Cultural Facilities Commission. It included the restoration of the ticket house and right field facade, the construction of the replica wall in right field, the addition of another acre to the plot for an all-purpose community field, and the installation of durable artificial athletic turf on the original diamond. A visitor center in the ticket house offers public meeting areas and historic displays on the upper level.

The project had been long rumored but wasn't undertaken until Cleveland mayor Frank G. Jackson put his political weight behind it. Jackson joined other city officials, local dignitaries, and citizens on a gray day in October of 2012 to officially break ground on the project and, citing his memories of playing on the

10. League Park

6601 Lexington Avenue
Cleveland, Ohio 44103
www.leaguepark.org

field as a child, predicted, "People will come to Cleveland. One of the historic places they will visit is here."

And so, a once-imperiled historic site that had once been the playground of baseball royalty like Babe Ruth, Cy Young, Joe Jackson, Ty Cobb, Hank Greenberg, Ted Williams, Walter Johnson, Tris Speaker, Lou Boudreau, Nap Lajoie, Joe DiMaggio, and Satchel Paige was restored to something more reminiscent of its former glory. As an added bonus, area youngsters now have a state-of-the-art recreational complex to utilize.

As for the park's life as a professional field, it began on May 1, 1891, when no lesser a man than Young himself pitched the Spiders past Cincinnati before a crowd of nearly 10,000. Like all stadiums prior to the turn of the twentieth century, League Park was a wooden structure, but it was rebuilt using steel and brick prior to the start of the 1910 season. By then the Spiders had disbanded and the American League Naps (soon to be rechristened the "Indians") were calling the park home.

The story of how the Spiders met their end is a colorful one. In their final season, they won only 20 of 154 games. They had actually been pretty good throughout the 1890s, finishing second in the National League three times to punch their ticket to the Temple Cup, a World

A street view of the restored Ticket House from East 66th Street

Series precursor. In 1898 they finished fifth in the twelve-team NL with a respectable 81-68 mark. But their fans had stopped supporting them, and during the following off-season, team owner Frank Robinson bought the St. Louis Browns. Robinson then transferred ownership of the Spiders to his brother Stanley and began relocating all of the talented Spiders to St. Louis through a series of lopsided trades and sales. Among the players the Brothers Robinson sent from Cleveland to St. Louis were future Hall of Famers Young and Jesse Burkett, along with every other Cleveland starter. Thus depleted, the Spiders made history in 1899. Fielding a team of semi-pro and minor-league players, they lost thirty of their first thirty-eight games, during what would prove to be their most successful stretch of the year. After drawing fewer than 200 fans per game during the first three months, they announced they would play most of their remaining games on the road. Playing just seven more times in Cleveland, the Spiders finished 9-25 at home and 11-109 on the road. They lost forty of their final forty-one. Their best pitchers were Jim Hughey (4-30) and Charlie Knepper (4-22). As for the Browns, who benefited from the influx of Spiders, they finished fifth, exactly where the Spiders had ended up the year before.

Fortunately, the Indians' tenure at League Park was not so inglorious. A decade and a half after the franchise arrived, League Park was renamed Dunn Field in 1916, in homage to team owner Jim Dunn. After Dunn's widow sold the team in 1927, it was renamed League Park. The field provided the setting for the Indians' 1920 World Series clincher against the Brooklyn Robins, Ruth's 500th homer, and Lajoie

A replica of The Great Wall in right field keeps balls in the field of play, just as it did in the park's heyday.

and Speaker's 3,000th hits. It was also where DiMaggio extended his record hitting streak to fifty-six games, and then saw it end the next night in 1941.

The park served the Indians through 1946, while also providing a home to the Negro League Bears and Buckeyes. The NFL Cleveland Rams also played at League Park between 1937 and 1945. From 1934 through 1946, the Indians actually split their home schedule between League Park and Municipal Stadium, hosting weekday games at 20,000-seat League Park and their more heavily attended Sunday and holiday games at the enormous stadium destined to become known as "The Mistake by the Lake."

After the Indians moved to Municipal Stadium on a full-time basis, League Park was partially demolished in 1951. Fortunately, though, the two-story ticket house was left intact, along with the right field line retaining wall and the field itself. Eventually, an Ohio historical marker was erected outside, reading:

League Park opened on May 1, 1891, with the legendary Cy Young pitching for the Cleveland Spiders in their win over the Cincinnati Redlegs. The park remained the home of professional baseball and football teams until 1946. In 1920 the Cleveland Indians' Elmer Smith hit the first grand slam home run and Bill Wamby executed the only unassisted triple play in World Series history. Babe Ruth hit his 500th home run over the park's short right field wall in 1929. With the park as home field, the Cleveland Buckeyes won the Negro World Series in 1945.

Even in an era when unusual outfield configurations were the norm, League Park was known for its eccentric dimensions. At the time of its reconstruction in 1910, several landowners beyond right field refused to sell their property to expand the field. As a result, the distance to the right field foul pole measured only 290 feet, while the distance to the left field pole was 385 feet. To give lefty swingers more of a challenge, the Indians erected a towering 60-foot-high fence in right. The lower half consisted of cement, while the upper portion took the form of a chain-link fence supported by steel poles. For decades, fans and outfielders held their breath whenever a fly ball was lofted to right. The ball could hit the lower portion of the wall and take a hard straight bounce off the cement, or it could hit the screen high above and drop gently to the warning track, or it could hit one of the support poles and careen into center field, or all the way into left, or maybe into right field foul territory.

Now you can visit League Park and even take a few hacks to see if you can reach the wall yourself. There aren't too many places left where you can dig in beside a home plate in the very spot where Babe Ruth once wielded his heavy lumber, so do take advantage of the opportunity.

11. The *Bull Durham* Movie Site

Historic Durham Athletic Park
428 Morris Street
Durham, North Carolina 27701

Not to be confused with Durham Bulls Athletic Park—the stadium that has served as home to the International League Durham Bulls since 1995—*Historic* Durham Athletic Park (or "the DAP") is one of the most recognizable ballparks in America, thanks to its starring role in the 1988 film *Bull Durham*. The park, you'll recall, provided the backdrop for the bush-league antics of washed-up slugger Crash Davis (played by Kevin Costner), rising star Nuke LaLoosh (played by Tim Robbins), and sultry baseball groupie Annie Savoy (played by Susan Sarandon). Today the old stadium looks much as it did when the movie was filmed in 1987, only slightly better, thanks to a multi-million-dollar renovation it underwent in 2008 and 2009. And it still sees plenty of use.

The DAP's trademark feature is its cylindrical ticket office, which is topped by a shingled conical roof. The structure makes the ballpark look like an oddly colored castle. Inside, the pale blue roof covers the infield grandstand, making for a cozy atmosphere. Don't bother looking for the snorting bull that blew smoke from its nostrils in the movie; it now resides a mile away on the interior concourse of Durham's new park.

The ballpark that Orion Pictures would make famous in the late 1980s originally opened in 1926 as El Toro Park. It was renamed Durham Athletic Park in 1933, then sat dormant in 1934 and 1935, when the Great Depression suspended operations of the local team. After the ballpark burned to the ground midway through the 1939 season, temporary seating was installed for the remainder of the year. The next winter, Durham completely rebuilt the park. At that time the steel-and-concrete structure that exists today came to be.

As for the team and players that called the DAP home for decades, the real Crash Davis played for the Durham Bulls in the 1940s and 1950s when the club was a member of the Carolina League. The team was named then, as it is now, for a locally made cigarette. During the late 1960s the Bulls merged with a team from nearby Raleigh to form the Raleigh-Durham Mets, who played half of their home games at Durham Athletic Park and half at Raleigh's Devereaux Meadow. The crowds were small at both locations, though, and in 1971 the team folded. The DAP sat without a tenant until 1980, when the Durham Bulls rejoined the Carolina League. The old park hosted the Bulls through the 1994 season, then yielded to the strains of age and time and bid the professional game adieu. The Bulls were still a Single-A team when they moved a mile south to their new yard, but in 1998 they joined the Triple-A International League.

As for *Bull Durham*, widely considered one of the best sports movies ever made, its effect on American film and sport cannot be overstated. Most of the game action was shot at the DAP, while other filming locations in North Carolina included Burlington Athletic Stadium, Greensboro's World War Memorial Stadium, and Fleming Stadium in the town of Wilson. The ballpark scenes were actually filmed in October and November of 1987 on turf that had to be spray-painted green due to the changing of the seasons; that explains why you can see the players' breath in many of the game scenes, even the ones supposedly taking place in midsummer. In any case, the movie grossed more than $50 million in North America, and after it received such rave reviews Hollywood rekindled its love affair with sports flicks, beginning a trend that continues to this day. Interest in minor-league baseball also skyrocketed in the wake of the movie's success, as a new generation of fans flocked to bush-league ballparks near and far. Ironically, the minor-league attendance boom of the early 1990s that was fueled by the movie led to the eventual replacement of many

Historic Durham Athletic Park with its familiar conical ticket house

of America's older minor-league stadiums, including Durham Athletic Park. But unlike the old yards in many cities, Durham's classic still stands as a monument to a simpler era.

In 2008 the City of Durham approved $4 million in bonds toward the preservation of the old park. Work began on the project in April of that year, transforming the park into a mixed-use professional and amateur facility. Over the next year, the project improved the field, concourse, and seating areas. Finally in August of 2009, the new-and-improved DAP opened. The next spring, on May 10, 2010, the Bulls hosted the Toledo Mud Hens for a regular season throwback game at their former home. The visitors prevailed 6–4 in the first minor-league game played at the DAP in more than fifteen years. The next year, the Bulls hosted the Indianapolis Indians at the DAP for another turn-back-the-clock affair, which they again lost. The so-called Back at DAP game has not taken place since, though, as Bulls management has cited the tremendous amount of work it took to facilitate a single game as the reason for discontinuing, or at least suspending, the spring game.

The original hope in renovating the park was that Minor League Baseball, which had committed to manage the facility, would use it as a training location for groundskeepers and umpires. There was also talk of turning the DAP into a minor-league baseball museum. But in 2011 the head honchos at bush league headquarters in St. Petersburg, Florida, decided the DAP wasn't proving to be as useful as they'd anticipated. Since then, the Durham Bulls have managed the stadium. The Bulls rent out the field for baseball camps and clinics, charity games, scouting events, and amateur tournaments, as well as for company picnics, weddings, concerts, festivals, barbecue cook-offs, and fund-raisers. The DAP also serves as the home park of the North Carolina Central University baseball team. The Eagles play in the Mid-Eastern Athletic Conference, beginning their season in February each year, and continuing until early May.

Although the ballpark gates are supposed to be locked when the park is not in use, you will often find them open during daylight hours. Even if the gates are closed, though, the inside of the park is visible from the gates on the third base side. And truthfully, if you're hoping to take a picture of yourself at this famous baseball movie site, you can get the money-shot you desire by posing in the shadows of the iconic ticket tower outside.

12. The National Baseball Congress World Series

Lawrence-Dumont Stadium
300 South Sycamore Street
Wichita, Kansas 67213
(316) 264-6887
www.nbcbaseball.com

The Little League World Series and College Baseball World Series may be baseball's most renowned amateur tournaments, but the National Baseball Congress (NBC) World Series is no less worthy of your attention. The NBC welcomes more than forty teams to Wichita each summer for a two-week extravaganza that includes more than eighty games. And for three days in the middle of the tourney, one of baseball's most unusual spectacles—a fifty-six-hour-long

Lawrence-Dumont Stadium has hosted the NBC World Series since 1935.

marathon called Baseball 'Round the Clock—treats you to seventeen consecutive games. This tradition rivals the surreal experience of watching a game in the middle of the night when the Alaska Summer League stages its annual "Midnight Sun Game" on the date of the summer solstice. In Wichita, the games just keep coming, hour after hour, day after day after day. During the nonstop action, you can slump down in your stadium seat for a quick nap, sprawl out in the aisles of historic Lawrence-Dumont Stadium to catch a few Zs during the darker hours of the late games, or sip coffee and pop M&Ms, refusing to miss a single pitch. Some fans grudgingly retire to a small village of tents on a grassy knoll outside the stadium, where you're welcome to set up camp too, if you'd like.

The teams that compete in this unique baseball bonanza are composed of the nation's top college baseball stars in some cases, but also of aging semi-pro players who simply want the chance to compete at the highest level they can. Other teams include former major leaguers looking to rekindle the glory of their youth.

The heroics of nearly 700 future or former major leaguers who have played in the NBC World Series are celebrated at the NBC Hall of Fame behind the outfield fence. The concourse behind the seats also offers a wealth of plaques and old photographs for you to peruse. This is a great place to learn about the exploits of NBC heroes like Barry Bonds, Joe Carter, Roger Clemens, Jacoby Ellsbury, Matt Garza, Jason Giambi, Paul Goldschmidt, Ron Guidry, Tony Gwynn, Whitey Herzog, Ralph Houk, Ian Kinsler, Billy Martin, Mark McGwire, John Olerud, Lyle Overbay, Albert Pujols, Tom Seaver, James Shields, Ozzie Smith, Don Sutton, Mark Teixeira, and Dave Winfield.

Satchel Paige was the star of the very first NBC World Series, which was played in 1935. The NBC was formed by local sporting-goods salesman Raymond "Hap" Dumont, who dreamed of creating a national tournament that would bring the country's best semi-pro and barnstorming teams to Wichita. Dumont had previously run a statewide event in Wichita at a ballpark on the banks of the Arkansas River, and after that park

Prior to the start of the NBC World Series, teams assemble on the field.

burned down, he convinced the city to build him a new park using WPA funding. The park was named for Robert Lawrence, a prominent local citizen who had died the year before. To headline the first NBC World Series, Dumont lured Paige to town with the promise of a $1,000 payday. And Paige didn't disappoint. The great hurler won four games, striking out sixty batters along the way, and led his team from Bismarck, North Dakota, to the title.

Fans of today's NBC World Series file into the same ballpark where Paige once dazzled their grandparents and great-grandparents. The delightfully old-timey ballpark, which was renamed Lawrence-Dumont Stadium in 1972, is notable for its many pillars that rise up from the grandstands to support the press box. It seats 6,400 fans. For years, it was one of the few ballparks in the world to feature a grass outfield and artificial turf infield. Then, in 2011, an extensive renovation outfitted the entire field with ATG Sports Industries' RamTurf, which is a huge improvement over the previous mixed natural and synthetic surface. Considering the wear and tear the field faces each year during this seemingly unending tournament, it is easy to understand why natural grass, in this case, wasn't the best option.

The NBC World Series begins in the last week of July and ends in the second week of August. Despite daytime temperatures in excess of 100 degrees, attendance averages more than 5,000 fans per day over the two weeks. A lower box seat for the entire tournament costs less than $200.00, while single-day tickets cost between $5.00 and $10.00. If you choose to enter the "Baseball 'Round the Clock Survivor Challenge," you check in with ballpark staff at least once per game at a random time that is announced over the PA system, then at the end of the seventeen-game marathon, you receive a free T-shirt, a free pass to the rest of the tournament, and gifts from the tournament's local sponsors.

If your summer work or travel plans preclude you from attending the NBC World Series, you should still make a point to visit Lawrence-Dumont Stadium at some other time to check out the many historic displays and soak up the atmosphere. The park doubles as the home park of the minor-league Wichita Wingnuts of the American Association of Independent Professional Baseball.

● ●

When it comes to honoring one of its own, Pasadena sure does right by local son Jackie Robinson. You can easily spend a morning or afternoon visiting the several tributes the city offers to the man who broke Major League Baseball's color barrier in 1947, thus paving the way for generations of Americans to enjoy a version of the national game that truly does include the best players in the land, not just the best Caucasians.

13. Pasadena's Jackie Robinson Trail

Various Locations
Pasadena, California 91109

Your first destination on the Jackie Robinson Trail should be his **Boyhood Neighborhood** (121 Pepper Street). The actual house that Robinson's mother, Mallie, bought in the early 1920s to serve as home to sixteen-month-old Jackie and his four siblings was demolished in the 1970s, but a plaque marking its location reads: "Jackie Robinson resided on this site with his family from 1922 to 1946." Robinson grew up here, attending nearby Muir Tech, now known as **John Muir High School** (1905 North Lincoln Avenue).

Next, you can visit **Jackie Robinson Memorial Field,** which sits within Brookside Park (360 North Arroyo Boulevard). This is where the Pasadena City College Lancers play their home games today. Robinson attended the school in the late 1930s—when it was known as Pasadena Junior College—then headed to UCLA in 1939. While in Los Angeles, Robinson's athletic prowess brought him national fame, as he starred on the Bruins' baseball, basketball, football, and track teams. He won twenty-four varsity letters, and then left UCLA midway through his senior year to enlist in the army for World War II. After completing his service and toiling in the Negro Leagues and minor leagues, Robinson became the first African American to play big-league baseball in more than half a century when he trotted out to first base at Ebbets Field on April 15, 1947. Today, this field named in his honor includes a plaque that reads: "Jackie Robinson Memorial Field. A scholar, an athlete, a trailblazer."

Next on your tour, you should visit the **Jackie Robinson Center** (1020 North Fair Oaks Avenue). The center isn't a museum—although it does display artwork and photographs that pay homage to its namesake—but rather is a multipurpose community center with a mission to enhance the lives of the "culturally, economically, and socially diverse population in the Northwest area of Pasadena." Certainly, this is a legacy that would make Jackie Robinson proud. The 18,000-square-foot facility opened in 1974. It offers health screenings, educational programs, legal counseling, addiction counseling, income-tax assistance, and recreational programs for local citizens in need of these important services. It is also the driving force behind several annual civic events, including Pasadena's Black History Parade and Festival, which takes place in February.

The center displays photographs and paintings of Robinson, many of which have been provided by the Baseball Reliquary. The center's most unusual piece is a replica of Robinson's longtime home park, Brooklyn's Ebbets Field. Confectionary artist William Robert Steele began the piece in 2001 under commission from the Baseball Reliquary. It was originally supposed to be constructed entirely out of cake frosting, but when it became apparent to Steele that frosting lacked the structural integrity to support a five-story stadium facade, two decks of seating, seven light towers, a right field scoreboard complete with a "Hit Sign, Win Suit" billboard, and the rest of the decorative flourishes that would be necessary to create a miniature version of Ebbets, the artist decided to also utilize other materials like wood, plastic, and clay. The resulting 50-by-39-inch-long, 15-inch-high model was unveiled during a special ceremony at the Jackie Robinson Center in May of 2002. Steele was on hand for the unveiling, of course, and happily signed a baseball to be inserted into the display case that now houses his model. Hard to believe though it may be, Steele, who learned his craft at the Baking School of Technology in Belfast, Northern Ireland, said that the baseball he signed that day was the first one he had ever held in his hands.

As for the center's artwork, Michael Guccione's oil painting entitled *Jackie Robinson Icon* stands out among the others, owing to its vivid depiction of Robinson as a modern-day saint. Wearing his Dodger blue, Robinson is ensconced

These massive busts of Jackie and Mack Robinson stand at Pasadena's Robinson Memorial Park.

by a foreground of brightly colored flowers. A linked-chain halo—symbolic of the chains that once restrained the African-American people—frames Robinson's head in the background, its links broken apart directly above the "B" on his Brooklyn cap.

The Jackie Robinson Center is open Monday through Thursday from 8:00 a.m. to 9:00 p.m. and Friday from 8:00 a.m. to 5:00 p.m. While you're visiting, you can also check out adjoining **Robinson Park** (1081 North Fair Oaks Avenue), which offers four basketball courts, a swimming pool, playground, and youth fields.

You should also spend some time across the street from Pasadena City Hall, where **Robinson Memorial Plaza** (100 North Garfield Avenue) honors Jackie and his older brother Mack, a star athlete in his own right, who won a silver medal in the 200 meters at the 1936 Berlin Olympics. The memorial takes the form of two gigantic bronze busts that depict the brothers' faces looking out at the city that was their home. Crafted by sculptors Ralph Helmick, Stu Schechter, and John Outterbridge, each head weighs 2,700 pounds and is 9 feet tall. Peach trees surround the plaza to acknowledge the Robinson family's time in Georgia, and granite benches offer etched quotations from the two brothers. The bench nearest Jackie's bust reads:

> Life is not a spectator sport . . .
> If you're going to spend your whole life in the grandstand just watching what goes on in my opinion you're wasting your time.

The bench near Mack's head reads:

> Athletes should recognize that once they establish themselves people will attempt to pattern their lives after their sports heroes.

If any athlete deserves to be remembered for his heroism—and not just on special occasions, but regularly—that athlete is Jackie Robinson, who was more than just a competitor on the various athletic fields and courts onto which he stepped but was a transformational figure in the life of our American society. For weaving reminders of Robinson's courage and grace into its civic landscape, Pasadena receives a well-deserved tip of the cap.

14. Babe Ruth's Grave

Twenty-five miles north of Yankee Stadium, the most celebrated player to ever don pinstripes—or any baseball uniform—lies buried. No baseball pilgrimage would be complete if you didn't pay homage to the man who revolutionized the game, turning it from a competition of station-to-station small-ball into one that included the game-changing potential of the long ball. George Herman "Babe" Ruth singlehandedly out-homered every other American

Gate of Heaven Cemetery
10 West Stevens Avenue
Hawthorne, New York 10532
(914) 769-3672
www.gateofheavenny.com

League *team* in 1920 and 1927, when he slugged fifty-four and sixty long balls, respectively. He went on to wallop 714 dingers in a career that made him one of the most recognizable people on the planet.

Although he was born and raised in Baltimore, Ruth stuck around the Big Apple after his retirement in 1937. He spent a year as the first base coach for the Brooklyn Dodgers, and then retired from the game for a second time in 1938. He spoke movingly before the Yankee Stadium crowd on Lou Gehrig Day in 1939, then addressed the masses a few weeks later in Cooperstown, New York, where the National Baseball Hall of Fame opened its doors for the first time. He played himself in the 1942 Gehrig biopic *Pride of the Yankees*. And he served as a larger-than-life goodwill ambassador for the sport he'd catapulted to ever-greater heights, making appearances at World Series and other public events.

Ruth and his second wife, the actress formerly known as Claire Hodgson, spent the summer months in New York and the winters on Florida's Gulf Coast. But Ruth's golden years were short-lived, as he waged and lost a three-year battle with throat cancer. He made his final appearance at Yankee Stadium on June 13, 1948, putting on a Yankees uniform one last time as part of a pregame ceremony commemorating the twenty-fifth anniversary of the stadium's opening. He was admitted to New York's Memorial Sloan-Kettering Hospital shortly after and passed away on August 16,

Babe Ruth's grave, adorned by a baseball and other trinkets pilgrims have left behind

1948 at age fifty-three. His body was laid in state at Yankee Stadium for two days, before being transferred to Manhattan's St. Patrick's Cathedral for funeral services. Afterward, he was buried in rustic Hawthorne, within the Gate of Heaven Cemetery. Claire would not join her husband for nearly three decades, until her passing in 1976.

You will find the Ruth memorial in Section 25 of this famous Catholic cemetery. Ruth and his wife occupy Plot 1115. There, a white monument depicts a life-size image of Jesus resting a guiding hand on the shoulder of a young boy. The epitaph on the left side reads, "May the divine spirit that animated Babe Ruth to win the crucial game of life inspire the youth of America." It is attributed to Cardinal Spellman, a prominent historic figure as a spiritual leader and sometime political player. On the right side of the memorial, the inscription reads, "George Herman Ruth 1895–1948" and "Claire Ruth 1900–1976."

Visiting Ruth's grave, you're apt to find that other pilgrims have delivered unto Ruth's plot an assortment of mementos meant to honor the slugger. On any given day, you might find Ruth's monument decorated with empty beer bottles, half-eaten hot dogs, baseballs, bats, baseball cards, Yankees hats, Yankees pennants, game programs from Yankee Stadium, and other pieces of pinstriped memorabilia.

While you're stomping around Gate of Heaven, you should also make a point to seek out the final resting places of two other men who devoted their lives to the game. Former Yankees second baseman and five-time Yankees manager Billy Martin is buried here, as well as former big-league umpire John McSherry.

Martin, who was as famous for butting heads with umpires as for his feuding with Yankees boss George Steinbrenner, died in a one-vehicle accident at the end of his driveway in Port Crane, New York, on Christmas morning 1989. It was an icy morning and Martin had reportedly been drinking. He was memorialized at St. Patrick's Cathedral, just as Ruth had been years before, and then laid to rest in Section 25, Plot 21, less than 150 feet from Ruth. Martin's gray granite marker offers a large engraved cross in the center, a depiction of Saint Jude on the left, and a quote from the deceased skipper on the right that reads, "I may not have been the greatest Yankee to put on the uniform but I was the proudest." The number 1—Martin's old uniform number—is chiseled into the right and left sides of the stone.

McSherry's stone, which can be found in Section 44, Plot 480, features the National League logo of an eagle spreading its wings with a baseball superimposed in the foreground. The design also includes an etching of a cap with an "N" on it, and an etching of an umpire's mask. McSherry died of a heart attack that he suffered on the field in the top of the first inning of the Reds season opener against the Expos on April 1, 1996. He was working as the home plate umpire that day and seven pitches into the game called for a time out. He walked slowly toward the Reds dugout, and then collapsed; understandably, the game was postponed.

You may visit these three graves between the hours of 8:00 a.m. and 4:30 p.m. each day, when the Gate of Heaven is open for visitors.

15. The Forbes Field Site

The University of Pittsburgh
230 South Bouquet Street
Pittsburgh, Pennsylvania 15213

While you'll find historic markers and plaques in cities across the country marking the sites where fabled ballparks of yesteryear once stood, Pittsburgh does the memory of its old yard one better, preserving a considerable stretch of Forbes Field's original outfield wall, as well as the old park's home plate in something approximating its original location.

The 12-foot-high redbrick outfield wall that once stood in left and left-center field at Forbes is now located on the University of Pittsburgh campus. The distance-from-home-plate markings—457 to the deepest point in left-center and 436 to center—still appear painted on the wall just as they were when the Pirates played their last games at Forbes, sweeping a doubleheader against the Chicago Cubs on June 28, 1970. Green cement pillars appear at regular intervals between the brick and mortar to provide support. The flagpole, which stood in fair territory in the outfield from the park's opening in 1909 through its final games, also remains. After the preserved stretch of the wall ends, a path of brick laid in the sidewalk and street continues to trace the outline of where the wall once stood, leading to a plaque in "left field" that marks the spot over which Bill Mazeroski's walk-off home run flew to propel the Pirates past the Yankees in Game Seven of the 1960 World Series. The actual stretch of wall over which the legendary homer flew stands outside PNC Park on its river walk.

While on the Pittsburgh campus, you should also check out the wooden re-creation of the arching Forbes Field entranceway that was built in the mid-2000s. And across the "Forbes Quad" in the lobby of Posvar Hall, you find the home plate that was used in Forbes's final season, encased beneath a protective layer of glass. Contrary to popular belief, the plate doesn't lie in its precise original location. According to researchers, the actual location was 81 feet away, within Posvar's economics library.

At the time of its opening, Forbes Field was considered one of the most ornate ballparks yet built. Before long its concrete-and-steel design became standard-issue in ballpark construction. Pirates owner Barney Dreyfuss was initially chastised by fans for building Forbes in a bustling downtown section of Pittsburgh, but those same fans were all smiles when the Pirates won their first World Series later that year, beating the Detroit Tigers four games to three. Over the ensuing decades, Forbes witnessed many memorable moments. On the final day of the 1920 season, the Pirates hosted the Cincinnati Reds for the only tripleheader in major-league history. Cincinnati won two out of three to clinch third place in the National League, while Pittsburgh dropped to fourth. On August 5, 1921, the first major-league game ever broadcast over radio was played at Forbes between the Pirates and Philadelphia Phillies; the Pirates won 8–5 as listeners tuned in to Pittsburgh's KDKA. On May 25, 1935, Babe Ruth slugged the final three home runs of his career at Forbes as a member of the Boston Braves. In 1951 the movie *Angels in the Outfield* was shot at Forbes.

But the most memorable moment of all occurred in the final game of the 1960 October

Each year on October 13, nostalgic fans gather in the shadows of the Forbes Field wall to listen to the broadcast of Bill Mazeroski's famous home run to win the 1960 World Series.

Classic. Although the heavily favored Yankees outscored the up-and-comers from the National League by an aggregate margin of 55 to 27 over the seven games, the Pirates prevailed, thanks to Mazeroski, who broke a 9–9 tie in the final frame with a long ball off Ralph Terry. The ball sailed over the head of helpless Yankees left fielder Yogi Berra—who was splitting catching duties with Elston Howard by that point—and crashed through the tree branches above the left field fence. Before "Maz" could reach home plate, a throng of fans had spilled onto the field, and a raucous celebration had begun. The win gave Pittsburgh its first World Series win in thirty-five years.

Pirates fans young and old still gather on the Pittsburgh campus on October 13 each year to mark the anniversary of the legendary homer by listening to a taped radio broadcast of the game. The tradition began in the 1980s when a local fan named Saul Finkelstein realized it would be kind of neat to listen to the historic game on the very grounds where it had taken place. Soon, Finkelstein's fall tradition had become a neighborhood's tradition. With each year, the crowds grew. For the fortieth anniversary of the legendary homer in 2000, Mazeroski himself turned out at the wall, along with more than 500 fans to listen to the old audio of NBC radio announcers Chuck Thompson and Jack Quinlan calling the game. Then, in 2010, for the fiftieth anniversary, Mazeroski joined a crowd of more than 1,000 nostalgic rooters to listen and witness the unveiling of a plaque in his honor at the site.

16. Green-Wood Cemetery

500 25th Street
Brooklyn, New York 11232
(718) 210-3080
www.green-wood.com

Some baseball landmarks are created through careful design and meant from the start to produce a meaningful fan experience—such as in the case of the many awe-inspiring baseball museums—while others like Green-Wood Cemetery come about serendipitously, following their own winding paths into the pantheon of baseball's hallowed grounds. Green-Wood was well on its way to becoming a baseball attraction long before baseball had even taken root in our collective consciousness as America's Game. Rather, the National Pastime was still in its infancy when Green-Wood began providing "lifetime memberships" to the game's early designers, players, managers, owners, umpires, and writers.

Almost 200 people who played leading roles in the game's invention and dissemination—including "father of baseball" Henry Chadwick, himself—began checking into this rolling hillside cemetery during the 1800s and early 1900s, planting the seeds for what is now regarded as a "true field of dreams," as baseball documentarian Ken Burns once described Green-Wood. Owing to its proximity to that baseball laboratory, Elysian Fields, the beautiful Brooklyn burial yard was a convenient resting place for scores of people who'd been associated with early club teams like the Knickerbockers, Atlantics,

and Excelsiors. Later, Brooklyn Dodgers owner Charles Ebbets was buried on one of the cemetery's wooded hillsides.

But before we get into detailing the exploits of the more notable baseball figures in Green-Wood, and the baseball-inspired headstones that mark their graves, some broader context regarding this National Historic Landmark is in order. The first thing you need to know about Green-Wood Cemetery is that it is *massive*, encompassing 478 rolling acres. The nearly 600,000 residents rest along scenic bluffs, in cascading valleys, and near glacial ponds. It is easy to see why Green-Wood was the most prestigious place to be buried for New Yorkers during the city's early era.

Green-Wood was founded in 1838 on the spot where the Revolutionary War's Battle of Long Island was fought. From its early days, the pastoral hills and wooded glens drew more than just the local deceased and their mourners. Green-Wood was one of the most popular American tourist attractions of the 1850s and 1860s, attracting a half-million visitors a year. Mind you, the Metropolitan Museum of Art would not open until 1872, nor the Statue of Liberty until 1886.

Aside from housing Chadwick (Section 131, Lot 32004), Ebbets (Section 129, Lot 35567), and other baseball visionaries, the cemetery also provides repose to such influential American figures as Boss Tweed (Section 55, Lot 6447), Leonard Bernstein (Section G, Lot 43642), Henry Steinway (Section 46, Lot 15388), and sundry other poets, authors, artists, actors, mobsters, war heroes, and politicians. Vaudevillian DeWolf Hopper (Section 31, Lot 5805), who rose to fame performing the Ernest L. Thayer poem "Casey at the Bat" some 10,000 times over a half-century career, is another notable resident, as is Charles Feltman (Section 199, Lot 32146), who is often cited as the inventor of that favorite ballpark treat, the hot dog.

You can learn more about baseball's murky nineteenth-century origins in the "Elysian Fields" chapter of this book, as well as about the roles played by Chadwick, Alexander J. Cartwright, and other "inventors" of the game. Chadwick, who'd grown up playing cricket in England, then moved to New York where he discovered "rounders," was a newspaper writer, who took to covering "base ball" in and around New York City in the 1850s. He wrote annual guides devoted to the sport, published statistics in the papers, and traveled nationally sharing the New York version of the game. Upon his passing in 1908, he was laid to rest beneath a stone that reads "Father of Base Ball." His marker was actually commissioned by Charles Ebbets; it incorporates a giant marble baseball at the top, as well as an early

catcher's mask and fielding glove. There are four bases arranged in a diamond around the main monument.

Duncan Curry (Section 189, Lot 18578), another early baseball visionary, is also buried beneath a stone here that reads "Father of Base-ball." He was a president of the early Knicker-bockers who worked alongside Cartwright to make a list of the game's formal rules. Another influential early player was Jim Creighton Jr. (Section 2, Lot 3384), who is said to have rein-vented the pitcher's role in the 1860s when he began throwing fastballs with the intent of evading the hitter's bat. Previously, the pitch-er's purpose had been to serve up the ball in a game that was primarily an offensive contest. Creighton died somewhat mysteriously at the height of his fame in 1862 at the tender age of twenty-one. According to lore, he hurt himself in

The main entrance to Green-Wood Cemetery

a cricket game, then tried to play baseball a few days later and aggravated some sort of internal injury that led to his demise. For years he laid beneath a tall marble monument that unfolded like a peeled lemon to reveal a baseball. More than 150 years after his death, though, the monument had fallen into complete disrepair. And so, in the fall of 2013, Green-Wood launched a campaign to raise the funds to recreate the original monument. Members of SABR-NY, including Keith Olbermann, led the effort, resulting in the unveiling of a new stone for Creighton in 2014. Peter J. Nash's book *Baseball Legends of Brooklyn's Green-Wood Cemetery* dubs the Creighton monument "baseball's first off-field tourist destination," citing a seminal trip to the monument made by the National Club from Washington, DC, in 1866.

Other baseball luminaries in the cemetery include Excelsior John B. Woodward (Section 72, Lot 10915), who went on to become a Union colonel in the Civil War; Knickerbocker Archibald Gourlie (Section 68, Lot 401), who was fined sixpence in 1845 for arguing with an umpire; brothers Sam, Joe, and Edward Patchen, who all played for the Star of Brooklyn club and rest in a shared crypt (Section 3, Lot 566); and Ebbets, who died of a heart attack in 1925 only to be followed to his grave by Dodgers co-owner Edward McKeever, who was said to have caught pneumonia while enduring the chilly April weather to attend Ebbets's burial.

The cemetery's main entrance at Fifth Avenue and 25th Street is open daily from 7:45 a.m. to 5:00 p.m. The gates at Fourth Avenue and 35th Street are open from 8:00 a.m. to 4:00 p.m. The entrances on Fort Hamilton Parkway and Prospect Park West are open from 8:00 a.m. to 4:00 p.m. on weekends. Before visiting, you can download a copy of the cemetery's digital map, which you can refer to on your mobile device. You can also get a print copy on the day of your visit from the guard booth at the main entrance.

17. The Hank Aaron Home Run Wall

Turner Field's Gold Parking Lot
755 Hank Aaron Drive
Atlanta, Georgia 30315

During most of its three decades as the home of the Braves, Atlanta–Fulton County Stadium offered little to distinguish itself from the other multipurpose stadiums of its era. For a time, shortly after its opening in 1966, the stadium featured a wigwam beyond its outfield fence that provided a home to resident mascot Chief Noc-A-Homa. And the stadium was always known as a hitter's paradise, owing to its altitude of more than a thousand feet above sea level. But for the most part, it was nondescript and forgettable. Surely, it would have faded into the furthest reaches of our collective memory bank by now if not for one glorious moment that forever stamped it as a baseball landmark.

On a damp night in April of 1974, Hammering Hank Aaron consecrated Atlanta–Fulton County Stadium as hallowed ground when he staked his claim to the most prestigious record in American

The stretch of wall over which Hank Aaron hit his 715th home run has been preserved in a Turner Field parking lot.

professional sports. In usurping Babe Ruth as baseball's all-time home-run king, Aaron ensured the stadium would never be forgotten. If you're a fan, chances are you can close your eyes and conjure the image of Aaron's monumental 715th big fly. You can see his quick swing, compact and powerful, and the ball sailing over the head of Dodgers left fielder Bill Buckner destined to land in the Braves bullpen. You can see the aging slugger's trot around the bases, faster than usual, as he tried to outrun a pair of overzealous well-wishers who had raced onto the field.

For most of us, Aaron's shot is frozen in time. It was a "baseball moment," yes, but it was more than that. It reached beyond the normal boundaries of sport to further speed along the cultural evolution of our nation. Not only had Aaron broken a record that for decades had been thought to be unbreakable, but he had done so amid an incredibly trying social atmosphere that had discouraged his progress at every step simply because he was a black man. With number 715,

Aaron silenced the bigots who had made threats on his life in the hope of ensuring that baseball's most glamorous record remained a white man's achievement. Aaron's homer sent the message that although the bigots might continue to assail the notion that all Americans deserved equal opportunities to succeed, ultimately their rancor would not deter the march of social progress.

Although Atlanta–Fulton County Stadium was demolished in the wake of Turner Field's opening next door in 1997, its memory—and the memory of what Aaron had accomplished on its lawn—lives on. A stretch of the left-center field fence over which Aaron's record-breaking home run flew stands today as a monument to this triumphant moment in history. The fence is located in the Gold Parking Lot across the street from Turner Field. In addition to housing the fence, the lot also traces the path of Atlanta–Fulton County Stadium's warning track and infield dirt in red brick and offers large metal plates where the bases once lay. The tall retaining fence that once rose behind the see-through mesh outfield fence and bullpens at the foot of the bleachers is also still in place, painted bright blue and bearing the words "Atlanta-Fulton County Stadium. Home of the Braves 1966–1996."

Aaron ended the 1973 season with 713 homers, leaving him just one short of moving into a tie with Ruth. On Opening Day of 1974, he drew even with the Bambino when his very first swing of the season resulted in a three-run homer in Cincinnati. Four days later, on April 8, 1974, Aaron stepped into the batter's box against the Dodgers' Al Downing in the second inning of the Braves' first home game and drew a four-pitch walk. His next at-bat came in the fourth inning with a runner on first and no outs. Aaron watched the first pitch bounce in the dirt for a ball, which caused the crowd of 53,775 expectant fans to groan audibly. With his next pitch Downing challenged Aaron with a high fastball, and Aaron swung. And the rest, as they say, is history.

Today a visit to the site where Aaron hit his record-breaking dinger is sure to bring goose bumps to your skin. Even when the asphalt and brick field has begun to fill with cars, you can step into the right-handed batter's box, take aim at the plaque atop the fence some 385 feet away that reads simply "Hank Aaron Home Run 715," and take a phantom swing. Then you can retrace Aaron's race around the brick base paths while imagining how he must have felt in the seconds immediately after he rewrote baseball's record books.

The Braves announced in 2013 that they would not be renewing their lease agreement with Turner Field upon its expiration at the end of the 2016 season. Braves management said the team would instead move to a new $672 million, 42,000-seat ballpark that was being designed for the Braves in Cobb County. Despite this looming change, the City of Atlanta maintained at the time that the Hank Aaron Home Run Wall would be preserved and incorporated into whatever redevelopment plan awaits Turner Field and its parking lots. Here's hoping that proves to be the case, because this is one baseball landmark that ought to stand forever.

The home plate from Atlanta–Fulton County Stadium and playing field, outlined in red brick, are preserved in the same parking lot that includes the Hank Aaron Home Run Wall.

As if beautiful Coors Field and the festive breweries and sports bars that surround it didn't present reason enough for you to visit Denver's Lower Downtown, a jewel of a baseball museum sits a half-block from Coors Field's main entrance. As the only national repository of artifacts exclusively devoted to preserving baseball's stadiums, the National Ballpark Museum has chiseled out a unique place for itself on the American hardball landscape that should endure for years to come.

The idea for a museum dedicated to baseball's parks was the brainchild of Denver native Bruce Hellerstein, who serves as the museum's curator. Hellerstein, who operates an accounting firm out of the same brick building on Blake Street where the museum resides, drew upon his knowledge of estate, gift, and trust planning when he donated his lifetime collection of ballpark memorabilia to a newly created nonprofit organization he established in 1999. A decade later, in 2010, he opened the museum on Blake Street. More than just being a lifelong fan of baseball, Hellerstein has traveled extensively over the past several decades visiting its yards and accumulating keepsakes. He also played an influential role in Denver's pursuit of the expansion franchise that would eventually become the Rockies in 1991. He served with other Denver businesspeople and civic leaders as a member of the Denver Baseball Commission, and then served on the Coors Field Design Committee.

So, what sorts of artifacts do you find on display at a ballpark museum? Well, in addition to an impressive pile of bricks from demolished stadiums, you find old wooden seats and turnstiles from no less than fourteen of the "classic era" parks, including Crosley Field, the Polo Grounds, and Tiger Stadium. Many of the seats are still affixed to the ornate ironwork that

18. The National Ballpark Museum

1940 Blake Street
Denver, Colorado 80202
(303) 974-5835
www.ballparkmuseum.com

appeared at the end of each row, displaying the home team's or ballpark's logo. You also find one of the original cornerstones from Forbes Field, as well as one of its arched windows, and one of its turnstiles. The Yankee Stadium drain cap in which rookie Mickey Mantle famously caught a spike and sprained his right knee in the second game of the 1951 World Series against the Giants is also on display, as are the giant "U" that hung from the original Yankee Stadium marquee, and a section of the 3-foot-high outfield fence that stood in right.

The museum also includes two of the original baseball globe lights that illuminated the famous Ebbets Field rotunda; the personal telephone from Red Sox owner Tom Yawkey's office at Fenway Park; the oversized blue exit sign that hung outside Tiger Stadium directing motorists to the corner of Michigan and Trumbull; part of the Tiger Stadium light tower off of which Reggie Jackson famously clanked a prodigious homer in the 1971 All-Star Game; and an Ernie Banks flag that once flew on the left field foul pole at Wrigley Field. But this is just a sampling of the more than a thousand items in the museum's collection. And Hellerstein isn't finished done collecting yet. He still has a few coveted ballpark relics on his list of items he'd like to

National Ballpark Museum founder Bruce Hellerstein

Another area of emphasis at the museum is Denver baseball history. The minor-league Denver Bears (who later became the Zephyrs and moved to New Orleans to pave the way for the Rockies to join the National League) played for decades at Bears Stadium. The park, which opened in 1948, was eventually rechristened Mile High Stadium in the 1960s, when it began serving as the home of the Denver Broncos. As one of the biggest venues in the minors, the facility would host more than 40,000 fans each Fourth of July, when it was a Denver tradition to go to the ballpark and then stick around for the postgame fireworks display. The Denver baseball artifacts include the pitching rubber from the final game at Mile High in 1995, a ticket stub from the first game at Bears Stadium in 1948, and a bench seat and sign from Mile High.

Prior to opening the museum, Hellerstein had been storing memorabilia in his basement. Some of the pieces in his collection were acquired at auction, while others were commissioned, and others were collected in the course of his ballpark travels. Today, he delights in leading visitors through the museum and telling them more about the various pieces. To find the museum, just look for the red and white "Gate B" sign that once hung outside Fenway Park (Hellerstein's favorite current big-league park), which today adorns the museum's attractive brick front on Blake Street. The 2,000-square-foot gallery and adjoining baseball library are open Monday through Saturday during the baseball season and by appointment during baseball's off-season. The museum keeps regular daytime hours during the season, and stays open later when the Rockies have an evening game. Check the website or call ahead for the exact times. Admission costs just $5.00 for adults, while children age ten and under are free.

acquire; at the very top of his list is a piece of the facade from the original Yankee Stadium, his favorite ballpark of all time.

If you sense a theme, you're right: Hellerstein loves the golden oldies that have attained almost mythic status through the years, and his collection reflects that. And that makes sense. As fans, we read about the legendary yards where baseball's most epic moments have played out, and occasionally we see them depicted in the latest baseball movies. Now we can get up close and personal with them, reviewing the actual signs, seats, historic game programs, ticket stubs, and other design flourishes that have been composited in this one convenient place to visit.

The National Ballpark Museum sits just a lazy fly ball from Coors Field.

Eventually, Hellerstein hopes to keep the museum open year-round, but first he needs to enlist enough volunteers and interns to keep it staffed. Judging from the track record he's established in collecting these fine relics, finding a place to display them, and creating a nonprofit organization to manage the enterprise, here's betting he surmounts this latest challenge.

In his autobiography, *My Turn at Bat*, Ted Williams expressed the passion with which he pursued batting excellence, writing, "A man has to have goals . . . and that was mine, to have people say, 'There goes Ted Williams, the greatest hitter who ever lived.'" Sure enough, the skinny kid from San Diego's North Park neighborhood fulfilled that ambition. Today most fans and historians agree that the "Splendid Splinter" was one of the best, if not *the* best all-around hitter to ever play the game. He hit for power. He

19. Ted Williams's Boyhood Home

4121 Utah Street
San Diego, California 92104

hit for average. And he played with a swagger and flair that made his exploits legendary even in his own time: He one-upped DiMaggio by batting .406 during the season in which Joltin' Joe notched his fifty-six-game hit streak; he homered against Rip Sewell's famous eephus pitch . . . in the All-Star Game . . . fresh off a return from military service; he slashed balls through Lou Boudreau's famous "Williams Shift"; he homered in his last big league at-bat.

More than just amassing baseball accolades (two Triple Crowns, six batting titles including back-to-back crowns at the ages of thirty-nine and forty, 521 home runs, a .344 batting average, an all-time-best .482 on-base percentage), Williams also took two time-outs at the peak of his greatness to serve in World War II and the Korean War. He didn't accept plum jobs doing PR appearances for the US armed forces either;

he flew a Navy fighter jet in World War II and later a Marine jet that was shot down in Korea. When Williams landed his flaming F-9 and emerged with hardly a scratch, it was called a "miracle." Then, he went back to work swatting home runs.

Sadly, there is no gravesite where fans can pay homage to this true American hero. Unlike other giants of the game like Babe Ruth and Jackie Robinson—who left behind headstones for us to visit—Williams left none. Upon his passing in 2002, his body was neither buried, nor cremated and spread over his beloved Florida Keys as he'd requested. Rather, at the behest of his eccentric son John-Henry Williams, it was shipped from Florida to a Scottsdale, Arizona, cryonics laboratory, known as the Alcor Life Extension Foundation, where a team of controversial scientists separated his

Growing up in this San Diego house, Ted Williams dedicated himself to becoming the greatest hitter who ever lived.

head from his body, pumped his remains full of antifreeze, and stored them in liquid nitrogen at minus 321 degrees Fahrenheit. The idea behind cryonics is to preserve the brain and other important organs so that future scientific advances might one day enable scientists to bring the deceased back to life. According to Ben Bradlee Jr.'s book *The Kid: The Immortal Life of Ted Williams*, Ted thought the premise was ridiculous, but his starry-eyed son thought there might be something to it. While a previous edition of *101 Baseball Places to See Before You Strike Out* included the Alcor facility as a slightly macabre spot to visit on your baseball pilgrimage, this edition of the book instead celebrates the place where Williams's rise to greatness began.

Along with his mother and his brother, the six-year-old Williams moved to this one-story bungalow on San Diego's Utah Street in 1924. He played sandlot ball in the neighborhood's streets and yards, played youth league ball at a neighborhood field, then headed to nearby Herbert Hoover High School, where he batted .583 as a junior and .406 as a senior. The eighteen-year-old Williams eschewed the big-league offers that ensued, opting instead to play 5 miles south of his Utah Street home for the Pacific Coast League San Diego Padres. After two seasons, Hall of Famer Eddie Collins, who was scouting for the Red Sox, convinced Williams to sign with Boston. The Red Sox organization shipped him to the Minneapolis Millers, for whom he won the American Association Triple Crown in 1938. The next season, "The Kid" landed in Boston.

Today, the house where Williams grew from boy to man looks much as it did in the 1920s and 1930s. Back then, the young Williams's passion for the game was fueled by his mother, May, who worked for the local Salvation Army, and by an uncle named Saul Venzor, who had played semi-pro ball. Today, there is no marker sanctifying this house as a baseball holy ground, nor is there a statue of the "Greatest Hitter Who Ever Lived" outside. The white house, with its white-and-blue awning, sits behind a chain-link fence and some overgrown branches. A not-quite-Fenway-green cement path leads from the sidewalk to the front steps.

The home is still a private residence, so be sure to respect the property owners' privacy when you visit. Someday, perhaps, it will be declared a National Historic Landmark and will be transformed into a Williams museum, but until then, we must pay our respects from the sidewalk outside. When Williams visited the house in 1992, he was welcomed by then-owner Terry Higgins. After visiting his old bedroom and posing for a picture on the front steps, "Teddy Ballgame" reportedly turned to Higgins and said, "Whatever you do, don't get famous. It's a pain in the neck."

During your visit to this modest baseball landmark, you should also schedule time to seek out the youth field where Williams first flashed his trademark swing. From Utah, follow Polk Avenue 2 blocks west, to North Park Community Park. The 8-acre park's baseball diamond is named **Ted Williams Field**. Here, you'll find a sign that reads, "Ted Williams Field. Officially named in honor of baseball's Hall-of-Famer by the Park and Recreation Board on November 16, 1990." This is one site where you may choose to linger. Bring a bat and bucket of balls, then step into the left-handed batter's box, dig your spikes (or sneakers) into the same red dirt where young Ted once batted, and take a few swings. Now, that's a whole lot more romantic than visiting the parking lot of a company that fills corpses with antifreeze while promising eternal life, isn't it?

20. Alexander Joy Cartwright's Grave and Honolulu's Historic Fields

Oahu Island
Honolulu, Hawaii

Baseball arrived in Honolulu in 1849, when Alexander Joy Cartwright Jr., the man some consider the father of baseball, relocated to what was then an upstart sugar-milling camp and put down roots. Cartwright served as Honolulu's fire chief from 1850 until the time of his death in 1863, and also founded the Honolulu Library. Before he died, Cartwright found time to lay out a baseball diamond where the locals took to the game immediately. Back then, Hawaii was its own kingdom and Cartwright's role as advisor to the ruling monarchy gave him a means to share his enthusiasm for the game and encourage its play.

Today, you will find Cartwright's rather understated grave at **Oahu Cemetery** (2162 Nuuanu Avenue). Although his headstone doesn't make reference to his role as a baseball visionary, you can usually find a pile of baseballs left at its foot, and it's not uncommon to find a Hawaiian lei draped over it.

More than half a century after Cartwright's death, Babe Ruth, Jimmie Foxx, Lou Gehrig, and other big-league stars of the 1930s headlined barnstorming tours to Honolulu, and when they arrived they were always sure to pay homage to Cartwright by visiting his grave. In those days, it was common for prominent big leaguers to embark on national and even international trips during the off-season, rather than taking second jobs like lesser players often did. In these pre–World War II days, these winter baseball sojourns often culminated in Japan, after stopping for a few games in Hawaii along the way. Later, the 1956 Dodgers played three exhibition games in Hawaii, as a team that included Jackie Robinson, Pee Wee Reese, Roy Campanella, Duke Snider, Don Newcombe, Don Zimmer, and Gil Hodges trounced the Maui All-Stars, the Hawaiian All-Stars, and the Honolulu Red Sox on successive days, before beginning Walter O'Malley's postwar "Goodwill Tour of Japan."

By 1961 Honolulu had its own professional team, the Hawaii Islanders, who played in the Triple-A Pacific Coast League. Located more than 2,500 miles from their nearest league rivals, the Islanders would often play eight-game series against the teams they visited, and likewise, when other league members made the long flight to Hawaii, they would stay for eight games. Over the years, the Islanders were affiliated with six major-league teams, including the Angels and White Sox, with whom they enjoyed two different stints. Today, the Islanders are best remembered as a Padres farm club, since their affiliation with San Diego lasted the longest—from 1971 through 1982. Tony Gwynn batted .328 for Hawaii in 1982, while Barry Bonds batted .311 in 1986. After twenty-seven seasons of shuttling back and forth to the mainland, however, the Islanders relocated to Colorado Springs following the 1987 season.

The final of three home parks used by the Islanders over the years—4,306-seat **Les Murakami Stadium** (1337 Lower Campus Road)—still sees regular use today as the home field of the University of Hawaii at Manoa baseball team. The park offers stunning views of the massive volcanic "tuff cone" named Diamond Head beyond its right field fence. It opened in 1984 as "Rainbow Stadium," prior to being renamed in honor of longtime University of Hawaii at Manoa baseball coach Les Murakami in 2002. The Hawaii Rainbow Warriors play in the NCAA Division I Big West Conference.

While the Rainbow Warriors have always enjoyed a good local following, the pro hardball drought did not last long. In 1993 the minor leaguers returned to Honolulu with the debut of the Hawaii Winter League. The developmental league played for five consecutive seasons, offering fans the chance to see teams composed of elite minor leaguers from the United States, Japan, and Korea. Future big leaguers like Ichiro Suzuki, Jason Giambi, Tadahito Iguchi, A. J. Pierzynski, Todd Helton, Mark Kotsay, Preston Wilson, and Honolulu native Benny Agbayani

all honed their skills in the league before it disbanded following the 1997 season.

The Winter League was resurrected in 2006 as a developmental league for top minor league prospects, unveiling a four-team format that included the Waikiki Beach Boys and the Honolulu Sharks using Les Murakami Stadium as their home field, and the West Oahu Cane Fires and North Shore Honu using nearby Hans L'Orange Field as their home. Unfortunately, the league fizzled out again in 2008, leaving all of the best prospects to play in either the Arizona Fall League or Caribbean Winter Leagues.

Fortunately, though, you will still find games being played at Les Murakami Stadium and Hans L'Orange Field when you visit Hawaii, thanks to their use as collegiate diamonds. While the

After helping launch New York City's love of baseball, Alexander Joy Cartwright brought the sport to the Hawaiian Islands, where he spent his final years.

Alexander Joy Cartwright's Grave and Honolulu's Historic Fields

Rainbow Warriors play their games at "The House that Les Built," the Hawaii Pacific University Sea Warriors of the NCAA Division II Pacific West Conference play at the park once known simply as Oahu Sugar Company Field.

As stunning as the outfield view is at Les Murakami Stadium, the setting at **Hans L'Orange Field** (94-1024 Waipahu Street) might be even more enchanting. On nights when Hawaii's famous purple "vog," or volcanic smog, sets the sky aglow at twilight, the backdrop for a game is surreal. A smokestack from the old Oahu Sugar Company rises up from a veneer of trees beyond the center field fence, adding a distinctive finishing touch on the view. The park seats 2,100 spectators in a small grandstand behind home plate and a bank of bleachers down the third base line. Given its proximity to the old mill, it is not surprising that it saw its first use as a recreational diamond for Oahu Sugar Company employees or that it is named in honor of the sugar miller who convinced management to turn under a couple of fields of sugarcane and build him and his friends a field in 1923.

As Americans living in the continental United States, most of us are only fortunate enough to visit the Hawaiian Islands once or twice and we usually arrive with rather lengthy itineraries. Whenever you visit the Islands, though, you should also make time to check out these two fields, both rich in history, steeped in civic pride, and visually delightful. If you're visiting in the springtime, you can even catch a college baseball game during your vacation.

As for the fields where Cartwright introduced the game to Hawaiians, at least one can still be visited today. **Cartwright Neighborhood Park** (Keeaumoku and Kinau Streets) was known as the Makiki Reserve back when Cartwright and his contemporaries were playing.

21. McCovey Cove

China Basin
Pier 38/The Embarcadero
San Francisco, California 94107

Wrigley Field has its rooftop bleachers looming behind the ivy and outfield bleachers. Fenway Park has its Green Monster Seats perched high atop its signature Wall. Kauffman Stadium has its 322-foot-long Water Spectacular. And Angels Stadium has its California Spectacular. But any debate concerning which major-league stadium offers the best aesthetic backdrop for a game must invariably arrive at San Francisco's AT&T Park. Your baseball travels just wouldn't be complete if you didn't experience a game here on the waterfront.

When it was constructed in the late 1990s, AT&T Park was built right up against the shores of an industrial channel known as China Basin. Right field and the bank of home-run seats overlooking it were both truncated due to the park's proximity to the water. As Giants fans readied for their new yard's grand opening at the start of the 2000 season, local sportswriter Mark Purdy wrote a column suggesting several colorful names for the waters into which he and others were already envisioning home runs splashing.

Fans afloat on McCovey Cove wait for home-run balls to splash down.

These included "McCovey Run" and "McCovey Channel," as well as "McCovey Cove," which Purdy attributed to fellow Giants beat writer Leonard Koppett. The latter nickname stuck, of course, and soon attained national recognition.

The tribute to McCovey is fitting. The lefty slugger played nineteen seasons with the Giants (1959–1973 and 1977–1980) in a Hall of Fame career that saw him belt 521 home runs, including one that once splashed down in a public swimming pool beyond the outfield fence of Montreal's Jarry Park. It is also fitting that Barry Bonds was the player who thrust McCovey Cove into the national baseball spotlight. McCovey, who had played with Bobby Bonds, is Barry's godfather and they have always been close. How significant was the younger Bonds in making McCovey Cove a household name? Of the Giants' first twenty-five homers to land in the salty water, Bonds hit twenty-three of them.

The oversized slugger chalked up his first splash landing on May 1, 2000, when he took the Mets' Rich Rodriguez deep; then Bonds hit eight more wet ones before Felipe Crespo became the second Giant to get wet on May 28, 2001. Two years passed before another Giants player not named Bonds or Crespo made a splash, as J. T. Snow finally added his name to the list of soggy sluggers in an interleague game against Minnesota on June 3, 2003. Through 2013, there had been a total of ninety-three splash homers in AT&T Park's history: sixty-three by the Giants and thirty by their opponents.

The shortest distance a fair ball must travel to splash down is 352 feet—307 to reach the foul pole and another 45 to clear the strip of land between the ballpark and water. That may not sound very far, but it's harder to reach the water than that distance would lead you to expect, because the outfield fence slants quickly away

An arched retaining wall separates the ballpark from the water.

from home plate as it heads toward center field. In right-center, a ball must carry 421 feet just to leave the yard, then another 50 feet to reach the water. A lefty slugger really has to yank one down the line to have a shot at making a splash.

Even though splash landings are rare, floating on McCovey Cove is a popular pastime for many Giants fans. The number of floating fanatics varies from game to game, depending on the start time, the weather, the day's opponent, and the water conditions. As a traveling fan, you should consider taking to the seas yourself when you visit San Francisco. You can watch one game from inside the park, and then the next day you can experience the game from the water. **City Kayak,** on the Embarcadero near the ballpark, offers kayak rentals year-round. During day games, you can rent a sea kayak and paddle on your own to McCovey Cove, which is just five minutes from the marina. During evening games, City Kayak offers escorted trips to and from McCovey Cove. The only items you need to bring are a

small smartphone to listen to the game, a telescoping fisherman's net just in case a long ball should splash down near you, some sunscreen, a windbreaker, and perhaps a change of clothes— just in case. From these calm waters you see the arched retaining wall that separates the ballpark from the sea, the backs of the right field foul pole and light banks, and the people seated in the upper deck around the infield. And every time a high fly ball or popup leaves a hitter's bat, you're treated to a fleeting glimpse of the horsehide.

You should also make a point to visit **McCovey Point** at China Basin Park. This public greenspace, behind the left- and center field fence, offers sweeping views of McCovey Cove, a statue of McCovey in the midst of a prodigious swing, a self-guided Giants History Walk, and plenty of room for a game of catch. There is also a plaque honoring the annual winners of the Willie Mac Award, designated each year to the major-league player who best embodies the spirit and leadership that defined McCovey's career.

Babe Ruth spent his early years in this Baltimore row house.

22. The Babe Ruth Birthplace and Museum

216 Emory Street
Baltimore, Maryland 21201
(410) 727-1539
http://baberuthmuseum.org

As you travel America's highways and byways, you will find several museums dedicated to celebrating the lives and times of the biggest stars America's Game has yet to produce. There are museums singularly focused on such baseball immortals as Ty Cobb, Cy Young, Ted Williams, Yogi Berra, Roger Maris, Joe Jackson, and Bob Feller, and they're all well worth visiting. With all due respect to those fine establishments, though, and to the amazing players whose lives they celebrate, you'll find no finer a player-specific museum than the Baltimore row house dedicated to honoring George Herman "Babe" Ruth.

The baby Babe entered the world on February 6, 1895, opening his eyes to the inside of this brick building that now serves as a museum in his honor. Growing up in the house, which was then leased by his maternal grandfather, Pius Schamberger, and at his father's nearby saloon, which was located where the right-center field bleachers at Oriole Park at Camden Yards now stand, the Bambino learned to cuss, gamble, and smoke. By age seven, he had grown so incorrigible that he was sent to St. Mary's Industrial School for Boys, a reform school on the outskirts of the city. There, Ruth was trained in shirt-making and carpentry. He gained the skills to succeed in either avocation, but was even more proficient on the baseball field. In 1914, Jack Dunn, owner of the International League Baltimore Orioles, discovered him. Because Ruth was only nineteen when Dunn offered him a pro contract, and because Ruth had been scheduled to remain in reform school until age twenty-one, the Orioles owner had to accept legal guardianship of him. When Ruth reported to his first spring training camp a few months later, the other players teased him, calling him Dunn's *baby*. The nickname eventually morphed into "The Babe."

Putting aside any paternal feelings he may have had for Ruth, Dunn sold the southpaw's contract to the Red Sox before the 1914 season was finished. And so, just five months after

The Canadian Baseball Hall of Fame and Museum has resided in this century-old stone building since 1998, but hopes to build a new larger building soon.

and ball signed by Babe Ruth are on display too, as well as the seat that marked the upper-deck landing spot of the longest home run in Olympic Stadium history, a blast by Willie Stargell. You'll also find Jenkins's 1971 Cy Young Award here, and the batting helmet Joe Carter was wearing when he hit his walk-off homer to clinch a Blue Jays victory over the Phillies in the 1993 World Series.

The exhibit space also pays tribute, of course, to the Hall's inductees, which included just over a hundred people as of this book's publication. Each year on a Saturday in late June, a new class of hall of famers is enshrined. The rules for eligibility stipulate that a player, coach, or front office executive must be retired for three years and that if they're not Canadian, they must have done something significant to advance baseball in Canada. Indeed, there are plenty of non-Canadians in the Canadian Baseball Hall of Fame. In most cases these are former Expos and Blue Jays—people like Roberto Alomar, George Bell, Gary Carter, Joe Carter, Andre Dawson, Tony Fernandez, Cito Gaston, Pat Gillick, Tom Henke, Tim Raines, Steve Rogers, Dave Stieb, and Tim Wallach. Robinson, who played for the International League's Montreal Royals in 1946, a year before he would break the major-league color barrier, and Lasorda, who pitched for the Royals from 1950 to 1955, and then from 1958 to 1960, are also members.

Canadian Baseball Hall of Fame 2013 Inductees (L–R): George Bell, Rob Ducey, Shirley Cheek (for her husband, Tom Cheek), and Tim Raines

The Hall also gives out the Tip O'Neill Award each fall, which is an annual MVP award for Canadian players. The award is not named for the American Speaker of the House who famously reached across the aisle to cut deals with Ronald Reagan in the 1980s. It is named for the Canadian Tip O'Neill who played for the St. Louis Browns back in the 1880s. O'Neill batted .492 in 1887 in an era when walks were being counted as hits. The award was founded in 1984, when Terry Puhl became the first recipient. Walker, who had so many great years with the Expos and Rockies, holds the record with nine O'Neill trophies to his credit.

The Hall is more easily accessed during the warmer half of the calendar year. In May it is open on Saturday from 10:30 a.m. to 4:00 p.m. and on Sunday from noon to 4:00 p.m. From June through the first week of October, it is open Monday through Saturday from 10:30 a.m. to 4:00 p.m. and on Sunday from noon to 4:00. Admission costs $7.50 for adults, $6.00 for senior citizens, or $3.75 for children age six through sixteen. You may also access the Hall during the latter portion of October through the end of April, but admission during that period is by appointment only and requires a minimum group of six people or a minimum payment of $30.00.

25. Carroll B. Land Stadium

Point Loma Nazarene University
3900 Lomaland Drive
San Diego, California 92106
(619) 849-2265
www.plnusealions.com/index
.aspx?path=baseball&tab=baseball

If you're a hard-core baseball fan, shortly after you flip your calendar from December to January and start to emerge from the winter holidays, you turn your attention to the upcoming season. The icy chill of winter may still prevail in your part of the country, and Major League Baseball's spring training games may still be two months away. But you begin to dream of the games to come. You imagine lazy days at the ballpark under warm summer sun. But why wait for summer or even spring, when you can take a late-winter trip to "America's Most Scenic Ballpark" to enjoy a game or two?

Although NCAA Division I baseball teams are prohibited from practicing before February 1 and don't begin playing actual games until mid-February, lower-level programs often begin their seasons much earlier. And that brings us to Carroll B. Land Stadium, where the Point Loma Nazarene University Sea Lions play in the NCAA Division II Pacific West Conference, and begin hosting regular season games during the first week of February each year. Here, you can sit back in sunny Southern California and take in a college baseball game at not merely one of the finer ballparks in the college baseball universe but at any level of play. Nestled among the seaside cliffs that overlook the Pacific Ocean, the stadium offers stunning views of the sparkling blue waves just beyond its outfield walls.

It's easy to see why the palm-adorned park is often referred to as "America's Most Scenic Ballpark." According to the university, the first to coin that term was a sportswriter for the *San Diego Union-Tribune*. In 1993, scribe Kevin Kernan was on campus to cover a volleyball tournament, and as he walked by the field he was awed by the view. He later wrote about the field and referred to it by that nickname in the *Union-Tribune* and in *Baseball America*. And that's the way the Point Loma Nazarene program has described its diamond ever since.

The field was originally part of the Cal-Western University campus, until Pasadena College relocated to San Diego in 1973 and took over the field along with the rest of Cal-Western's facilities. Pasadena College baseball coach Carroll B. Land made the move along with the team he'd been guiding since 1961, and Mr. Land played a leading role over the next three decades in renovation efforts that would install dugouts, improve the outfield walls, expand the seating areas, and add concession stands and restrooms to what was then known as Crusader Field. Land would serve the Pasadena College/Point Loma Nazarene University baseball program for thirty-nine years before retiring from the head coaching post in 1998 to accept full-time responsibilities as Point Loma Nazarene's athletic director. At that time the university decided to rename the baseball field in his honor.

Whether you find yourself in Southern California during February through early May, when the Sea Lions play home games that usually begin in early afternoon, or during the summer months, breathtaking Carroll B. Land Stadium warrants a visit. After checking out

Point Loma Nazarene University outfielders can barely hear the crack of the bat over the din of the nearby waves crashing to shore.

the view from the infield seats on the third base side, head for the observation deck atop the nearby athletic training facility to better enjoy the convergence of the field's green grass and the ocean's blue water. It is truly a sight to behold.

● ●

Follow the trail of bronze bats adorning Louisville's Main Street, and you will soon find yourself standing in the shadows of the biggest baseball bat in the world. The Louisville Slugger Walk of Fame leads you to the barrel of the 120-foot-tall, 68,000-pound bat that stands outside the most famous baseball-bat company in the land. The giant Louisville Slugger is made of steel, but painted to resemble the wood grain of a real bat. It rises quite a bit higher than the five-story brick building against which it leans, its altitudinous handle serving as a beacon for

26. The Louisville Slugger Museum and Factory

◇◇

Hillerich & Bradsby Company
800 West Main Street
Louisville, Kentucky 40202
(877) 775-8443
www.sluggermuseum.com

The giant bat outside the Louisville Slugger Museum and Factory rises more than five stories into the sky.

hardball pilgrims in search of the Louisville Slugger Museum and Factory. The massive bat is a to-scale replica of the 34-inch stick once wielded by "The Sultan of Swat" himself, Babe Ruth.

Inside the museum, you can check out the Louisville Slugger into which Ruth carved sixty notches in 1927—one for each of the sixty home runs he hit that year. You also find exhibits tracing the evolution of the bat, offering examples of the very weapons famous sluggers like Ty Cobb, Ted Williams, Mickey Mantle, and Johnny Bench once used to assail major-league pitching, as well as models swung by more recent stars like Cal Ripken Jr., Ken Griffey Jr., Derek Jeter, and David Ortiz.

Another oversized attraction at the museum is a 12-foot-wide baseball glove made of 450-year-old Kentucky limestone. Children can

sit and play in the glove, which weighs 17 tons and could only be installed after the museum's front doors were removed.

Appropriately, the museum also tells the story of the Hillerich & Bradsby Company's founding, detailing the humble beginnings of a local woodworking shop that grew to become the most prolific bat maker in the land. Believe it or not, Hillerich & Bradsby was founded long before baseball had taken root as America's Game. Back in 1856, German immigrant Fred Hillerich opened the shop to make bedposts, bowling pins, and butter churns. Two decades later, young Bud Hillerich began working as an apprentice in his father's shop. When the old man wasn't looking, Bud used the equipment in the family shop to make baseball bats for him and his friends to use on the local field. One day Bud made a special bat to help his favorite player out of a horrific slump. Pete "The Old Gladiator" Browning was the star of the American Association's Louisville Eclipse, but was really struggling at the plate. Browning was willing to try anything to change his luck, even accept a bat from a local kid who swore his handmade lumber would do the trick. So on a warm spring day in 1884, The Old Gladiator stepped to the plate with one of Bud's models on his shoulder. And the rest, as they say, is history.

Soon, Browning was rapping hits all over the yard. He went on to bat .336 that season and never swung a bat made by anyone other than Bud Hillerich over the remaining ten years of his career. By then word had spread, and many other major leaguers were swinging Louisville Sluggers, including Pittsburgh Pirates star Honus Wagner, who helped cement Hillerich & Bradsby's place in the game when he signed an endorsement deal with the company in 1905. Cobb signed a similar contract in 1908.

More than just learning about the evolution of the bat and about the history of the leading bat manufacturer, you can also take a tour of the factory, which operates in the same building. On the tour, you learn how planks of white ash and maple harvested from the company's 6,500 acres of forest in Pennsylvania and New York are lathed into the best bats in the business. Hillerich & Bradsby sells nearly two million bats per year to major leaguers, minor leaguers, and amateurs. According to the company, the typical big leaguer goes through about a hundred bats each season, custom ordering hardwood to account for the weight, length, barrel,

and handle dimensions that best suit his style. You can peruse the signatures of the thousands of big leaguers whose names have been burned onto Louisville Sluggers, as their names are displayed en masse in the museum's lobby on its Signature Wall. There is also a batting cage where you can take a few hacks using the bats once swung by the best hitters of all time.

The museum that tells the story of this uniquely American success story is open Monday through Saturday from 9:00 a.m. to 5:00 p.m., and Sunday from noon to 5:00 p.m. Admission costs $12.00 for adults and $7.00 for children age six through twelve. Factory tours run every day but Sunday, and every fan who takes the tour receives a miniature souvenir bat. For an additional fee, you can also design and personalize your own full-sized bat.

Even if your trip to Louisville occurs during the dead of night, or during some other time when visiting the museum is not possible, you should make a point to take a stroll along the **Louisville Slugger Walk of Fame.** It begins at Louisville Slugger Field—where the Pacific Coast League's Louisville Bats play—on East Main Street and continues for a full mile, until it ends at the Louisville Slugger Museum and Factory. It honors sixty players, most of whom were not only big-league stars but eventual Hall of Famers, all of whom swung Louisville Sluggers. For each player, there is a bronze bat leaned against a storefront, sidewalk bench, or other piece of the urban landscape, together with a bronze home plate noting the player's accomplishments. It is a unique, if somewhat selective, tribute to some of the game's best ever.

27. The World Wiffle Ball Championship

Channelside Park Wiffle Ball Complex
Main Street and McCormick Boulevard
Skokie, Illinois 60076
www.skokieparks.org/world-wiffleball-championship

It's Game Seven of the World Series . . . bottom of the ninth inning . . . down by three runs . . . bases loaded . . . two outs . . . a three-two count . . . the pitcher winds . . . you swing. . . .

Unless your name is David Ortiz, Kirk Gibson, Joe Carter, Bill Mazeroski, or Bobby Thomson, you will only dream of experiencing the adrenaline rush of standing in a batter's box in a packed stadium under such dramatic circumstances. But chances are you projected yourself into this imaginary role at least fifty times when you were a kid, probably as the shadows of your dad's garage rendered the backyard too dark to see, obscuring the fluttering plastic ball that had provided you and your friends with an evening of enjoyable competition. And chances are your imagination has wandered in this direction at least a few times *since* you were a kid, when you and your buddies or family members played a game of Wiffle Ball.

Since its invention in Shelton, Connecticut, in 1953, Wiffle Ball has made dreamers of us all. The game was the perfect antidote for a rapidly urbanizing America that no longer provided every neighborhood with 5 acres of open space suitable for hardball, or with eighteen like-minded individuals to facilitate a game even if such a field existed. With its plastic ball perforated on one side and its 30-inch-long yellow plastic bat, Wiffle Ball introduced us to a baseball-like game that could be played in a fraction of the space and time needed for a real game. Furthermore, it reduced the number of players required for a game to two. And it eliminated the need for cumbersome and expensive equipment like bats, extra balls, gloves, bases, and catcher's gear.

As many as nineteen games at once take place during the opening rounds of the World Wiffle Ball Championship.

Nate Hansen prepares to take a mighty rip during the 2013 World Wiffle Ball Championship.

Through the decades, we have made Wiffle Ball a regular part of our recreational lives, bringing it along on camping expeditions, trips to the beach, company picnics, and other excursions. While the game's casual players number in the millions, it has also engendered a cult following of yellow-bat-toting gamers, who view it not so much as a game but as a sport. With a trip to the northern suburbs of Chicago, you can pay homage to this unique variation of the National Pastime and to the legion of athletes who choose to play it for keeps . . . as well as for fun. The oldest and largest Wiffle Ball tournament in the country takes place in Skokie, Illinois, where it is organized by the Skokie Park District under the direction of Jim Bottorff, who cofounded the annual summer extravaganza in 1980.

Until 2013, the tournament had been based in Mishawaka, Indiana, though it has also held regional tournaments through the years in Baltimore; Indianapolis; Los Angeles; Eugene, Oregon; Barcelona, Spain; and Skokie. Now, the World Wiffle Ball Championship takes place over the course of the second weekend in July at Skokie's 20-acre Channelside Park. Three of the park's soccer fields are reconfigured to produce nineteen Wiffle Ball diamonds, suitable to accommodate players from across the United States who travel to Skokie for the event. Each team consists of four or five players, who fork over a modest entry fee for the privilege of testing their mettle against the best Wiffle Ballers on the planet.

The tournament's slogan is "Where the kids play with the kids-at-heart," and on the first day of the event, the matches bear this out. Anyone over the age of ten is eligible to participate, and, as a single-division open event, the tournament's brackets might match a squad of twelve-year-olds against a team of middle-aged men, or you might see five guys playing against five women. Sometimes fathers wind up playing with (or against) their sons or daughters. Usually the teams that move on to the finals on Sunday are composed of men in their twenties or early thirties, but on that first day all participants, young and old, dream of a world title.

The tournament was born in the summer of 1980, when Bottorff and his childhood friend Larry Grau were working summer jobs for the Mishawaka parks department but at different ends of the city. The two teens hatched a plan so they could spend more time hanging out together during the workweek. They unified their two youth sports camps by creating a Wiffle Ball league for the kids they counseled; then they staged a big tournament at the end of the summer. For several years the two founders kept the tournament going as a regular summer event. Even after they moved away from Mishawaka, they and several of their old friends would reunite to play Wiffle Ball once a year in their hometown. As the tournament became a national event, other Mishawakans kept it going. A Mishawaka family services agency organized the twenty-five-year-old World Wiffle Ball Championship from 2005 to 2012. Then, in 2013, management of the tournament reverted back to Bottorff, who moved it 120 miles west, to near his home in Chicago.

The brand of Wiffle Ball that tournament participants play should not be confused with the version of Wiffle Ball known as "line ball" that most of us play. These games take place on fields with 6-foot-high outfield fences 85 feet from home plate, bases 40 feet apart, and pitchers' rubbers 30 feet from the plate. The players run the bases, unlike backyard line-ballers, and observe rules that allow for "pegging," so long as the runner is not struck above the neck. A batted ball returned to the pitcher before the batter reaches first base counts as a force-out no matter where the pitcher is standing. Games are scheduled for six innings, but the forty-five-minute time limit or fifteen-run mercy rule sometimes ends them sooner.

Watching nineteen games unfold all at once on the first day of the tournament is truly a sight to behold. It's sort of like the first days of the NCAA Division I basketball tournament in March, when the action is fast and furious and you don't even know where you should be directing your attention. There may not be a crack of the bat to hear, and the players may not "flash the leather," but there are plenty of home runs to see, plenty of diving catches, plenty of baffling trick pitches, and plenty of late-inning heroics as players dig into the batters' boxes with their games and seasons on the line. It's every Wiffle Baller's fantasy, and it plays out over and over again on this one special weekend each summer in Skokie, Illinois.

A home run sails over an outfield fence adorned with pennants commemorating the winners of past World Wiffle Ball Championships.

Built in 1922 and added to the National Register of Historic Places in 1997, Henley Field's life as a functional professional ballpark appeared to be in the distant past as the twenty-first century dawned. Although the days when the Detroit Tigers had used it as their Grapefruit League home from 1934 through 1965 were distant memory, the park was at least aging gracefully, serving as home to the Lakeland High School Dreadnoughts and Florida Southern College Moccasins. Then, something rather amazing happened: The baseball gods breathed new life into the old park, granting it one magical throwback season.

As Lakeland embarked upon a $10 million project to renovate and expand Joker Marchant Stadium, the very facility that had replaced Henley Field as Lakeland's spring training and minor-league hub in 1966, the city realized it would need a temporary home for its Florida State League Lakeland Tigers. The work on Joker Marchant would take all of the summer and fall of 2002, and the local minor-league team needed a place to play. Re-enter Henley Field, which received a $250,000 renovation prior to the 2002 season to make it a viable temporary home for the Tigers' Class A team. After not hosting a professional game since 1965, the field that had once seen Babe Ruth, Joe DiMaggio, Ted Williams, and other stars of baseball's glory era on its lawn welcomed future big leaguers like Jeremy Bonderman, Brian Moehler, and Jason Frasor for a season of Florida State League ball. Thus, the local fans that huddled in Henley's cozy grandstand each night were treated to a version of the minor-league game the way it used to be. And they loved it.

Today, you can still watch the Florida Southern Moccasins play at this charming old ballpark. Florida Southern is more often cited for its golf

28. Henley Field

1125 North Florida Avenue
Lakeland, Florida 33805
http://fscmocs.com/sport
.asp?sportID=1

alumni (Rocco Mediate, Lee Janzen), but its baseball team is a perennial Division II powerhouse too. The team entered the 2014 season under the head coaching of alum and former big leaguer Lance Niekro with nine national championships to their credit. In addition to Niekro, who was a second-round pick in the Major League Baseball draft in 2000, Florida Southern has also sent plenty of other players on to professional baseball, including familiar names like Rob Dibble, Matt Joyce, and Brett Tomko. In the first decade of the 2000s, the grandson of Hall of Famer Al Kaline—who had played at Henley Field during the first several spring trainings of his long career with the Tigers—joined the Moccasins. An infielder, Colin Kaline was drafted by the Tigers in the twenty-sixth round of the 2011 MLB draft but has yet to make it to the major leagues.

Arriving at Henley Field today, you are met with an attractive exterior that takes the form of earth-tone yellow stucco. After buying tickets at one of the old-fashioned ticket windows on either side of the main entrance, you pass through the narrow arched entrance to the grandstand. Inside, there is room for just 800 people on the metal bleacher benches that were added as part of the 2002 renovation. All of the benches are covered by the low grandstand roof, so there's

After not hosting a professional game since 1965, Henley Field came out of retirement to serve as home to the Class A Lakeland Tigers during the 2002 season.

no need to worry if you're headed to the park on a rainy night. And all of the seats are further protected from any harm that might become their patrons by a see-through backstop screen that spans the entire front of the grandstand.

Henley Field is named for Clare Henley, the Lakeland druggist who convinced the city to buy the land upon which the ballpark was built. According to local lore, the property was owned by a dentist named Pike Adair, and Mr. Henley simultaneously convinced Adair to sell his vacant lot, and the city to buy the land and construct the park. Then Henley lured the Cleveland Indians to

Lakeland to make Henley Field their spring training home. The Indians made spring trips to Lakeland from 1924 through 1927, then Henley Field was without a big-league spring training tenant for a few years before the Tigers arrived in 1934. Mr. Henley eventually came to own several pharmacies in the area and would sell game tickets at his stores. In 1952, after Lakeland was well established as a Grapefruit League bastion, the city honored Mr. Henley by renaming "Athletic Field," as it was originally known, "Clare 'Doc' Henley Ball Park," which was later condensed to Henley Field.

This book would not be complete if it did not include a chapter encouraging you to explore the best ballpark neighborhood in the bigs. Whether you find yourself in the Windy City during the heat of summer, when tickets to the Wrigley Field bleachers fetch several times face value on the black market, or during the chill of winter when "The Hawk" whips off Lake Michigan making baseball season seem ages away, you should be sure to visit the streets surrounding America's second-oldest big-league park. What the North Side lacks in public parking, it more than makes up for in pubs, sports bars, and restaurants that embrace baseball's lovable losers, the Chicago Cubs. No matter the time of year, people of good cheer can be found congregating to tip back a few frosty mugs and talk a little baseball.

There are dozens of watering holes and restaurants worthy of your attention in Wrigleyville. Almost all of them display collections of Cubs memorabilia, and many feature menu items creatively named after beloved local players. This chapter highlights a handful of these hangouts, but you should visit for yourself to decide which Wrigleyville joints are your personal favorites.

The Cubby Bear (1059 West Addison Street) has welcomed thirsty fans to the corner of Addison and Clark—kitty-corner to Wrigley Field's distinctive red marquee—since opening as the Cubs Pub in 1946. It has gradually expanded to the point where its 30,000 square feet of floor space today offer seventy-five flat-screen TVs and five projection screens. If there's an out-of-town game you're hoping to see, you will find it on at least one of the tubes here. When the Cubs are playing an afternoon game, they open the doors at 10:00 a.m. to serve Old Style beer and Chicago-style hot dogs (a wiener topped with diced onion, tomato, relish, pickle, mustard, and

29. Wrigleyville

Neighborhood Surrounding
Wrigley Field
1060 West Addison Street
Chicago, Illinois 60613

peppers on a steamed poppy seed bun) to start you off right.

Another classic Cubs haunt, **Murphy's Bleachers** (3655 North Sheffield Avenue) began as a hot dog stand called Ernie's Bleachers in the 1930s, and then became Ray's Bleachers in 1965, and then Murphy's Bleachers in 1980, when it was bought by Jim Murphy. It is located at the corner of Waveland and Sheffield, just outside the entrance to the Wrigley Field bleachers. The beer garden is a great place to watch the crowd gather on game day, or to score tickets from a fellow patron who has decided to spend the next few hours at Murphy's, rather than in the hot sun across the street. As an added attraction, Murphy's houses a small Cubs museum that showcases, among other items, a miniature replica of Wrigley Field.

If you're looking to shake the dust off your lumber, you can visit **Sluggers** (3540 North Clark Street), which has several batting cages within its large second-floor game room. That's right, indoor batting cages at a bar! Why don't we find this in every city? According to legendary Cubs fan Ronnie Woo Woo, who can often be found cutting a rug at Sluggers, local son John Cusack used to take batting practice upstairs on a regular basis before he made it big in Hollywood.

Fans wait for home-run balls on Waveland Avenue during batting practice.

Goose Island Brew Pub (3535 North Clark Street) is another popular pre- and postgame hangout. Here's betting you'll enjoy its large mural that depicts several of the game's all-time greats playing the game they loved. While marveling at the likenesses of Hank Aaron, Joe Jackson, Walter Johnson, and Babe Ruth, you can sip pints of their delicious microbrew.

Merkle's Bar and Grill (3516 North Clark Street), named for the New York Giants rookie whose baserunning blunder paved the way for the Cubs to narrowly win the National League pennant in 1908, is another excellent choice, as it offers a festive atmosphere and nice collection of memorabilia.

You should also sample the famous deep-dish pizza at **Giordano's Famous Stuffed Pizza** (140 West Belmont Avenue), where the pies are made with the marinara on top of the mozzarella. The hot dogs and Italian dipped beef at **Clark Street Dog** (3040 North Clark Street)

should also be on your Wrigleyville checklist, along with a precautionary bottle of Tums. **The Wiener Circle** (2622 North Clark Street), which also specializes in Chicago-style hot dogs, is another great place to grab an afternoon treat.

Finally, no trip to Wrigleyville would be complete without your visiting the ballpark for a game, tour, or simply to trace its perimeter, which is adorned by statues of Cubs greats Ernie Banks, Ron Santo, Billy Williams, and longtime broadcaster Harry Caray. Should you opt to take the $25.00 ballpark tour—offered daily from March through September between 11:00 a.m. and 3:00 p.m. when the Cubs are on the road or playing an evening home game—you get to walk through the stands and onto the field. On non-game days, you even get to visit the Cubs clubhouse and dugout. For more information, visit the Tours page on the Cubs website at http://chicago.cubs.mlb.com/chc/ballpark/tours/index.jsp?content=daily.

Baseball fans received some disappointing news in early 2007 when it was announced that the Ted Williams Museum and Hitters Hall of Fame would be closing its doors for the final time at its diamond-shaped facility in Hernando, Florida. Unfortunately, the museum had experienced a decline in visitors at its out-of-the-way location in the north-central part of the Sunshine State, where Williams spent his later days. When "The Kid" was alive, it had attracted prominent players, past and present, and other prominent Americans like Muhammad Ali, George H. W. Bush, Bob Costas, Curt Gowdy, and Bobby Orr, who brought with them crowds of baseball fans. But after Ted's passing in 2002, the project that had been so close to Williams's heart since its opening in 1994 could no longer draw enough celebrities and fans to sustain its operations.

Within just a few days of announcing it would be closing, though, the museum issued another press release, this one to announce that it had brokered a deal with the Tampa Bay Rays to move to Tropicana Field its plethora of artifacts chronicling Williams's life in baseball, the military, and as a fisherman. And so in March of 2007 the Ted Williams Museum and Hitters Hall of Fame began its second life on the Trop's outfield concourse. No lesser a star than Mariano Rivera, whose Yankees were spending spring training in nearby Tampa, cut the ribbon on the date of the new facility's grand opening. And just like that, an already excellent baseball museum became even more convenient to visit than ever before. Sure, the museum is only open when the Rays have a home game, but your ballpark admission is also good for entrance to the museum. And the museum hosts special events outside of the baseball season when you can sometimes visit.

30. The Ted Williams Museum and Hitters Hall of Fame

Tropicana Field
1 Tropicana Drive
St. Petersburg, Florida 33705
www.tedwilliamsmuseum.com

Within its designated space on the right side of the Trop's rotunda, the museum showcases such novelties as Williams's minor-league contract to play for the Minneapolis Millers, a 150-pound stuffed tarpon that he caught on fly equipment in the Florida Keys, his golf clubs, his rifle, pictures of him in his World War II flight gear, and exhibits honoring the great stars of the Negro Leagues and Williams's friend Sadaharu Oh, the Japanese home-run king.

The centerpiece of the museum is the Hitters Hall of Fame, which celebrates the accomplishments of the twenty greatest hitters (other than Williams) who ever lived, as well as the achievements of more recent hitters who have since been added to the exclusive group. The original twenty whom Williams chose are Babe Ruth, Lou Gehrig, Jimmie Foxx, Rogers Hornsby, Joe DiMaggio, Ty Cobb, Stan Musial, Joe Jackson, Hank Aaron, Willie Mays, Hank Greenberg, Mickey Mantle, Tris Speaker, Al Simmons, Johnny Mize, Mel Ott, Harry Heilmann, Frank Robinson, Mike Schmidt, and Ralph Kiner. Each is honored with a display case of memorabilia and photographs. Among the more than fifty subsequent inductees are old Red Sox friends of Williams like Dom DiMaggio, Carlton Fisk, Dwight Evans, Carl Yastrzemski, and Jim Rice, as well as the barred-from-Cooperstown

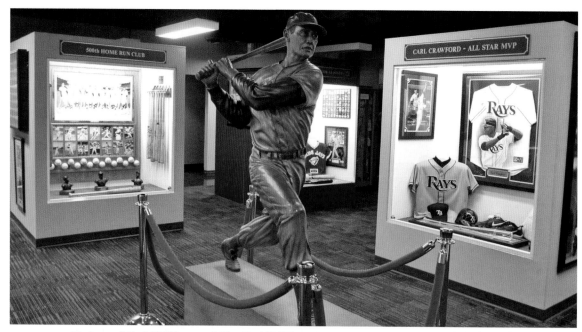

Statue of Ted Williams at the Ted Williams Museum and Hitters Hall of Fame

Pete Rose and more recent stars like Ryne Sandberg and Roberto Alomar.

Upon moving to the Trop, the Museum began inducting pitchers to its Pitching Wall of Great Achievement, thus opening its doors to hurlers as well as batsmen. Several pitchers have since been inducted. Other highlights of the museum include a Cy Young exhibit that showcases memorabilia from Rays star David Price's 2012 American League Cy Young Award–winning campaign; a Triple Crown exhibit that honors Miguel Cabrera—the latest player to lead his league in batting average, home runs, and runs batted in—as well as other trifecta winners like Mantle and Williams; and a "League of Their Own" display that honors the women who played in the All-American Girls Professional Baseball League in the mid-1900s when the men were away at war.

The museum opens two hours before each Rays home game and stays open through the sixth inning. It also hosts several special events annually, ranging from autograph signings, to charity auctions, to ceremonies honoring special players who are visiting town. The yearly induction ceremony—usually held in early February—serves as a one-night elixir to local fans who can't wait for pitchers and catchers to report to their spring camps in the coming month. Recent years have seen stars like Wade Boggs, Price, Ben Zobrist, Chris Archer, and Alex Cobb headline the induction festivities. The more than a thousand people who attend are treated to a white-tablecloth dinner served on the Trop lawn. They enjoy a night of baseball talk, and get to mingle with the current and former players on hand. The class of 2014 included hitters Craig Biggio, Johnny Damon, and Frank Howard, and pitchers James Shields, Dwight Gooden, and Jim "Mudcat" Grant.

Williams's daughter Claudia Williams also visited the Museum during 2014 to sign copies of her memoir, *Ted Williams, My Father,* during a Rays' game.

In March of 2012, a month before Boston celebrated the one hundredth anniversary of Fenway Park's opening, Fort Myers opened the most awe-inspiring replica yet of Fenway's famed Green Monster. Although knock-off Monsters have stood for years in backyards across New England and even at minor-league ballparks in cities like Portland, Maine, and Greenville, South Carolina, where Red Sox minor-league affiliates play, fans knew from the start that the big green wall at the Red Sox new spring training complex in Southwest Florida was in a class by itself.

The Fort Myers Monster contributes to a ballpark effect so amazingly like the one at Fenway that you'll almost wonder if you're in Beantown. And yet, it's different in one very important way: In Boston, the Wall has seats on its very top, offering a bird's-eye view of the game. In Fort

31. The Fort Myers Monster

JetBlue Park at Fenway South
11500 Fenway South Drive
Fort Myers, Florida 33913
(888) 733-7696
www.leeparks.org/facility-info/facility-details.cfm?Project_Num=0050

Myers, they have those, but they also have seats *inside* the towering green edifice.

That's right, behind a protective mesh screen, you find three rows of the most unusual seats in professional baseball. You can actually watch the game from inside the wall. Struck

The big green wall in Fort Myers rises 6 feet higher than the one at Fenway Park in Boston.

The replica of Fenway Park's famous Green Monster at JetBlue Park in Fort Myers offers a seating area inside the wall.

balls that hit below or above the long viewing window carom off the wall and back toward the infield. Balls that hit the mesh either fall harmlessly down onto the left field warning track where they are in play, or not-so-harmlessly come crashing through the netting into the seating areas where they eventually come to rest as ground-rule doubles.

Built as the centerpiece of a multi-field Grapefruit League facility that cost $77.8 million, JetBlue Park offers you the chance to experience many of the other traditions fans enjoy at regular season games in Boston too. You can eat a Fenway Frank, drink a Sam Adams, high-five Wally the Green Monster, rock out to "Sweet Caroline" in the eighth inning, and watch a game played on a field that traces the same footprint as the Fenway lawn. Aside from the local Monster beginning its ascent 310 feet from home plate, just like in Beantown, the park replicates

Fenway's right-center-field triangle, which measures 420 feet from the batter's box, right field bullpens that lie 380 feet from home, and even its quirky Pesky Pole in right, which stands just 302 feet from home plate. The Red Sox' retired numbers even hang on the facing of the right field grandstand, appearing in their familiar Fenway location and order, reading from left to right: 9 (Ted Williams); 4 (Joe Cronin); 1 (Bobby Doerr); 8 (Carl Yastrzemski); 27 (Carlton Fisk); 6 (Johnny Pesky); 14 (Jim Rice); 42 (Jackie Robinson).

There are subtle differences though, besides the obvious incongruity of there being fans sitting inside the trademark green wall. One big difference is that the Fort Myers Monster tops out at 43 feet high, whereas the one in Boston climbs *only* 37 feet, 6 inches above the field. Another aspect of the Fort Myers Monster that's similar to but different from *the* Monster is its scoreboard. The manually operated board on the facing of the Fort Myers Monster is the very one that displayed the game's line-score at Fenway from the 1970s until 2001, when a new Fenway board was installed. But unlike at Fenway, there is no room inside the Fort Myers Monster for a scoreboard attendant to update the score from inside the wall. At JetBlue, the attendant sits in foul territory while the game is in progress, then treks onto the warning track with a stepladder during lulls in the game to quickly update the numbers. One of the very first games ever played at JetBlue was an exhibition between the Red Sox and Northeastern University. After the Red Sox won 25–0, the scoreboard attendant estimated that he had dragged his ladder out some one hundred times over the course of the evening!

In case you're wondering, JetBlue—which ferries snowbirds from Boston's Logan International Airport to Southwest Florida Airport each

March aboard jets bearing oversized imprints of the Red Sox logo—paid $1 million for naming rights to the park in a deal that runs through 2020. Outside the park, a tail fin from an actual JetBlue jet rises like a monument.

Not only will you find opportunities to visit JetBlue during March, but the stadium and its several practice fields are used for various tournaments and youth competitions throughout the summer and fall. One interesting league that utilizes JetBlue and a handful of other spring training venues offers senior citizens the chance to relive the glory days of their youth. The Roy Hobbs Baseball World Series uses JetBlue Park in October and November. Vintage Division players must be over age sixty-five but younger than seventy; Timeless Division players are seventy to seventy-five; and Forever Young Division players are over seventy-five. Attending one of these games allows you more time and freedom to explore JetBlue Park than attending a sold-out spring training game, but you won't get to sing along to "Sweet Caroline" or to participate in some of those other Red Sox rituals.

• •

Baseball's blue highways lead to a wide range of sculptures related to the Grand Old Game. These days, practically every big-league park offers at least a few life-size statues of the home team's former stars. You can find Ted Williams outside Fenway Park in Boston, Kirby Puckett outside Target Field in Minneapolis, Stan Musial outside Busch Stadium in St. Louis, Willie Mays outside AT&T Park in San Francisco, Roberto Clemente outside PNC Park in Pittsburgh, and Bob Feller outside Progressive Field in Cleveland. Some cities and teams go to even greater lengths to fuse baseball and art, moving beyond realistic tribute pieces into the realm of abstract works that make their own statements about the special place the game holds in the hearts and minds of local connoisseurs.

Outside Safeco Field in Seattle, for example, you'll find a giant bronze baseball mitt with a hole in the middle to symbolize the ball. Outside Coors Field in Denver, you find an ornate arched entryway decorated with colorful sculptures that trace the evolution of the ball in all of its many forms, from tetherballs to meatballs, to crystal balls, to mothballs, to Christmas-tree

32. *Batcolumn*

⟨⟩

600 West Madison Street
Chicago, Illinois 60661

balls, to dozens of sports balls, including, of course, baseballs. Outside Comerica Park in Detroit, you are greeted by giant concrete tigers that lurk above the entrance gates. And throughout Marlins Park in Miami you find works by world-renowned artists on display, as well as ballpark fixtures—like the colorful home-run sculpture in left-center field—that reflect the aesthetic vision of Jeffrey Loria, who before he bought the Marlins made his millions as a professional art dealer.

To visit the granddaddy of all baseball sculptures, though, you should set your compass for the Windy City, where there stands a 101-foot-tall, 20-ton, shiny metal baseball bat. The massive monument stands in neither of the city's two famous baseball neighborhoods, but rather almost exactly midway between them, in front of the Harold Washington Social Security Administration building. Known as *Batcolumn*, the piece was commissioned jointly by the Art in Architecture Program of the United States General Services Administration and the National Endowment for the Arts. It was created by Swedish artist Claes Oldenburg.

Oldenburg, who spent part of his childhood in Chicago during the 1950s when his father was stationed in the city as a Swedish diplomat, began the sculpture in 1975 and completed it in 1977. His other works, which can be found in cities around the world, include an oversize hot dog, a giant clothespin, a big lipstick tube, a massive toothbrush, and an enormous ashtray. His hallmark was transforming otherwise mundane objects into massive pieces of pop art.

But there's nothing mundane about a baseball bat, and Oldenburg did well to create in *Batcolumn* a work that captures the essence and power of the slugger's best friend. Even when viewed from blocks away, there's no doubting that this tapered metal column that grows ever higher and wider in a web of intricate steel latticework is a baseball bat. *Batcolumn* ranks right up there with the 120-foot-tall bat that breaks the skyline in Louisville, Kentucky, as the most striking (if you'll excuse the pun) of baseball landmarks.

A plaque on the piece's concrete base reads:

> For his commission to create a public sculpture for the Social Security Administration building, Claes Oldenburg selected the baseball bat as an emblem of Chicago's ambition and vigor. The sculpture's verticality echoes the city's dramatic skyline, while its form and scale cleverly allude to more traditional civic monuments, such as obelisks and memorial columns.

Whether or not you find yourself reflecting on the ways in which *Batcolumn* resembles "more traditional civic monuments, such as obelisks and memorial columns," upon standing in its shadows, you're sure to find a trip to see it worthwhile. After your visit, here's guessing you'll never again look at your 34-inch softball bat or 30-inch Wiffle Ball bat the same way.

The 101-foot-tall *Batcolumn* has stood in Chicago since 1977.

There are several compelling reasons why any lover of the game, its history, and its old parks should make a special effort to visit the home of the Pawtucket Red Sox. First, McCoy Stadium presents you with one of the few remaining opportunities to visit a fully functioning stadium built by President Franklin Delano Roosevelt's Works Progress Administration, which set to work millions of unemployed people during the Great Depression. The park's charming covered grandstand, which is supported by steel pillars that rise up sporadically from the grandstand seats, dates back to 1942. Sitting under the roof on a warm summer's night will bring you back to an earlier time in the game's history when ballparks of this kind were common.

More than that, McCoy—which has been home to the top team in the Red Sox minor-league

33. McCoy Stadium

◇◇

1 Columbus Avenue
Pawtucket, Rhode Island 02860
401-724-7300
www.milb.com/index.jsp?sid=t533

system since 1973—possesses a rich history, the details of which are well represented by colorful displays on its concourses, which turn it into a sort of living baseball museum. These exhibits celebrate the International League Triple Crown that Jim Rice won as a member of the "PawSox" in 1974, the batting title Wade Boggs claimed in 1981, the classic pitcher's duel between Yankees prospect Dave Righetti and New England native Mark Fidrych in 1982, the perfect game Bronson Arroyo pitched in 2003, and so on.

Claiming the most space of all on the concourse, though, is a seemingly endless line score that tells the story of the longest game in professional baseball history, which since 1981 has been McCoy Stadium's claim to fame. That year, the Pawtucket Red Sox and Rochester Red Wings locked horns for a thirty-three-inning game that began on a chilly night on the Saturday before Easter Sunday. The game began at 8:25 p.m. After the Red Wings carried a 1–0 lead into the bottom of the ninth, the PawSox scored a run on a wild pitch to send the game into extras. Twelve innings later, and well after midnight, the Red Wings took a 2–1 lead in the top of the twenty-first. But in the bottom of that

Mural of former Pawtucket Red Sox and Boston Red Sox first baseman Carlos Quintana

McCoy Stadium's covered grandstand dates back to an original opening in 1942.

inning, the PawSox knotted the game on a double by Boggs. And the innings kept rolling along, while the fans kept shivering, nodding off, and then eventually heading home to bed. On the orders of the league president, the game was finally suspended at 4:07 a.m. on Easter morning after thirty-two innings.

A few months later, in June, the teams resumed play at a time when the big leaguers were on strike. With nearly 6,000 fans on hand and the national media attention focused on Pawtucket, Rhode Island, it took just eighteen minutes and less than one full inning to settle the epic affair. Pawtucket's Dave Koza knocked a bases-loaded single into left field in the bottom of the thirty-third to score Marty Barrett and give the PawSox a 3–2 win. Future Hall of Famers Boggs and Cal Ripken Jr. went 4 for 12 and 2 for 13 in the game, respectively. Future big leaguer Bob Ojeda, meanwhile, who pitched the top of the thirty-third, got credit for the win. In all, twenty-five future major leaguers played in the marathon, which included 219 at bats, 882 pitches, and 60 strikeouts, and took eight hours and twenty-five minutes to complete.

In case you're wondering, the longest major-league game ever was a twenty-six-inning tie played between the Brooklyn Robins and Boston Braves at Braves Field in 1920. There have also been two twenty-five-inning games, including one played by the White Sox and Brewers at Comiskey Park in 1984, and one between the Mets and Cardinals at Shea Stadium in 1974.

As if the chance to learn more about the longest professional baseball game still wasn't enough to lure you to Pawtucket, McCoy Stadium also offers one of the most impressive decorative flourishes in all of the minors. Adorning the concourses and entranceways, you find dozens of 3-by-6-foot murals of former PawSox who went on to make good in the majors, ranging from Don Aase to Bob Zupcic and nearly a hundred players in between. The PawSox began the tradition of honoring their notable alumni this way in the early 1980s when a team employee painted the giant likenesses of Boggs, Rice, Carlton Fisk, Bruce Hurst, John Tudor, Cecil Cooper, Fred Lynn, and Roger Clemens right onto the cement walls of McCoy Stadium's spiraling first base entrance ramp. When a renovation in the early 1990s necessitated that the paintings be sandblasted away, the PawSox commissioned a local artist to re-create nearly fifty of them on movable 4-by-8-foot panels.

In the early 2000s, though, another renovation added railings to the entrance ramps to make them wheelchair-accessible. This made the paintings too large to return to their original locations. The PawSox donated several of the paintings to the Pawtucket Armory Association at that time, and they were auctioned off to raise money for an arts-education center. After fans complained in the mid-2000s about the paintings' absence, however, the PawSox decided to restore and rehang dozens of the oldies still in storage, as well as to use digital technology to blow up some of the other old ones and to mount them along entrance ramps and concourses throughout McCoy. The team has not only returned the old favorites—like Oil Can Boyd, Butch Hobson, Sam Horn, and Steve Lyons—to the stadium walls, but has added the images of more recent Pawtucket stars like Jonathan Papelbon, Nomar Garciaparra, and Kevin Youkilis as well. No other minor-league team does as classy a job of honoring its legends, and for that reason, among all the others, McCoy Stadium is a thoroughly mesmerizing place to visit.

• •

Many of our most amazing baseball landmarks hardly have a chance of catching us by surprise. In Louisville and Chicago, for example, you can see those massive faux baseball bats from blocks and blocks away. In Boston, you need only drive into town on the Mass Pike or take a stroll along the banks of the Charles River to locate Fenway Park and its towering Green Monster. Elsewhere in the baseball universe, however, you do sometimes stumble upon a pot of baseball gold in a seemingly unlikely place, like a shopping mall.

Thanks to its unique location, the Roger Maris Museum in Fargo, North Dakota, is one of the game's least heralded and yet most accessible gems. You walk through the checkout line of Sears and into the main gallery of the West Acres Mall. You pass a Payless Shoe Store, and then a Nails Pro, and then you're confronted with the entrance of a wonderful little museum that makes you suddenly feel like you're twelve years old again and sitting on your grandpa's porch listening to the familiar twang of the local play-by-play announcer as twilight fades to full night and the game wends its way

34. The Roger Maris Museum

West Acres Shopping Center
3902 13th Avenue South
Fargo, North Dakota 58103
(701) 282-2222
www.rogermarismuseum.com

through the middle innings. Anytime the mall is open—which is every day of the year except for Easter, Thanksgiving, and Christmas—you can visit this surprisingly comprehensive tribute to a hometown hero the local folks never forgot.

Contrary to popular belief, Roger Maris was not born in Fargo—he was born in Hibbing, Minnesota—but his family moved to Fargo when his father was offered a position with the Great Northern Railroad, and he grew up in this lovely city, which was lauded then, as it is now, for being a friendly and entirely pleasant place to live. Back in the glory days of his youth, Roger Maras (as his name was then spelled) was a star football, track, and basketball player for Fargo Shanley High School. He only fiddled with baseball during the summer months, when he strapped on spikes for the local American Legion club. Football was his primary passion. After setting a high school record for the most return touchdowns in a game, bringing back four kickoffs against Devils Lake High to lead Shanley to a 32–27 victory in 1951, Maris earned a football scholarship to the University of Oklahoma but spent less than a semester there, before returning to Fargo and his high school sweetheart Pat Carvell, whom he would eventually marry.

On the heels of his American Legion success, Maris signed a $15,000 minor-league contract with the Cleveland Indians in 1953 and by 1957 he was in the big leagues. By 1960 he'd bounced from Cleveland to Kansas City to New York. And by October 1, 1961, as we all know, he'd turned in the greatest season for a power hitter the game had yet seen, bashing sixty-one long balls to overtake Babe Ruth's single-season record. Asterisk or no asterisk, it was an amazing feat.

What many fans fail to remember is that besides hitting those sixty-one dingers and winning the American League MVP Award that season, Maris had won the MVP the prior year too. More than being a one-hit (or sixty-one-hit)

Banners at the Roger Maris Museum commemorate each of Maris's record sixty-one home runs in 1961.

wonder, he made four consecutive All-Star teams from 1959 through 1962 and played in seven World Series in the 1960s as a member of the Yankees and Cardinals.

After retiring in 1968, Maris followed his old Cardinals' boss Gussie Busch's lead and got into the beer business, founding a Budweiser distributorship in Gainesville, Florida, where he and Pat settled. But he always retained his ties to Fargo. When he was approached in the early 1980s by museum developer and eventual curator Jim McLaughlin about contributing some of his keepsakes to a museum, the modest gentleman in him was reluctant to accept the honor. He finally yielded under the conditions that the tribute be—and always be—highly accessible and completely free to visitors. As such, the museum was designed to be open during all hours that the mall is open.

Since 1984, the museum has displayed an impressive collection of artifacts from all phases of Maris's sports career. You find photos and relics from his high school and American Legion days, his minor-league career—which included stints in Fargo-Moorhead, Keokuk, Tulsa, Reading, and Indianapolis—and his time with the Indians, Royals, Yankees, and Cardinals. The timeline tracing Maris's accomplishments and milestones is colorfully adorned by home-plate-shaped red-white-and-blue banners overhead that mark the date and location of each of Maris's sixty-one homers in 1961.

The exhibits related to Maris's Yankee days include a replica of his locker at Yankee Stadium, a massive bronze facsimile of the monument that stands to honor Maris in Yankee Stadium's Monument Park, and a theater that allows you to watch highlights of Maris's exploits from the relative comfort of actual 1960s-era Yankee Stadium seats. Both of Maris's MVP trophies are on display, as are his "Sultan of Swat" crowns from 1960 and 1961. A portrait of Maris posing with a bat in his Yankee uniform is another highlight, among the many baseball cards, bats, balls, photos, and trophies.

Sadly, Maris died of lymphoma in 1985 at age fifty-one. But he is remembered throughout this friendly city, where a celebrity golf tournament is still played in his name each June to raise money for the causes he held dear; Sanford Hospital welcomes patients to the Roger Maris Cancer Center; and a billboard stands on US 10 declaring "Fargo's Roger Maris" the "Legitimate Home Run King."

Maris's plot at **Holy Cross Catholic Cemetery** (1502 32nd Avenue North) is also worth a visit while you're in Fargo. There, a diamond-shaped headstone showcases the silhouette of Maris's swing, beside the caption, "61/61."

35. Historic Dodgertown

3901 26th Street
Vero Beach, Florida 32960
(772) 569-4900
http://historicdodgertown.com

After serving as the spring training home of the Brooklyn and Los Angeles Dodgers for more than six decades, the all-inclusive player-retreat Walter O'Malley and Branch Rickey created in the 1940s bid adieu to the spring game midway through the 2008 Grapefruit League season. But the tropical complex and quaint ballpark at its heart remain intact, thanks to a venture led by former Dodgers owner Peter O'Malley and former Dodgers pitchers Hideo Nomo and Chan Ho Park. Today, the 79-acre complex is a baseball camp that hosts an umpire school in the winter, college and high school baseball tournaments in the spring, and adult baseball camps in the summer.

You can visit Historic Dodgertown any time of year to stroll its scenic walkways named for the Dodgers greats. And you can visit Holman Stadium, which hosted the Dodgers and their March foes from 1953 until 2008.

Dodgertown was the brainchild of Rickey, the baseball visionary who also played an instrumental role in positioning Jackie Robinson to integrate the game. At a time when most big-league teams maintained affiliations with twenty or more minor-league clubs, Rickey envisioned a "baseball college" where he could bring together all 600 players in the Dodgers organization to teach them the finer points of "Dodgers baseball." He also wanted to create a

safe place—even in the Jim Crow South—where emerging African-American stars like Jackie Robinson, Don Newcombe, and Roy Campanella could train alongside their white teammates.

In 1949, Rickey brokered a deal with Vero Beach mayor Bud Holman to rent a decommissioned naval air base in the Atlantic coast town. Under Holman's direction, Vero Beach hastily chiseled baseball diamonds into abandoned airstrips and converted the military barracks into dormitories. Over the ensuing decades, Rickey and O'Malley turned the initially spartan site into a posh resort, building a movie theater, tennis courts, basketball courts, two golf courses, and a swimming pool for the players and their families. O'Malley also added such decorative flourishes to the complex as streetlights bearing illuminated baseball globes, an orange grove, and a heart-shaped pond that he presented to his wife, Kay, one year on Valentine's Day.

Other features of the complex developed more organically, like the patch of grass off Don Drysdale Way that came to be known as "Campy's Bullpen" after a wheelchair-bound Campanella made a spring habit of working there with young Dodgers catchers. A blue-and-white sign marks the spot where the legendary backstop would sit in the shade and bark out instructions to the youngsters.

But the centerpiece of Dodgertown was, and still is, Holman Stadium—one of the most delightful little ballparks pro ball has ever known, simply because there is so little about it that resembles a professional park. The field is surrounded not by walls but by a man-made hill that traces the perimeter of the diamond. Behind home plate and along the baselines, stadium seats are set right into the hills. Spectators would sit in the shade of the live oak trees growing between the seats, while the players would sit on uncovered

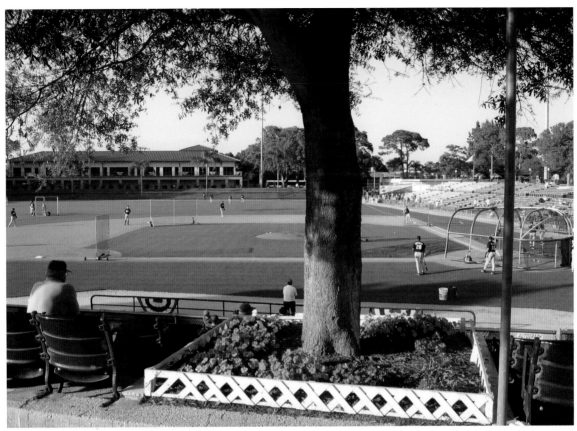

At Holman Stadium the big leaguers sat on uncovered benches instead of in dugouts, and the fans looked for spots beneath the live oak trees that grew in the stands.

benches at field level along the baselines. That's right, as recently as 2008 big leaguers were using this facility that more closely resembles an American Legion baseball field than a major-league or even collegiate one. The spring baseball scribes would rough it too, plying their trade in a wooden press box barely big enough to hold a dozen people. For years there wasn't an outfield fence, just a small hillside, but eventually a low stretch of chain-link was installed, like the kind you see at Little League fields.

As idyllic as this setting was and is, it is easy to see why the big-league game eventually passed it by for the glitz, glamour, and creature comforts

of modernity. And it's forgivable that the Dodgers abandoned the facility and their longstanding tenure in the Grapefruit League when they moved to a new $120 million complex that had been created for them to share with the White Sox in Phoenix. First, it made sense for a team that plays in Los Angeles to spend spring training closer to home, instead of subjecting its players and fans to cross-country flights. Second, Camelback Ranch, the team's new facility, has more modern facilities. And third, Camelback seats more than twice as many fans (about 13,000) as Holman Stadium.

After the Dodgers pulled their Florida State League team out of Vero Beach in 2007, relocating their Class A prospects to the California League, the big leaguers returned to Vero for one final truncated Grapefruit League season the next spring. They played their last Grapefruit League game on March 17, 2008, wearing green caps in honor of St. Patrick's Day. Before the game, Hall-of-Fame Dodgers manager Tommy Lasorda stood in full uniform, addressing the crowd from a microphone on the field. "We're going to leave," he said, "but we're not leaving our memories." Then, after the Dodgers fell to the Astros 12–10 before a sell-out crowd that stayed until the very last pitch, the Dodgers headed west to play the remainder of their spring schedule in the Cactus League, using the A's spring park, Phoenix Municipal Stadium, as a temporary home.

After the Dodgers' departure, Vero Beach made an effort to lure another big-league team to the complex that the Dodgers had been leasing for years. There was talk of the Orioles possibly moving to Vero, but that fell through when the Baltimore club signed a lease with Sarasota. That was when Peter O'Malley stepped in with a plan to transform the complex his father had built into a camp for amateur teams and tournaments. He enlisted the help of his two former players, Nomo and Park, and a handful of other investors, and Vero Beach Sports Village was born. Frank McCourt, the Dodgers owner at the time, refused to let the Dodgers name be attached to the complex. Then in 2013, after McCourt had sold the Dodgers in disgrace, O'Malley petitioned Dodgers president Stan Kasten for permission to call the camp Dodgertown once again, and received the licensing rights to "Historic Dodgertown."

You'll find that not much has changed since the Dodgers left town. Peter O'Malley has kept it looking much as it did during his childhood, when he and his sister Terry would stomp around the orange grove with the children of the Dodgers players and coaches. What you will notice is that the complex sees nearly year-round use now, as starry-eyed youths, collegians, and adults play and practice on the very fields once graced by giants of the game like Pee Wee Reese, Robinson, Drysdale, Sandy Koufax, and Fernando Valenzuela.

36. The Water Spectacular at Kauffman Stadium

1 Royal Way
Kansas City, Missouri 64129
http://kansascity.royals.mlb.com/kc/
ballpark/information/index
.jsp?content=moreinfo

No tour of America's baseball landmarks would be complete if you didn't visit the best ballpark accoutrement of them all. Sure, the Diamondbacks have their outfield swimming pool, the Rays have their "touch tank" full of fish, and the Reds have their riverboat smokestacks, but those flourishes don't mesmerize the eyes and soothe the soul like the Royals' amazing water fountain does. Designed by team founder Ewing Kauffman to play off Kansas City's "City of Fountains" nickname, the Water Spectacular at Kauffman Stadium stretches an amazing 322 feet, beginning above the fence in right field and running all the way into left-center. Paid for by Kauffman himself, who sank $1.5 million into its construction in the early 1970s, it remains the largest privately funded fountain in the world.

The Kauffman Stadium fountains shoot water high into the air as players warm up on the field between innings.

But it's more than just a fountain; it's also a waterfall. The water cascades down 10 feet, from an upper pool to a midlevel pool, then cascades down another 10 feet to a third pool below. While the players and fans are concentrating on the game, the water unobtrusively trickles down the black facing between the levels. There's a reason why rich people build small waterfalls in their living rooms, and why the rest of us have a "waterfall" setting on the white-noise/sleep-aid machines we buy for our nightstands. The fans nearest the waterfalls—a 2009 renovation added three sections of outfield seats above and below the water, as well as a Fountain bar, and a patio where you can stand and watch the game—hear the most tranquil of ballpark sounds. And no matter where you're sitting in the park, you see the water glimmering in the sun, or beneath the ballpark lights, as your backdrop to the game. It's present, but not distracting: just the right kind of ballpark accent. Then, between innings, the Water Spectacular becomes much more than just an accent. It becomes a fountain, shooting water from the middle pool several stories into the air. At night, colored lights shine on the water, creating an effect that truly is . . . well . . . spectacular!

The $250 million renovation the Royals completed between 2007 and 2009 made the Water Spectacular so much more accessible to us fans than it had been previously when there was no seating in the outfield. Now, you can walk right up to the waterfalls and feel the mist when the geysers erupt. Besides adding the walkway and seats, the project also installed a festive outfield plaza that makes it possible for you to encircle the entire field via the first level concourse. On the plaza, statues honor George Brett, Frank White, and Dick Howser. Not far away, a kids' area offers a baseball-themed minigolf course, a carousel, a miniature diamond with 100-foot home-run fences, batting cages, video games, and more.

The **Royals Hall of Fame** in straightaway left field home-run territory is another highlight of the renovation. The 7,000-square-foot emporium replaced a small hall of fame display case that used to stand on the first level concourse behind home plate. To access this colorful museum, you walk through a tunnel like the one that runs from the Royals clubhouse to the dugout. Once there, you find lockers set up to honor Brett, White, and Howser, the 1985 World Series trophy, a giant No. 5 sculpture made of a bat and 3,154 baseballs (one for each of Brett's career hits), White's Gold Glove Award trophies, a replica of the Royals dugout, and displays honoring the minor-league Kansas City Blues and Negro League Monarchs.

Farther afield, a stroll along the first level concourse eventually takes you to Section 127 behind home plate, where Seat 9 in Row C is colored red, amid a sea of otherwise Royal blue stadium chairs. The **Buck O'Neil Legacy Seat** honors Mr. O'Neil, the late Negro Leagues star who became a household name after Ken Burns's wonderful PBS documentary *Baseball* introduced him to modern fans. O'Neil was an advocate for Kansas City's Negro Leagues Baseball Museum in his later years, as well as a goodwill ambassador for the game in general.

Whether visiting the O'Neil seat, circling the concourse in pursuit of a ballpark treat, or settling into your upper level seat, you can see the Water Spectacular, a signature ballpark feature that's been wowing visiting fans and players for generations.

• •

37. Chappell's Restaurant and Sports Museum

323 Armour Road
North Kansas City, Missouri 64116
(816) 421-0002
www.chappellsrestaurant.com/
chappells/hours.asp

Just a short ride from Kauffman Stadium, you can peruse what is almost certainly the largest collection of sports memorabilia housed in any bar or restaurant in the United States. Since opening in 1986, Chappell's Restaurant and Sports Museum has steadily expanded its physical dimensions and sports collection to the point where it now includes more than 10,000 items. Clearly, the place is a labor of love for owner Jim Chappell, a longtime friend of former Kansas City and Oakland A's owner Charlie O. Finley, who delights in leading first-time visitors from wall to wall, while providing background information on his collection's most interesting pieces. So popular has this unique restaurant/museum been through the years, that in 2013 Mr. Chappell was inducted into the Missouri Sports Hall of Fame in recognition of his extraordinary career as a "sports museum entrepreneur."

Some of the artifacts on display date back to Mr. Chappell's boyhood days, when he first started

Memorabilia adorns the walls and ceiling at Chappell's Restaurant and Sports Museum.

collecting. Others have been purchased since the restaurant opened. There's a pair of boxing gloves that Muhammad Ali autographed; more than 1,000 football helmets, including the three that Joe Montana donated—one each from his days with Notre Dame, the San Francisco 49ers, and the Kansas City Chiefs; Olympic torches from two different Olympic Games; the trunks worn by Sylvester Stallone in *Rocky*; Super Bowl rings; team pennants; antique athletic equipment; scores of autographed jerseys; and more.

For traveling baseball fans, Chappell's most interesting item is the 1974 World Series trophy, a gift from Finley, who apparently had trophies to spare after his rough-and-tumble A's won their third title in a row, beating the Dodgers. Also noteworthy are baseballs autographed by dozens of diamond kings like Babe Ruth, Ty Cobb, and Dizzy Dean; vintage baseball uniforms; a beautiful LeRoy Neiman painting of George Brett that is autographed by both the artist and the subject; Chesterfield cigarette posters featuring Ted Williams and Stan Musial—and that's just the tip of the iceberg. All of the available wall and ceiling space is covered with sports memorabilia. Even the men's and women's bathrooms are laden with location-appropriate sports keepsakes. The ladies' room, for example, displays a copy of the *Sports Illustrated* cover story "The Lady is an Ump," as well as a Vassar College pennant, and photos of Chris Evert and Martina Navratilova.

Your best bet is to visit during the middle of the day or early evening, before it gets too crowded, then to order a cold drink and amble around for a while before settling at a table or on a barstool. That's one of the nice things about

Chappell's: It is laid out in a way that leaves room for you to wander without getting in the way of the staff or other patrons. There is no admission charge if you just want to check out the sports artifacts and depart, but you'll likely find it impossible to leave without dropping a few dollars on one of the trademark menu items, like the filet mignons wrapped in bacon, delicious Kansas City strip steaks, and crispy curly fries.

Chappell's, which has been cited as one of the best sports bars in the country by the *Chicago Tribune*, *USA Today*, and *Sports Illustrated*, attracts visitors from around the country. It is open Monday through Thursday from 11:00 a.m. to 10:00 p.m. and on Friday and Saturday from 11:00 a.m. to 11:00 p.m. It has been the weekly meeting site of a college class on sports memorabilia, taught by a local professor from Northwest Missouri State, and it was recently the setting for a book by a local author who partnered with Mr. Chappell to recall some of the more interesting sports conversations that took place within its walls during its first quarter-century of operation. *Conversations at Chappell's* (2012) by Matt Fulks and Jim Chappell describes Chappell's as a "sports version of the Hard Rock Cafe, the Louvre, and Grauman's Chinese Theatre rolled up in one." Whether or not you're familiar with the Louvre or Chinese Theatre, here's betting Chappell's will indeed awe you with its rich tapestry of memorabilia.

38. The Midnight Sun Game

Growden Memorial Park
Wilbur Street
Fairbanks, Alaska 99701
www.goldpanners.com

In keeping with a tradition that began in 1906, Fairbanks ushers in the start of summer by playing a baseball game in the middle of the night. The game begins at 10:30 p.m. on the night of the summer solstice and usually doesn't end until sometime after 1:00 a.m. the next day. The kicker is that the Alaska Goldpanners and their opponents play this game, in its entirety, without needing to turn on the ballpark lights. No, they don't use one of Charlie Finley's Day-Glo baseballs from the 1970s; it actually stays that light in Fairbanks on the longest day of the year.

The Goldpanners bill themselves as the "farthest north baseball club on the face of the earth." That has a downside: The summers are short; the winters are brutal. The upside is that Growden Park, which lies only 160 miles south of the Arctic Circle, is bathed in near perpetual daylight throughout the second half of June.

The Goldpanners play in the four-city, six-team Alaska Summer League, which attracts some of the best collegiate players in the land: players from "outside" or "down south," as Alaskans say, who spend a summer on the Last Frontier burnishing their baseball skills against other top-notch competition before returning to their respective universities.

All summer long, the games are compelling and the atmosphere unique. Games are routinely played under surreal skies, infused with pink and blue hues, even when the clock says they should be going dark. But this game, when the sun dips below the northern horizon for only about an hour before rising again, is

Players line up on the field prior to the start of the 2014 Midnight Sun Game.

extra special. It is an annual rite of summer in the "Land of the Midnight Sun." For more than a century, local residents have headed to the local ballpark to celebrate the arrival of their glorious summer. The game is a celebration, joyous and life-affirming.

When the sun dips out of sight in the middle innings, there is enough indirect light for the two teams to continue playing. At midnight, they halt the game and have a short ceremony on the field. There have been stadium lights surrounding rustic Growden Park since 1964, when Fairbanks became the first Alaska town to install them, but they have never been turned on during this game. That held true even in 2011, when heavy rains and gale-force winds caused the game to be suspended in the eleventh inning, with the Goldpanners and California's Oceanside

Waves knotted at 1–1. When play resumed in that 106th playing of the Midnight Sun Game at 6:00 p.m. on the night of June 22, the 'panners plated a run in the bottom of the 13th to prevail.

Although the Alaska Goldpanners and this special game now go hand in hand, the team has "only" been associated with this unusual rite of summer for about half of its history. Throughout its first half-century, the Midnight Sun Game utilized several different Alaska fields and involved an ever-revolving cast of teams. But ever since the Goldpanners were founded in 1960, they have hosted the game.

The very first Midnight Sun Game was played between two local bars, the California Bar and the Eagles Club, whose players nicknamed themselves the "Drinks" and the "Smokes," respectively. The two teams played nine innings at an amateur field in Fairbanks as June 21 turned to June 22, and when they were finished both the players and 1,500 spectators agreed that the game should become an annual tradition. Accordingly, bar teams and military teams squared off on the eve of the solstice in the decades to follow.

Since the start of its affiliation with the Goldpanners, the game has given future major leaguers like Tom Seaver, Dave Winfield, Dave Kingman, Terry Francona, Dan Plesac, Harold Reynolds, Jason Giambi, Jacque Jones, and Adam Kennedy the chance to showcase their skills in one of the most unusual baseball spectacles on the planet. The Goldpanners' opponent in the game changes from year to year, and with the home crowd firmly behind them they usually win; through 2014, they had a record of 44-11 in Midnight Sun Game competition.

As for Growden Memorial Park, little about it has changed since 1960. It seats just 3,500, but typically hosts a standing-room crowd for the big game. The largest crowd in its history turned out in 1967 to watch a Goldpanners team featuring Bill Lee and Bob Boone bow to a team from Kumagai-Gumi, Japan, that had recently been crowned Japan's national champions. There were 5,200 at the tiny park that day. More than four decades later, Lee returned to Growden Memorial Park to pitch in the 2008 game. The stunt attracted a crowd of 4,900.

Growden is a fun place to visit on any day of the thirty-five-game Alaska Summer League season. The experience is extra special, however, on the one day a year when the home team doesn't take the field for the top of the first until 10:30 p.m. On this night without darkness, the jovial fans don visors and sunglasses, drink beer, and eat hot dogs, and when the clock strikes midnight, the game stops so they can sing the "Alaska Flag Song." It is surreal enough simply to be sitting outside in broad daylight at midnight; add a baseball game to the equation, and the experience becomes nothing short of mind-blowing.

Interestingly, the Growden Park grandstand contains some of the stadium chairs and benches that once appeared at Sick's Stadium, the home of the Pacific Coast League Seattle Rainiers and American League Seattle Pilots. The only knock on the park is that it has an artificial turf infield

The sun dips below the horizon for only an inning or two during the annual playing of the Midnight Sun Game in Fairbanks.

(the outfield grass is real), but this is forgivable, considering how quickly winter turns to summer in Alaska.

Another Alaska Baseball League field that deserves a visit during your once-in-a-lifetime baseball trip to the Forty-Ninth State is **Herman Brothers Field** (Glenn Highway, Palmer). Located on the Alaska State Fairgrounds, the home park of the Mat-Su Miners offers a view of the looming snowcapped Chugach Mountains from its small grandstand. The effect is really something to see.

The Alaska Baseball League begins play in the second week of June and continues through the final week of July. The league champion travels to Wichita, Kansas, to participate in the National Baseball Congress World Series, which hosts its own series of midnight games during its "Baseball 'Round the Clock" extravaganza. Of course, the folks in Wichita have to turn on the ballpark lights at Lawrence-Dumont Stadium when they play *their* late games.

• •

Just a mile from Fenway Park, you find a bronze statue of Cy Young, depicting the great hurler on the mound, staring in to read a sign from an imaginary catcher as he readies to deliver a pitch. The statue is located on the spot where the pitcher's mound once rose in the middle of the diamond at the Huntington Avenue Grounds, an early home of the Boston Pilgrims, who would eventually become the Red Sox. The site is significant for several reasons but most notably for being the spot where in 1903 the first game of the very first World Series was played.

While it is true that previous postseason series, such as ones that pitted the National League's regular season champion against its runner-up and ones that saw the National League's champ play the American Association's champ, had at times been referred to by the sporting public as the "World Series," the 1903 tilt between the Pilgrims and Pittsburgh Pirates represented the first postseason clash between the regular season winners from the National League and fledgling American League. And more than that, the series took place at a time when several of the rules that historians would later point to as markers of the beginning of baseball's "modern era"

39. The Site of the First World Series Game

The Huntington Avenue Grounds
Northeastern University
400 Huntington Avenue
Boston, Massachusetts 02115

had just been established. In 1903, for example, the three-year-old American League accepted a rule that the National League had adopted earlier and began counting foul balls as strikes. Nonetheless, it would still be years before the arrival of such modern baseball staples as the lively ball, uniform numbers, webbed gloves, dugouts, and relief pitchers. And back in those days, fans were still allowed to stand behind rope barriers in the outfield once the seats filled up, as they often did during that first October Classic.

The first World Series was not without its controversy. After Young and his Pilgrims lost three of the first four games—including the very first, in which Young was defeated 7-3—

Cy Young threw the first pitch of the very first World Series game at this location in 1903.

Boston rebounded to win the best-of-nine match in eight games. But the finale, played in Boston on October 13, was witnessed by the smallest crowd of the series. While gatherings of 16,000 to 18,000 had turned out at the Huntington Avenue Grounds for the first three games in Boston, only 7,455 spectators filed into the ballpark stands for Game Eight. That was because Boston's "Royal Rooters" had decided to boycott the game after arriving home from the away games in Pittsburgh only to discover that Pilgrims management had sold their usual block of seats to ticket scalpers. Nonetheless, Boston prevailed 3–0 behind the pitching of Bill Dinneen, a hard-throwing right-hander who won three of his four starts in the series while posting a 2.06 ERA.

It is Young's likeness, not Dinneen's, however, that has stood in a courtyard at Northeastern University since its unveiling on October 1, 1993—the ninetieth anniversary of the first World Series game. And fittingly so. The immortal Young, who went 2-1 with a 1.85 ERA in his only World Series, won 511 games during his twenty-two-year career. Dinneen won 170 and lost 177 over his twelve seasons. Young also authored the first perfect game in American League history from the Huntington Avenue Grounds mound, blanking the Philadelphia A's 3–0 on May 5, 1904.

The statue is located outside Churchill Hall along a footpath named World Series Way. It shows Young with his socks pulled up high, the collar of his Boston jersey neatly laced together below his chin, and with his five-fingered glove resting on his left thigh. At its base an inscription reads, "At this site in October 1903 baseball's winningest pitcher led Boston to victory in the first World Series." Sixty feet, six inches from where Young toes the rubber, a bronze home plate is laid in the grass.

Not far from this shiny version of Young, a plaque on the exterior of Northeastern's Cabot Center reads:

> Huntington Avenue American League Baseball Grounds, on which in 1903 four games of the first World Series were played. The Boston Americans defeated the Pittsburgh Nationals five games to three. This plaque is located approximately on what was then the left field foul line. Erected May 16, 1956.

Inside the building, a **World Series exhibit** on the second floor offers a small collection of old photos and wool jerseys from those earliest days of Boston baseball.

The Huntington Avenue Grounds grandstand was built in two months' time in 1901 at a cost of $35,000. Like all parks of the day, it was wooden, and never more than a smoldering cigarette butt away from catastrophe. Its outfield playing surface consisted of sand and weeds. And fans and players were constantly subjected to the plumes of smoke that billowed into the park from the rail yard next door. The ballpark lasted eleven years before being replaced by the much larger, concrete-and-steel Fenway Park in 1912. As for the World Series, it has enjoyed greater staying power, enduring times of poverty, illness, war, and civil strife while chiseling out its own special place in American culture. Only two autumns have passed without a World Series since 1903. After the Pilgrims won the American League title for a second consecutive season in 1904, John McGraw, the cantankerous manager of the National League champion New York Giants, refused to play them. Then in 1994, baseball's acting commissioner Bud Selig canceled the World Series due to a labor dispute between the owners and players. Other than that, the World Series has been a continuous rite of fall for us, ranking right up there with heading back to school, picking apples, and trick-or-treating.

· ·

During the heyday of the Negro Leagues, Pittsburgh stood above all other American cities as the undisputed hub of the "black baseball" universe. The Steel City was home to not one but two of the finest Negro Leagues teams in the land—the Homestead Grays and the Pittsburgh Crawfords. Both clubs offered fans the chance to witness the daily heroics of some of the best ballplayers—of any era, creed, or color—to ever lace up a pair of spikes. Today, all these decades later, the memories of both teams remain alive at various sites you may explore in and around the

40. Pittsburgh's Negro Leagues Trail

Multiple Locations
Pittsburgh, Pennsylvania

Steel City. Statues, historic markers, and relics of an era past pay homage to the men who made Pittsburgh a Negro Leagues hub.

Fans visit statues of Negro Leagues stars and learn more about their accomplishments via computer kiosks found throughout PNC Park's Highmark Legacy Square.

The Grays were founded in 1910 by a man named Cumberland Posey, who played for the team and managed it. Originally, the Grays played at West Field in the suburb of Munhall, but as they grew more popular, they often played weekend games at Forbes Field. Later they began "hosting" some of their games at Griffith Stadium in Washington, DC, while playing their Pittsburgh schedule at Greenlee Field in the city's Hill District. Greenlee doubled as the home of the Crawfords, who originally played at Ammon Field but switched to Greenlee after legendary Pittsburgh club owner Gus Greenlee bought the team and footed the cost of the $100,000 stadium. That park opened in 1932 and quickly drew praise as the finest black-owned ballpark in the land

(at the time it was common for Negro Leagues teams to simply use the home stadium of the nearest big-league or minor-league club).

Throughout most of their days, the Negro Leagues comprised a loosely organized and ever-changing assortment of teams that played against one another while also playing barnstorming games against semi-pro teams; thus, definitive team records and individual-player statistics related to the Negro Leagues are hard to quantify. This much is certain though: The brightest of Pittsburgh's many stars was a barrel-chested catcher often referred to as "the black Babe Ruth." Josh Gibson began his career with the Grays in 1929, switched to the Crawfords in 1930, and proceeded to belt seventy-five home runs in 1931. After being part of what many historians consider the best black club ever—the early 1930s Crawfords, which featured four other future Hall of Famers in Satchel Paige, Cool Papa Bell, Oscar Charleston, and Judy Johnson—Gibson rejoined the Grays in 1937, to join forces with another future Cooperstown inductee, Buck Leonard, to lead the Grays to nine consecutive Negro National League titles. Although it is uncertain exactly how many home runs Gibson hit between 1929 and 1946, most debates concerning his long-ball prowess begin around the 800 mark. Tragically, his career, and life, ended abruptly in January of 1947, just a few short months before Jackie Robinson would break Major League Baseball's color barrier. The great slugger, who had suffered from a brain tumor and battled substance-abuse problems, died of a brain hemorrhage at age thirty-five.

Today, you can visit several of Gibson and his contemporaries' old stomping grounds. Only fragments of a glorious past remain, but if you look closely enough, you will find them. A plaque marks the former site of **Ammon Field** (2217 Bedford Avenue) reading:

> Joshua (Josh) Gibson (1911–1947), Hailed as Negro League's greatest slugger, he hit some 800 home runs in a baseball career that began here at Ammon Field in 1929. Played for the Homestead Grays and Pittsburgh Crawfords, 1930–46. Elected to the Baseball Hall of Fame, 1972.

Amateur baseball is still played near the plaque at what is now called **Josh Gibson Field.**

The field was refurbished in 2008 through a $292,000 project led by the Josh Gibson Foundation, which is headed by Gibson's grandson.

Another historic marker stands outside the site of the **Crawford Grill** (2141 Wylie Avenue), recognizing the nightclub that Gus Greenlee once owned for the role it played in black social life in the 1920s, 1930s, and 1940s. Inside, old photographs pay tribute to the jazz legends and ballplayers that passed through the Crawford's doors. Still another marker, on **Amity Street** near the Fifth Avenue ramp, remembers the Grays and their era of dominance.

More than any other old Negro Leagues park in greater Pittsburgh, **West Field** (Main Street, Munhall) still retains much of its original form, existing as a dilapidated monument around a field that is today the home of the Munhall–West Homestead Baseball Association's Colt League. The old bleachers, dugouts, locker rooms, and light towers remain. And the center field fence is more than 700 feet from home plate. This is one of those sites where you can show up with a bucket of balls and a bat and take a few hacks.

Another highlight of any tour of Pittsburgh's Negro Leagues mementos is PNC Park's **Highmark Legacy Square.** You find this interactive tribute inside the Left Field Gate of the Pirates' home park. Stunning bronze statues of seven players are accompanied by interactive kiosks that allow you to learn more about each player and his respective teams. Giant oversized bats hang above the statues, displaying each player's name. Captured in bronze are Bell, Charleston, Gibson, Johnson, Leonard, Paige, and Smokey Joe Williams.

41. The Jack Norworth Memorial

◇◇◇◇◇◇◇◇◇◇◇◇◇◇◇◇◇◇◇◇◇◇◇◇◇◇◇◇◇◇◇◇◇◇◇◇◇

Melrose Abbey Memorial Park
2302 South Manchester Avenue
Anaheim, California 92802
(714) 634-1981
www.melroseabbeyfh.com

Less than a mile from Angel Stadium of Anaheim you can pay your respects to the songsmith who penned the lyrics to the most influential baseball song ever written at one of the newest and most overdue monuments to the game's pop culture.

Vaudevillian Jack Norworth scribbled the words to "Take Me Out to the Ballgame" while riding a New York City subway car in 1908. He went on to perform the ditty thousands of times as he traveled the country as an entertainer over the next half-century. Along the way, he spread enthusiasm for America's Game, encouraging countless fans to embark upon their own ballpark adventures. In his later years, Norworth settled in Laguna Beach, California, where he founded the Laguna Beach Little League in 1952. He was honorary president of the league until he died in 1959 at age eighty. Today, the team that wins the Laguna Beach Little League championship each year is awarded the Jack Norworth Trophy, which is the original trophy that the Cracker Jack Company presented to Norworth at the Los Angeles Coliseum in 1958 to celebrate the fiftieth anniversary of his writing the song.

At the time of his death, Norworth was laid to rest beneath a humble marker in this small Anaheim cemetery. Long after his burial though, his song continued to delight crowds during the seventh inning of baseball games across the country. Finally, in 2010, a group of local baseball fans stepped to the plate and installed a proper monument to Norworth, honoring his impact on baseball's rise to popularity and his contribution to the ballpark experience we still enjoy today.

The story goes something like this. In April of 2010, author Chris Epting was signing copies of his book *Los Angeles's Historic Ballparks* at a Huntington Beach Barnes and Noble. A gentleman by the name of J. P. Myers, of Diamond Bar, California, was in the store that day and was fascinated to hear Epting talk about the area's old baseball grounds. He was surprised when he heard Epting mention that Norworth was buried not far from his home and even more surprised when he learned how understated Norworth's burial marker was. Myers launched a Facebook crusade to raise interest in and money for a proper memorial for Norworth. Within three months, Maria and Charles Sotelo of High Desert Monuments of Hesperia, California, had stepped to the plate to donate a memorial, and AOL and another private donor had volunteered more than $4,000 for a new plot for the marker in Melrose Abbey Memorial Park. Because no living relative of Norworth could be found to approve an addition to his actual burial plot, the monument is about 100 feet from his actual grave, which you can also find in the cemetery.

On July 11, 2010, players, parents, and officials from the Laguna Beach Little League joined Myers, Epting, and other area fans for an unveiling of the new Norworth memorial. Score one for the power of social media, eh? Adding prestige to the event, the ceremony was attended by Hall of Fame pitcher Rollie Fingers. Mr. Fingers, who flew in from Las Vegas for the event, told the crowd, "As a kid growing up playing Little League, we knew that song. This is long overdue for him

After writing "Take Me Out to the Ballgame" as a younger man, Jack Norworth settled in Laguna Beach, California, where he founded the Laguna Beach Little League.

. . . You mention the words 'Cracker Jack,' and you automatically think about the song he wrote."

The story of how Norworth came up with the idea for the song is almost as improbable as the serendipitous turn of events that resulted in the creation of this new marker to honor him. Amazingly, Norworth had never been to a professional baseball game when he wrote "Take Me Out to the Ballgame," and he wouldn't attend one for another thirty-two years. But inspiration struck the twenty-nine-year-old entertainer as he rode the New York City subway one day. He saw a poster advertising a game at the Polo Grounds and hastily scribbled lyrics onto a piece of paper. His friend Albert Von Tilzer set the words to music, and Norworth's wife, Nora Bayes, performed the vocals. Before long, the song had become a smash hit, first on the vaudeville circuit and then on vinyl.

You surely know the chorus, but you might wonder what the full song was about. Well there were two versions—the original written in 1908, and a later one written in 1927. Both concern young ladies—Katie Casey in the first, Nelly Kelly in the second—who are obsessed fans. In the first verse her gentleman caller comes for her, suggesting they go to a Broadway show (or to Coney Island in the second version). But being the fan she is, Katie/Nelly pleads instead to go to a baseball game. In the second verse, she is at the game, first heckling the umpire and then imploring the home crowd. In the midst of a tie game, she encourages her fellow fans to sing the chorus in the ballpark stands.

The song's staying power is testament to its appeal. It's just a shame that big-league parks don't take an extra minute or two to play the full song during the seventh inning stretch so fans can

interest in the team after his friend passed away. Under his stewardship, Tiger Stadium's signature upper deck was constructed, and it was renamed Briggs Stadium (it was renamed Tiger Stadium in 1960). His is the only other aboveground tomb at Holy Sepulchre, but it isn't guarded by any cats.

There are hundreds of cemeteries across the United States that lay claim to housing at least one former major leaguer and scores that offer repose to Hall of Famers and former big-league team owners. To visit them all would be impossible. But you should make a point to stop by Southland, Michigan, where you can make like you're on safari and check out the prowling tigers, as well as the ones in repose.

• •

47. The Tiki Seats at Bright House Field

601 North Old Coachman Road
Clearwater, Florida 33765
(727) 712-4300
www.threshersbaseball.com

Since Bright House Field opened in 2004, the Clearwater Threshers—a Class-A Philadelphia Phillies affiliate—have led the twelve-team Florida State League in annual attendance year after year. The Threshers attract upwards of 175,000 fans per season, more than doubling the annual attendance of some league rivals. Upon setting foot inside Bright House Field, it is easy enough to figure out why the Threshers draw so well. Built in the Spanish Mission architectural style, Bright House is an absolute gem. Its sunken playing field and 360-degree concourse enable you to walk circles around the entire diamond while only losing sight of the action briefly when you step behind the batter's eye in straightaway center. And its Tiki Seats are among the very best specialty viewing locations in the game.

You find this special seating area in the left field corner, within a steeply rising pavilion that offers long tables with accompanying barstools. The effect is something like that created by the Green Monster Seats at Fenway Park in Boston, only in Clearwater the seats are much closer to ground level so you can actually see the action right up to the left field fence, unlike in Boston. The five rows offer sixty stools in all, which are available on a first-come, first-served basis, both during baseball's spring training season when the Phillies use the park and during the minor-league season. These primo home-run-territory seats sit beneath an authentic 50-foot straw-thatch tiki hut, like the kind you see at nearby Clearwater Beach.

But the Tiki Seats only take up a portion of left field home-run territory, leaving plenty of room for a massive outfield seating lawn behind a see-through mesh outfield fence that allows you to watch the game as you recline on the grass. Nowadays outfield lawns or seating "berms" are sprouting up at minor-league ball-parks across the country, but when Bright House unveiled its lawn upon its opening in 2004, it was ahead of the curve.

Even if you don't arrive early enough to score one of the Tiki Seats, you can still settle on the lawn and partake in the left field revelry—which includes frozen drinks, live music in the pregame and postgame hours, lawn games,

The Tiki Seats are the most coveted seats in the house at Bright House Field.

and nightly contests for fans. The party crowd almost always spills onto the seating lawn, as men and women tote bottles of beer in buckets of ice to their picnic blankets, then plop down to watch the game. This is perhaps the trendiest spot in all of the minor leagues. Need proof? Consider that stadium management opens Bright House Field for Happy Hour every Wednesday at 5:00 p.m. all season long, even on nights when the Threshers are on the road. That's right, the locals enjoy hanging out at the ballpark, listening to live music, mingling, and yes, drinking, so much that they show up whether there's a game or not. Well, there is *a* game on these nights technically, just not a baseball game. For $5.00 you can enter the nightly corn-hole contest and compete to win a raft of prizes. Of course, like any baseball

location that serves as a functional ballpark, the experience is much better when there is a baseball game!

On game days and non-game days, Bright House also serves a veritable menu of Philadelphia-based culinary treats that Gulf Coast fans have come to know and love through the years. This tip of the cap to the home team's association with the Phillies includes offerings from Delco's Steaks, Rita's Water Ice, Herr's Potato Chips, TastyKakes, and Victory beer. Another nod to Philadelphia can be found in the form of a life-size statue named *The Ace* that stands outside the stadium's West Gate, depicting Hall of Famer Steve Carlton, who pitched for the Phillies from 1972 to 1986. The architecture of the park also reflects some of the design aspects of the Phillies' regular season home, including the blue stadium chairs and meandering outfield fence that offers lots of nooks and crannies.

If you're thinking that Bright House goes to greater lengths to tap into its big-league parent team's culture and fan experience than most minor-league parks do, you're right. Bright House opened in March of 2004, a month before Citizens Bank Park in Philadelphia. Both parks were designed by the ballpark experts at Populous (formerly HOK Sport), who worked in tandem with the architectural firm Ewing Cole of Philadelphia. It was the intention all along to give Clearwater fans a taste of Philly, and also to give the park a distinctly Floridian flair. On both counts, Bright House Field is a smashing success.

48. The Billy Goat Tavern

430 North Michigan Avenue
Chicago, Illinois 60611
(312) 222-1525
www.billygoattavern.com/index.php

When the Boston Red Sox won the 2004 World Series and finally silenced talk that Babe Ruth had placed a hex on his former team after being sold to the Yankees in 1919, Boston passed the mantle of baseball's most star-crossed team on to the Cubs. Sure, the Cubs' world championship drought had been longer-running than the Red Sox' all along, but because the Red Sox had come close to winning the big kahuna so many times, only to have their hopes dashed in increasingly heartbreaking fashion, their "Curse of the Bambino" was more prominent in fans' and sportswriters' minds than the Cubs' "Curse of the Billy Goat."

All that changed though, when the Red Sox swept the Cardinals in the 2004 October Classic and thus ended a drought that had begun after Ruth led Beantown to a World Series win in 1918, shortly before being jettisoned to New York. Suddenly the Cubs and their decades-long stretch of futility—which dates to their back-to-back world championships in 1907 and 1908—took center stage. The Cubs' woes were further underscored when the crosstown White Sox, who'd gone without a title since 1917, ended their skein the very year after the Red Sox ended theirs.

In any case, those happy developments for other teams contributed to the "Curse of the Billy Goat" gaining more national traction. According to Chicago lore, a local barkeep named William "Billy" Sianis is responsible for the Northsiders' enduring misery. And today, you can visit one of the many Billy Goat Tavern locations owned by the Sianis family to embrace the tongue-in-cheek hex.

The story of how the curse originated goes something like this: Billy Sianis adopted a goat after the animal jumped off a passing truck outside his downtown Chicago saloon one day in the early 1940s. He named the creature "Murphy," and kept it at the bar as a house mascot. Murphy was friendly and tame, and the life of the party on many nights. Naturally, then, when Sianis found himself the proud holder of two tickets to Game Four of the 1945 World Series between the Cubs and Tigers, he opted to make Murphy his "plus one." On the morning of October 6, the odd pair set off down West Madison Street, heading for Wrigley Field. The Cubs were leading two games to one in the series and both man and beast were eager to see them take a commanding 3–1 lead in the best-of-seven affair.

But when Sianis arrived at the turnstiles with his goat standing handsomely beside him, he was told that no animals were allowed in Wrigley Field. Sianis demanded to speak with whoever was in charge of the joint and soon found himself facing none other than team owner Philip K. Wrigley. When the Cubs owner only reiterated Wrigley Field's humans-only policy, Sianis asked "Why?" and Mr. Wrigley reportedly said, "Because the goat stinks." It was then that Sianis, a Greek immigrant well versed in the ancient art of the stink-eye, proclaimed, "Them Cubs, they ain't gonna win no more."

Never mind winning a World Series, the Cubs have only won one World Series *game* since that turning point in franchise history. They lost three out of the final four contests against the Tigers to drop the 1945 Series, and haven't returned to the October Classic in more than seven decades since: this from a team that prior to the goat incident had won ten National League pennants. Hmm, think Cubs fans were a bit hasty in riding Steve Bartman out of town after his interfering with a foul pop along the third base line precipitated the Cubs' National League Championship Series meltdown against the Marlins in 2003? It would seem that greater forces than a souvenir-crazed twenty-six-year-old may have conspired to thwart the Cubs!

Today, the Billy Goat Tavern website provides a daily update on how long it has been since the Cubs last won the World Series. The widget shows years, months, and days since the team's last title, alongside the words "Who Stinks Now?" The site also directs you to the

According to Chicago lore, Billy Goat Tavern founder Billy Sianis cursed the Cubs when his goat Murphy was denied entrance to Wrigley Field during the 1945 World Series.

several different Billy Goat Tavern locations in Chicago and one in Washington, DC. At any of these shops you can enjoy a tasty meal while perusing old photos and newspaper clippings related to "the Curse."

If you're only going to visit one Billy Goat Tavern location, you should set your sights on the one set below street level on North Michigan Avenue about 4 miles south of Wrigley Field. The Billy Goat's signature franchise since 1964, this Chicago landmark has welcomed into its cozy dining room such prominent Americans as George H. W. Bush, George W. Bush, Bill and Hillary Clinton, Al Gore, Jay Leno, Bill Murray, Harrison Ford, John Cusack, Charlton Heston, Frank Sinatra, Ronnie Woo Woo, and John Belushi, who based his famous "Cheeseborger, Cheeseborger" skit on *Saturday Night Live* on the antics of an overzealous Billy Goat Tavern employee.

Although "the Curse" has given the Billy Goat Tavern plenty of free publicity and contributed to its prospering all these years, the Sianis family and the lovable losers of the National League Central have long since made their peace. On Opening Day of the 1984 season, Sam Sianis, the nephew of Billy and owner of today's Billy Goat establishments, was invited by the Cubs to walk on the Wrigley Field lawn with a goat believed to be a direct descendant of Murphy. After Sam said that all was forgiven, the Cubs had a strong season that saw them advance to the NLCS. After winning the first two games of the best-of-five series against the Padres, though, they lost the final three games and missed out, once again, on a chance to play in their first World Series since 1945. Apparently the Opening Day gesture was not enough to satisfy the ghosts of old Billy and Murphy after all.

So, as long as the Cubs keep losing, fans and pundits will keep referencing "the Curse" as one explanation for their almost preternatural pattern of failure. And customers hungry for some good eats served with a side of baseball myth will continue to frequent the Billy Goat Tavern.

Locations

Billy Goat Tavern—Original
Near Tribune Towers and Wrigley Building
430 North Michigan Avenue at Lower Level
Chicago
(312) 222-1525

Billy Goat Tavern—Navy Pier
Navy Pier—Outdoor Seating
700 East Grand Avenue
Chicago
(312) 670-8789

Billy Goat Tavern Inn
1535 West Madison Street
Near the United Center
Chicago
(312) 733-9132

Billy Goat Tavern II
330 South Wells
Chicago
(312) 554-0297

Billy Goat Tavern
60 East Lake Street
½ block west of Michigan Avenue
Chicago

Billy Goat Merchandise Mart
222 Merchandise Mart #Fc-2
Chicago
(312) 464-1045

Billy Goat—Airport
O'Hare Airport
Terminal 1, Concourse C
(773) 462 -9368

Billy Goat
164 Randhurst Village Drive
Mount Prospect, IL
(847) 870-0123

Billy Goat—DC
500 New Jersey Avenue Northwest #1
Washington, DC
(202) 783-2123

A trip to Yankee Stadium offers you the chance to visit not one but two of baseball's most intriguing places. Aside from housing the latest incarnation of Monument Park, which receives treatment elsewhere within this book, the latest Yankees' monolith provides access to a top-notch museum. Yes, this is a *Yankees* shrine, not one dedicated to the game writ large. Seeing as the Yankees have been baseball's most successful and influential team through the generations, you'll likely find yourself moved by its collection even if you consider yourself a Yankee-hater. Sure, Babe Ruth spent his glory years as a *Yankee* hero, but don't you see him more broadly as a hero of the game? The same goes for Lou Gehrig, Joe DiMaggio, Mickey Mantle, and several others who through their success, intrinsic characteristics, and placement in time came to embody certain American ideals. For DiMaggio, the Streak and his brief marriage to Marilyn Monroe made him larger than life. For Gehrig, his own Streak and then the terribly sad but brave way he bid the game adieu captured America's fascination. Mantle and Roger Maris gave us the great home-run race of 1961. And so on.

If the new Yankee Stadium falls short of recreating the magic of the original Monument Park, it goes a long way toward making up for the disappointment through this wonderful 3,600-square-foot museum. Where else, outside Cooperstown, can you gaze upon seven World Series trophies? That's the hardware from all seven of the team's world championships since 1977.

One of the most interactive exhibits is the Ball Wall, which showcases upwards of 900 baseballs signed by former Yankees players, coaches, broadcasters, and front office personnel. Big names like Ruth, Gehrig, Phil Rizzuto, and

49. The New York Yankees Museum

Yankee Stadium
1 East 61st Street
Bronx, New York 10451
(646) 977-8687

Joe McCarthy are represented, as well as lesser lights, like Jose Canseco, A. J. Burnett, Butch Hobson, Andy Stankiewicz, and Bob Wickman. A handy touch-screen "ball finder" allows you to scroll through the names to find the location of each person's ball. Then you can walk over and check out the person's autograph.

The museum also includes a unique approach to honoring a great moment in team history. Matching statues depict Yogi Berra squatting behind home plate and Don Larsen delivering a pitch from a bronze rubber 60 feet, 6 inches away. More than half a century later, Larsen's perfect game in the 1956 World Series remains the only perfecto in postseason history, and it seems appropriate to celebrate it in such innovative fashion. The home plate in front of Berra serves as a marker, detailing the events of the game.

An exhibit dedicated to controversial Yankees owner George Steinbrenner, who owned the team from 1973 until his death in 2010, includes pictures of him from his childhood at Culver Military Academy, pictures from his glory days at the Yankees' helm, and all of his World Series rings. The "Lead, Follow, or Get the Hell Out of the Way" sign from his desk and the Tony Award he won in 1970 for a Broadway musical he coproduced titled *Applause* are other curios.

Thurman Munson's locker, which sat unassigned at the old Yankee Stadium from the time of his death until the time of the ballpark's closing in 2008, is also on display, as is the home plate from the last game at old Yankee Stadium and the jersey Derek Jeter was wearing on July 9, 2011, when he tallied his 3,000th hit with a home run off Tampa Bay's David Price.

In recent years, the Yankees have shown a willingness to broaden the scope of the museum, if only slightly. In 2011, for example, they added a "Latino Living Legends" display, honoring six living Hall of Famers of Latino descent—Roberto Alomar, Luis Aparicio, Rod Carew, Orlando Cepeda, Juan Marichal, and Tony Pérez—none of whom played for the Yankees.

The museum is open to ticket holders during Yankee games. But don't fret if you're visiting New York when the Pinstripes are out of town, or in the middle of the winter. The Yankee Stadium Tour takes you to both Monument Park and the Yankee Museum. Tours run about an hour in length, with new groups departing daily beginning at noon and continuing every twenty minutes until 1:40 p.m. You can buy a tour pass through the phone or Internet by contacting TicketMaster, or you can purchase a pass at any of the Yankees Clubhouse Shops in Manhattan or at the Yankee Stadium ticket window on the day of your tour. The cost is $25.00 for adults, and $23.00 for senior citizens and children.

A statue of Don Larsen delivers a pitch to this statue of a squatting Yogi Berra at the Yankees Museum.

After spending nearly three decades behind the center field fence at Shea Stadium, the Mets Home Run Apple now resides outside Citi Field's main entrance. It stands as a delightfully kitschy, campy, cheesy reminder of a less aesthetically sophisticated era in the life of the Grand Old Game that also brought us such atrocities as those popsicle-orange Astros jerseys, the shorts Bill Veeck's White Sox once wore, Day-Glo orange baseballs, and the mechanical rabbit A's owner Charlie O. Finley commissioned to pop up behind home plate and deliver fresh baseballs to the home plate ump. If you're of a certain vintage, you can think back and recall those freewheeling days when the players wore lamb-chops and 'fros, the managers were colorful older gents who played hunches rather than sabermetrics, and whenever a Mets player went yard at Shea, a giant fiberglass apple arose from a 10-foot-tall black magician's hat in center field.

The Home Run Apple was so ridiculous that fans came to love it.

The unique home-run celebration made somewhat oblique reference to a lucky turn of events in 1966 that helped pave the way for the Miracle Mets of 1969 to win the World Series. But it wasn't born until early 1980, when the Mets changed hands and the newly installed ownership group commissioned the hat and apple to be made by a New Jersey company

The original Home Run Apple from Shea Stadium is a popular spot for fans to snap pregame photos.

The original Mets Home Run Apple from Shea Stadium now welcomes visitors to Citi Field.

that specialized in floats for the annual Macy's Thanksgiving Day parade. The Home Run Apple was installed that spring as part of an ad campaign that decreed "The Magic is Back," in an attempt to reinvigorate the flagging franchise's fan base. The idea of a lucky Mets hat dates, of course, to the post-draft lottery that baseball commissioner Spike Eckert conducted in 1966, as teams vied for the services of former University of Southern California pitcher Tom Seaver. "Tom Terrific" was originally drafted and signed by the Atlanta Braves, but because Seaver signed his contract after the next year's USC season had begun, Eckert voided it, saying the Braves' exclusive bargaining period had expired. The commissioner then said any team willing to match the Braves' offer should submit a bid. When the Mets, Phillies, and Indians

all submitted matching offers, their names were thrown into a hat to determine Seaver's future team. Yes, the workings of the commissioner's office really were that primitive in those days! And when it came time for the drawing, the Mets' entry was the one plucked from the hat. As a rookie in 1967, Seaver won sixteen games. He won sixteen more in 1968. Then, in 1969, he won a "miraculous" twenty-seven, including a game apiece in the NLCS and World Series, which the Mets won against the Braves and Orioles, respectively.

When plans were unveiled in the 2000s to finally replace Shea Stadium with a new facility that more closely resembled a baseball park, Mets fans were in near unanimous support of the plan. But a small contingent of local rooters rallied to the cause of saving the Home Run

Apple from the wrecking ball that would shortly level Shea. Mets management, to its credit, listened to the fans. Even though a new Home Run Apple was built to serve the same purpose as its predecessor in center field of Citi Field, the old Apple was preserved. When Citi opened in 2009, the original Apple could be found just inside its bullpen gate. Then, the next spring, the Apple was moved outside the park, to its current location. Adorned by a lush bed of petunias, marigolds, and lilies, the big piece of fruit is one of the first things you see as you exit the Willets Point subway station and make your way toward Jackie Robinson Rotunda. This is the perfect spot to pose for a picture with the stadium in the background.

Not far away, the **Mets Hall of Fame and Museum** includes a classy plaque gallery that honors favorite sons like Gary Carter, Dwight Gooden, Keith Hernandez, Gil Hodges, Ralph Kiner, Tug McGraw, Seaver, Casey Stengel, Darryl Strawberry, and Rusty Staub. The 1969 and 1986 world championship trophies are on display next to a TV that plays an endless loop of Mookie Wilson's ground ball going through Bill Buckner's legs in Game Six of the 1986 Series.

If you're looking for another unique place to pose for a picture, you can elbow up beside the statue of baseball-headed mascot "Mr. Met" that stands in the museum. Admission is free before, during, and after Mets home games, provided you have a game ticket. On the other hand, the Home Run Apple just outside the ballpark gates is always available for your viewing and photographing pleasure. You can even hop up into the flower bed that surrounds it and rap your knuckles against its red fiberglass skin!

• •

When the topic of baseball's most colorful characters comes up, most fans agree that Yogi Berra's name belongs at the top of the list. And that's saying something. After all, we're talking about a game that has given rise to such legendary oddballs as Dizzy Dean, who once bought a service station in Bradenton, Florida, on a whim and spent an entire spring training pumping gas; Jimmy Piersall, who once ran around the bases backwards after hitting a home run; Mark Fidrych, who carried on detailed conversations with baseballs before throwing them; Bill Lee, who spent an entire season referring to his manager, Don Zimmer, as "the gerbil" in his conversations with Boston sports reporters; Steve "Psycho" Lyons, who once dropped his drawers in front of 25,000 fans so he could shake the dirt out of his underwear after

51. The Yogi Berra Museum and Learning Center

Montclair State University
8 Yogi Berra Drive
Little Falls, New Jersey 07424
(973) 655-2378
www.yogiberramuseum.org

diving into a base; and scores of other unique characters.

As for the former Yankees catcher whose goofy persona inspired Hanna-Barbera to create a cartoon bear in his likeness in the 1950s, and who decades later costarred in commercials with celebs like Yao Ming and the AFLAC Duck,

The Yogi Berra Museum sits beside Yogi Berra Stadium on the campus of Montclair State University.

Berra has earned his persona as an eccentric not so much by what he's *done* as by what he's *said*. The man oft-referred to as the "master of the malapropism" is credited with coining such familiar phrases as: "It ain't over till it's over"; "It's déjà vu all over again"; "Ninety percent of the game is half mental"; "You can observe a lot by watching"; "When you come to a fork in the road, take it"; "The future ain't what it used to be"; and "Nobody goes there anymore, it's too crowded."

More than just being a comedic and surprisingly insightful observer of human nature, Berra was, of course, also a stellar ballplayer. In fact, he was one of the best catchers to ever strap on the "tools of ignorance." He earned his pinstripes and plaque in Cooperstown by slugging 358 home runs and batting .285 over an

eighteen-year career that included a record fourteen World Series.

Much like the man himself, there is more to the Yogi Berra Museum and Learning Center than you might initially assume. Yes, the museum includes the requisite exhibit detailing Yogi's impact on American culture and fun with the English language, providing the backstories related to some of his more famous and outrageous quotations. And yes, it features plenty of memorabilia from Berra's career—including all ten of his World Series championship rings and the mitt he used to catch Don Larsen's perfect game in the 1956 World Series. It also offers the expected nods to the Yankees mystique—including a video history of baseball with a very heavy focus on the Bronx Bombers' role therein. But the museum also provides interesting educational exhibits related to the way the game used to be played back in the 1800s and early 1900s; a tribute to the All-Century Team that was named in 1999; a collection of dolls modeled after famous players like Willie Mays, Jackie Robinson, and Babe Ruth; an ever-changing assortment of artifacts borrowed from the National Baseball Hall of Fame; and educational programs designed to foster sportsmanship and good citizenship in the many youngsters who visit the museum by the busload on field trips from school, with Little League teams, or through their involvement with community youth programs.

For a Yankees fan, or any fan of the game, the museum is well worth the $6.00 cost of admission for adults or $4.00 for children under the age of 18. It is open Wednesday through Saturday from noon to 5:00 p.m., and Mr. Berra can sometimes be found on the premises. The old catcher, who was awarded an honorary doctorate from Montclair State University in 1996, has lived in Montclair since his playing days. He originally uttered his "fork in the road" saying when giving a dinner guest directions to his house. As it turned out, either branch of the fork led to his home, so Yogi's directions, like most of the things he has said through the years, kind of made sense after all.

As an added bonus, you can catch a ballgame during your Berra adventure, as there's a professional ballpark right next door to the museum. **Yogi Berra Stadium** is home to the Division III Montclair State Red Hawks during the spring and to the unaffiliated New Jersey Jackals of the Can-Am League during the summer. The 3,700-seat facility opened in 1998, the same year as the museum. In addition to its cozy grandstand, it offers room for another 1,500 fans on its right field lawn. On days when the Jackals have a home game, the museum stays open until 7:00 p.m.

Through the years baseball culture has often bled into popular culture, infusing literature, theater, music, television, and film with source material for creative ventures that have garnered mainstream popularity. The examples of this effect range from the Broadway musical *Damn Yankees*, to John Fogerty's song "Centerfield," to Chad Harbach's novel *The Art of Fielding*, to any of the baseball movies of recent decades, including *Bull Durham*, *Field of Dreams*, *Major League*, and *Moneyball*. Usually, the inspiration flows from the game into pop culture. Rarer are the instances when the game itself is shaped by forces at work in mainstream popular culture. One such example of this phenomenon may be found in Albuquerque, New Mexico, where the longest-running US sitcom ever has played a role in shaping the

52. *The Simpsons* Statues

Isotopes Park
1601 Avenida Cesar Chavez Southeast
Albuquerque, New Mexico 87106
(505) 222-4058
www.milb.com/content/page.
jsp?ymd=20081103&content_
id=41346586&sid=t342&vkey=team1

identity of a minor-league club. Today, you can even rub elbows with the show's by-now-iconic characters when you visit the local park.

Bart Simpson nearly "had a cow" when the Isotopes scored nine runs in the fifth inning of a 2014 game against the Salt Lake Bees at Isotopes Park.

The story of how *The Simpsons* played a role in naming the Albuquerque Isotopes goes something like this: In just the second year of the animated series' long life, a 1990 episode titled "Dancing Homer" introduced a minor-league team named the Isotopes that played in the Simpsons' fictional Springfield, and established Homer Simpson's bona fides as a fan of bush-league ball. In the episode, Homer attends a game and launches into a goofy dance routine that appears on the Jumbotron as the camera pans the crowd. After Homer fires up his fellow fans and catalyzes a winning streak for the home team, he finds himself thrust into the role of Isotopes mascot and, predictably, calamity ensues.

Fast-forward more than a decade to another baseball-infused Simpsons episode titled "Hungry, Hungry Homer" that ran in 2001. This time, Homer catches wind that the Isotopes are secretly planning a move to Albuquerque. But before the team can pull a Seattle Pilots–style disappearing act, Homer takes action, chaining himself to a pole outside Duff Stadium and beginning a prolonged hunger strike. By the end of the episode, Homer manages to shed light on the nefarious plan and ensure that the Isotopes will remain in Springfield. As for Albuquerque, it sets its sights instead on pilfering the Dallas Cowboys from their home city.

The hilarity of "Hungry, Hungry Homer" and its depiction of Albuquerque as the would-be team-poaching villain of the Southwest were still fresh in fans' minds a year later when the owners of the Calgary Cannons of the Pacific Coast League announced they would be moving to Albuquerque. When a poll was put before readers in the *Albuquerque Tribune* to help name the new team, which would start play in 2003, a whopping 67 percent of the 120,000 respondents suggested that the team name be the Isotopes. Noting that Albuquerque did indeed have a connection to the nation's nuclear industry, team ownership accepted the fans' decision and even introduced a mascot named Orbit. Since then, whenever the "Hungry, Hungry Homer" episode runs in syndication, the Isotopes' online merchandise store is inundated with orders.

Throughout beautiful Isotope Park's first several seasons, fans chuckled at the team name's reference to the popular television series, but the Simpson family didn't have an actual presence. That changed in 2010 after Isotopes general manager John Traub accidentally happened upon a set of "life size" matching statues depicting a reclining Homer holding a remote control (later repainted to resemble a pair of baseball

"Dancing Homer" takes a breather.

game tickets) and Marge holding a big bucket of popcorn.

Traub and his wife, Liz, spotted the statues during a trip to Los Angeles to watch the Dodgers' 2009 playoff series against the St. Louis Cardinals. When the Traubs found them, Homer

and Marge were adorning the exterior of a La Brea Avenue antiques store called Nick Metropolis Collectable Furniture. After a lengthy negotiation that included Isotopes' team president Kevin Young, the shop owner agreed to part with his animated friends. The next challenge involved finding a way to transport Homer and Marge from Los Angeles to Albuquerque. After trying out three rental vehicles that proved too small, the Traubs were able to wedge the statues into a Ford Expedition. And so, Homer and Marge made the trip east, got a much-needed bath and refurbishing at a local salvage yard, and then were declared ready for the big time. The next spring Isotopes fans were delighted to find them sitting on matching benches on the Isotopes Park concourse.

Predictably, the benches immediately became popular places for local rooters to plop down and pose for photos with the field in the background. In the years since, statues of Bart and Lisa Simpson have been added to the Isotopes Park collection.

A visit to Isotopes Park, fondly referred to as "The Lab" by local fans, offers you the chance to consider how far-reaching the effect of the game is on our culture—after all it has inspired several *Simpsons* episodes, not just those two—but also on how the game has been impacted by popular culture through the years as well.

53. The Shoeless Joe Jackson Museum and Baseball Library

356 Field Street
Greenville, South Carolina 29601
(864) 346-4867
www.shoelessjoejackson.org/
index.php

Regardless of whether he could "say it wasn't so" when asked on the steps of a Chicago courthouse to refute allegations that he and seven of his White Sox teammates had conspired to fix the 1919 World Series, Joe Jackson was one of the greatest hitters to ever live. And his hometown of Greenville, South Carolina, chooses to remember him for his grace on the field, where he accumulated the third-highest lifetime batting average, rather than for the circumstances surrounding his premature departure from baseball.

Although Jackson was never convicted of a crime, baseball commissioner Kenesaw Mountain Landis toed a hard line with the so-called "Black Sox," barring them all from baseball in 1921. Jackson was thirty-one years old at the time and the owner of a gaudy .356 average over thirteen seasons. He would play semi-pro

The Joe Jackson Museum provides a rare glimpse into Jackson's life after his years in the game.

ball under a number of assumed names over the next several years before returning to his boyhood home of Greenville in 1929. He opened a liquor store in town and could be found behind its counter until he suffered a heart attack and passed away in 1951.

A tour of the many Jackson landmarks in Greenville begins at the **Shoeless Joe Jackson Museum and Baseball Library,** which opened in 2008, in the house where Jackson was born and raised, and where he returned to spend his later years with his wife, Katie. Although this is the actual redbrick house in which Jackson lived, it does not sit at its original location. When Jackson lived in it, the house was located at 119 East Wilburne Avenue. It was disassembled in 2006, and over the next couple of years reassembled closer to downtown. It now resides in Greenville's West End, not far from **Fluor Field,** home of the South Atlantic League's Greenville Drive.

In addition to providing you with a peek into the very rooms where Jackson spent his life, the Museum includes signed balls, old photos, newspaper clippings, framed photos of the actors who portrayed Jackson and his White Sox teammates in the movie version of *Eight Men Out*, and other artifacts from Jackson's years in Greenville and in baseball. You'll find one of Jackson's weather-beaten fielder's mitts, and his 1917 World Series ring here. Jackson batted .304 (7 for 24) in that first World Series of his career, helping to guide the White Sox to victory over the Giants. Interestingly, he performed even better at the plate in the fateful 1919 Series, batting a robust .375 (12 for 32) against the Reds. In the gift shop, you'll find, rather curiously, a set of Shoeless Joe Poker Chips for sale, as well as a Shoeless Joe Cookbook that provides the details on how to prepare some of the slugger's favorite meals.

This statue was crafted inside Greenville's City Hall while townsfolk observed the sculptor's lengthy project.

The museum is currently operating on a shoestring budget. It is staffed by local volunteers, and open to the public on Saturday from 10:00 a.m. until 2:00 p.m. Admission is free, though donations are happily accepted.

While you're in town, you should make a point to also visit **Shoeless Joe Jackson Memorial Ballpark** (406 West Avenue), where Jackson honed his legendary swing and first wielded the 48-ounce bat he famously called "Black Betsy." Jackson was just thirteen years old when he played his first semi-pro game on this field that now bears his name. In those days the field was called the Brandon Mill Ballpark, and it was where Jackson was discovered and signed to his first professional contract by

Connie Mack. A plaque marking the historic significance of the location is inscribed with the words:

> As a thirteen-year-old, Joe Jackson earned a position on the Brandon Mill Team. He possessed a talent so uncommon that legends grew from his deeds. His home runs were known as "Saturday Specials," his line drives "blue darters." His glove "a place where triples die." Shoeless Joe was the greatest natural hitter ever to grace the diamond, and was such an inspiration that Babe Ruth chose to copy his swing. He was banished from baseball for his complicity in the 1919 Black Sox scandal, yet his memory still moves across the conscience of America.

Today, a vintage baseball game is played on this field every other summer, sponsored dually by the Jackson Museum and Royston, Georgia's Ty Cobb Museum. In odd years, the summer throwback game is played in Greenville; in even years, it takes place at Ty Cobb Field in Royston. The players are amateurs who hail from the local communities.

Not far from the field, at **West End Market** a bronze statue depicts Jackson finishing one of his prodigious left-handed swings. His tiny glove is tucked neatly into one of his back pants pockets. The statue, which incorporates bricks from Comiskey Park into its base, was sculpted by Doug Young, who made it in the lobby of the Greenville City Hall in 2002 while members of the public observed his work.

After visiting the hallowed grounds where Jackson's baseball career took flight amid so much hope and glory and this rendering of Jackson in his prime, you can follow Pendleton Street to the place where Jackson sought refuge after he was banished: the site of his **liquor store** (1262 Pendleton Street). According to Ken Burns's documentary *Baseball*, Cobb once stopped into the store to buy a pint of whiskey while passing through Greenville and was saddened to find a broken-down Jackson behind the counter. "Don't you know me?" Cobb asked his old rival, and Jackson replied, "Sure, I know you. But I wasn't sure you wanted to know me. A lot of them don't."

A final point of interest along Greenville's Joe Jackson trail is the Jackson grave at **Woodlawn Memorial Park** (Wade Hampton Boulevard). Jackson's tombstone is nothing fancy, but it is easy to find thanks to the baseballs, bats, white socks, and other memorabilia that pilgrims leave behind. The inscription on the stone does not refer to Jackson as "Shoeless Joe," a nickname he earned early in his career after removing a pair of tight-fitting spikes and batting barefoot, but as "Joseph W. Jackson."

Together these Greenville landmarks memorialize a great player and by all accounts a decent human being, who unfortunately got involved with the wrong crowd and out of greed or ignorance, or both, made a decision he would regret for the rest of his life. The game has known no figure more tragic than Joe Jackson, who had all the talent in the world but no place left to showcase it, and a visit to Greenville does much to remind us of the temptations we face in life and of the price to pay if we make poor choices.

Outside George M. Steinbrenner Field—the Yankees' towering 11,000-seat spring training home—you find a palm-adorned replica of Yankee Stadium's famed Monument Park. Tampa's Monument Park embraces the spirit of the monument- and bronze-laden area beyond the outfield fence in the Bronx, if not the exact look. Located just outside Steinbrenner Field's main entrance, it consists of pinstriped plaques that display the uniform numbers of the Yankees' heroes whose numbers have been retired by the team. Beneath the numbers, blue placards offer quotations from the players themselves, summaries of their accomplishments, and general words of praise about them.

Lou Gehrig's marker reads, "Lou was one of the most prolific Yankee hitters of all time. From 1923–1939. His skills and inner strength were things of beauty on the ball field and earned him the nickname, 'The Iron Horse.'"

Babe Ruth's reads, "From 1920–1934. Single-handedly lifted baseball to new heights with his unlimited talent and unbridled love for the game. His enormous contributions to baseball and the Yankees made him the most celebrated athlete who ever lived."

Joe DiMaggio's reads, "I want to thank the good Lord for making me a Yankee."

This well-landscaped attraction debuted in 1996, when the City of Tampa opened what was soon christened "Legends Field" on a plot abutting the home stadium of the NFL's Tampa Bay Buccaneers. The baseball complex was built at a cost of $30 million to lure the Grapefruit League Yankees away from their longtime spring roost in Fort Lauderdale. Yankees owner George Steinbrenner kept his year-round home in Tampa, and was a driving force in facilitating the move. In 2008, Tampa's ballpark was renamed in his honor.

54. Tampa's Monument Park

George M. Steinbrenner Field
One Steinbrenner Drive
Tampa, Florida 33614
(813) 875-7753
www.steinbrennerfield.com

After Mr. Steinbrenner's death in 2010, the Yankees installed a 600-pound life-size marble statue of him on a 3-ton granite base outside the entry steps to Steinbrenner Field. Depicting him in a smartly fitted business suit, and wearing his 2009 world championship ring, the piece is a duplicate of a statue that stands inside Yankee Stadium. A plaque on the base reads, "A great philanthropist whose charitable efforts were mostly performed without fanfare, he followed a personal motto of 'the greatest form of charity is anonymity.'"

Aside from Tampa's Monument Park and the statue of the "Boss," Steinbrenner Field reflects many other similarities to Yankee Stadium. Not far from the entrance gates, you encounter a massive souvenir and apparel shop that quickly recalls the in-your-face merchandising that assails you as you walk along the concourse of any level of the Yankees' regular season home. The Legends Room bills itself as the largest repository of Yankees gear in the Southeast, and it seems like a fair bet that the claim is correct. The shop is open year-round, Monday through Friday from 10:00 a.m. to 5:30 p.m., and Saturday from 10:00 a.m. to 3:00 p.m. If you're a Yankees rooter looking for a keepsake, rare autograph, or game-worn jersey from a current

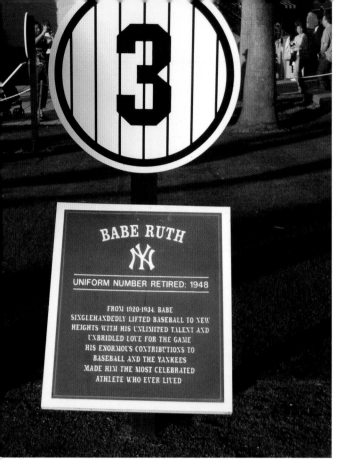

The Babe Ruth plaques at Tampa's Monument Park

with field dimensions that mimic the ones in the Bronx. The home-run porch in right field is just 314 feet from home plate; the fence in straight-away center measures 408 feet; "Death Valley" in left-center measures 399 feet; and the left field foul pole is 318 feet from home plate. Decorative white arches and filigree extend high above the Steinbrenner Field roof, mimicking the facade that rings the upper level of the new Yankee Stadium and which ran above the right field bleachers at the previous incarnation of Yankee Stadium. Another likeness is the outfield video board, which as in the Bronx is oversized, to put it mildly. And lest anyone forget which is the home team, giant blue windscreens rise above the top row of seats, offering one letter apiece to spell Y A N K E E S.

After hosting a full slate of Yankees home games during March, Steinbrenner Field serves as the regular season home of the Florida State League Tampa Yankees. In addition, a small ballpark adjacent to the main stadium, NY Yankees Community Field, is the home diamond of the Hillsboro Community College Hawks. The Yankees also host a wood-bat high school tournament at Steinbrenner Field each November for teams from Hillsboro and Pinellas Counties. But even on days when no games are scheduled, the Yankees' complex is worth visiting for a taste of the Bronx mystique in Southwest Florida.

or former star, there's a good chance you'll find it here.

The similarities between the Yankees' regular season and spring training homes are abundant inside Steinbrenner Field as well, beginning

As bad as baseball's PED Era was, it never threatened the game's very existence. As the revelations that many of the sport's biggest stars of the early 2000s were products of chemical enhancement came to light, most of us expressed our displeasure even as we continued turning out at the turnstiles and tuning in on the television, radio, and Internet. Surely, this dark period for the game has been an unpleasant one, but how many of us have been so outraged that we actually considered giving up the game?

And so, the most damning black eye the game has yet endured remains the one involving the eight Chicago White Sox players who allegedly conspired with gamblers to fix the 1919 World Series against the Reds. The federal court case against Joe Jackson and his teammates may have proven inconclusive in the eyes of the law, but it revealed that baseball's playing field had often been anything but level during the first two decades of the twentieth century. The game's very integrity was at stake. But fortunately, the Gamblers Era, if you will, came to an end in Chicago.

While the Cook County Criminal Courts Building no longer serves as a courthouse, it still stands in Chicago, preserved as a National Historic Landmark. It represents the place where baseball lost its innocence, and also the place where it finally fought back against the wise guys who had infiltrated its ranks. It was here that a horrified nation learned the details of the Black Sox Scandal and of the ensuing cover-up that involved signed confessions by three of the accused players—Jackson, Eddie Cicotte, and Lefty Williams—mysteriously disappearing. It was here that the growing rift between baseball's owners and players came to light; here that the notion of the game as solely that, a game, and not a business, was finally dispelled; here that a jury ultimately found all eight accused players

55. The "Black Sox" Trial Courthouse

Cook County Criminal Courts Building
54 West Hubbard Street
Chicago, Illinois 60654

not guilty in the eyes of the State of Illinois, only to see the verdict overruled by the game's first commissioner, Judge Kenesaw Mountain Landis, who banned the eight for life.

Today a plaque beside the courthouse door reads, "This Romanesque style building, which housed the Cook County Criminal Courts for 35 years, was the site of many legendary trials, including the Leopold and Loeb murder case and Black Sox scandal. . . . Dedicated on June 9, 1993, Richard M. Daley, Mayor."

Baseball myth holds that this is where a young fan implored Jackson to profess his innocence with a cry of "Say it ain't so," only to watch through teary eyes as his idol sadly shook his head and said, "Yes, kid, I'm afraid it is." In fact, this exchange never took place. According to Jackson and others who watched him descend the courthouse steps after testifying before a grand jury on that September day in 1920, there were no children present, just a few adults, including reporter Charley Owens of the *Chicago Daily News*, who later penned the article that included the details of this supposed encounter, perhaps as a way to personify the betrayal and hurt the nation felt upon learning that one of the game's brightest stars was suspected of purposely losing the most hallowed of baseball contests, the World Series.

The trial held in this building forced baseball to finally address its festering gambling problem.

A signed confession by Joe Jackson mysteriously disappeared from the evidence room of the Cook County Criminal Courts Building before the start of the 1921 Black Sox Trial.

Over the next eleven months the courthouse provided the stage for a court case that deeply wounded the psyche of the nation but ultimately left the national game on sounder footing than it had ever been before. Even though the missing confessions (years later they would turn up in the possession of White Sox owner Charlie Comiskey) helped ensure the players' acquittal, the undeniable connection the trial exposed between the players and many shady characters from the gambling underworld convinced Landis that they were guilty enough in his book. His unequivocal expulsion of them, and his subsequent refusal to consider their pleas for reinstatement during his remaining twenty-four years in office, discouraged other cheats and would-be cheats, while also helping to restore public faith in the game.

Today, a visit to the Cook County Criminal Courts Building, or "Courthouse Place" as it is also called, serves as a reminder that though the government can play a role in maintaining baseball's credibility—just as it did in orchestrating the congressional hearings that helped shine a light on the PED Era—in the end the game must police itself.

● ●

56. Los Angeles Memorial Coliseum

3911 South Figueroa Street
Los Angeles, California 90037
www.lacoliseum.com

As part of the Dodgers' efforts to commemorate the fiftieth anniversary of their move west, from Brooklyn to Los Angeles in 1958,

they played an end-of-spring-training exhibition against the Red Sox at Los Angeles Memorial Coliseum on March 29, 2008. The spectacle was the first baseball game at the Dodgers' original West Coast home since September 20, 1961, when Sandy Koufax beat the Cubs 3–2, pitching all thirteen innings in a Coliseum finale that just didn't want to end. The next season, the Dodgers moved to Dodger Stadium.

No one pitched thirteen innings when the Red Sox and Dodgers squared off for a throwback game at the Coliseum in 2008, but the game was notable for setting a new world record

On March 29, 2008, the Dodgers hosted David Ortiz (batting) and the Red Sox for an exhibition game at the LA Coliseum.

for the biggest crowd ever to attend a baseball game. Some 115,300 people watched the Red Sox defeat the Dodgers 7–4 that night, breaking the previous mark of 114,000 that had witnessed a game at a cricket grounds in Australia during the 1956 Olympics.

Before the Dodgers' return to the Coliseum, pundits and players alike had joked that the exhibition would result in a football-like score, owing to the fact that the lopsided diamond that had been carved onto the football grid placed the left field foul pole just 201 feet from home plate. There was, however, a 60-foot-high screen— promptly dubbed the "Screen Monster"—in left field, making it a bit more difficult for hitters to reach the seats. In the end, there were only four long balls—two by each team.

While the game was a hot ticket, most people who witnessed it agreed afterward that the Coliseum really wasn't cut out to host base-ball. And that was pretty much the consensus an earlier generation of fans had reached, when the Dodgers spent their first four seasons in Los Angeles playing at the facility. But the cavern-ous home of the University of Southern Califor-nia Trojans football team is still worth your visit today to connect with the dawning of West Coast big-league ball and to check out the plaques on either side of the main entrance, many of which celebrate the Coliseum's baseball past.

The Coliseum was originally constructed in the early 1920s and then underwent an expan-sion so that it could accommodate the 1932 Olympics. During the next few decades it served

This tree was a tiny seedling when Babe Ruth planted it during a tour of the Hawaiian Islands in 1933.

celebs who planted them give you a chance to connect with the history of the island and with the broader cultural and political history of the United States.

Ruth's tree resides across the street from the Hilo Hawaiian Hotel. Although it was just a twig when the aging slugger's two rough hands gently patted down the soil around its slender trunk, it now stands as an expansive monument to the Sultan of Swat.

The story of how the Hilo Walk of Fame and Banyan Drive came into existence dates back to a few months before Ruth's visit, when filmmaker Cecil B. DeMille arrived in Hawaii to film scenes for his stranded-adventurer movie *Four Frightened People*. The Hilo Park Commission asked DeMille and some of the actors from the movie to plant trees to commemorate their work on the island. Ruth followed suit later in the year, then President Franklin Delano Roosevelt in 1934, then Amelia Earhart and King George V during separate visits in 1935. A road was added between the trees, and before long hotels began sprouting along it. Richard Nixon planted a tree in 1952, long before he became president, then after it was lost in a tsunami, First Lady Pat Nixon returned to the islands during his term in office to replace it. Supreme Court justice Earl Warren planted a tree, as did Chinese premier Sun Fo, musician Louis Armstrong, and a host of other notable people.

For the most part, the banyans have held up. Among all the types of trees Hilo might have chosen to withstand the decades, the banyan was a wise choice. Banyans are believed to live as long as a thousand years and can grow to more than 656 feet in diameter (that is not a typo!). There is something mystical and unusually reassuring about standing beside a living tree and knowing that a person who had an important impact on American culture or politics was responsible, at least in part, for its existence. If you hail from subtropical climes yourself, you can even pilfer some of the figs that sometimes fall from the trees to take home and plant. Who knows, you might just sprout and cultivate a little bit of Ruth's legacy in your own backyard!

Although it lost its place in minor-league baseball when the Southern League Chattanooga Lookouts moved to a new downtown ballpark at the start of the 2000 season, historic Joe Engel Stadium is poised to remain an important part of the Chattanooga landscape for a good long time. In 2009, the ancient park was placed on the US National Register of Historic Places. Also that year, the Engel Foundation was formed to see to the stadium's preservation. A couple of years later, Engel Stadium was deeded by the city of Chattanooga and Hamilton County to the University of Tennessee at Chattanooga (UTC).

It's a good thing they kept this old park standing as long as they did, because it sure came in handy when it came time to film the Jackie Robinson biopic *42*. After identifying it as an apt stand-in for Brooklyn's Ebbets Field, a crew from Legendary Films arrived in 2012 to retrofit the stadium to resemble Robinson's old home. The studio went so far as to deconstruct the dugouts and install a 40-foot-long "green screen" in the outfield to obscure the fence. The angle of the playing field itself was also altered for the film, as was the configuration of the lower seating bowl and the outfield scoreboard.

When the filming was finished, the folks from Hollywood left Engel Stadium a little bit better off than they had found it, funding the restoration of the original aesthetic elements that had been altered, and making much-needed improvements to the roof, plumbing, and electrical infrastructure.

This is a baseball location that surely deserves to be preserved and treasured. It possesses as colorful a history as any still-standing bush-league yard of yesteryear.

The story of how Engel Stadium carved out its unique place in the game begins in the

58. Joe Engel Stadium

1130 East Third Street
Chattanooga, Tennessee 37403
www.engelfoundation.com

1920s, when Washington Senators owner Clark W. Griffith sent former big-league pitcher and vaudeville entertainer Joe Engel to Chattanooga to construct a new ballpark for one of Washington's minor-league clubs. Engel coordinated the ballpark project and then decided he liked Chattanooga so much he wanted to stay and run the team. The park opened in 1930, and Engel immediately began applying the lessons he'd learned in his post-baseball career as an entertainer to his management of the Lookouts. Among his many publicity stunts were a raffle that awarded a $10,000 house to a lucky fan; a trade in which Engel sent Lookouts shortstop Johnny Jones packing to the team in Charlotte in exchange for a 25-pound turkey that Engel then served to the local sportswriters; a pregame elephant hunt that took place on the outfield lawn; a midgame ostrich race in the outfield; and the installation of a barber's chair behind home plate.

The most famous Engel gimmick of all, though, and the one that put Chattanooga on the national baseball map, occurred on April 2, 1931. That spring Engel signed a seventeen-year-old girl named Jackie Mitchell to a contract just prior to the New York Yankees visiting for an exhibition game. When the big leaguers arrived, Engel sent the 5-foot-5-inch 130-pound Mitchell to the mound. All the young lady did was strike out the first two batters she faced: Babe Ruth

Joe Engel was crowned "King of Baseball" by *Time* magazine in 1940.

and Lou Gehrig. Then she walked Tony Lazzeri on five pitches and was removed from the game. Within a matter of days, grainy black-and-white footage of this extraordinary feat was playing at movie houses across the country, and fans in faraway cities were debating whether the two strikeouts had been staged or legitimate.

Forward thinking as always, commissioner Kenesaw Mountain Landis saw need to quickly stifle talk of the female whose wicked sidearm sinker had humbled two of baseball's brightest stars. "The Judge," as he was called, promptly declared there was no place for women in baseball and voided Mitchell's contract. So much for progress. Chattanoogans still talk about the historic moment, though, as each generation of local fans passes down the story to the next.

The ballpark that was Engel's promotions laboratory today offers a classic redbrick facade and cozy grandstand full of wooden seats tucked beneath a roof supported by exposed steel girders. Beneath the stands you find your way lit by antique iron lamps that were added during an early 1990s renovation that restored the ballpark to its 1930s glory. For several decades the field's most distinguishing feature was its sheer size. Throughout its days as a minor-league venue, Engel Stadium's center field fence measured a distant 471 feet from home plate. Recently though, an intermediary fence less than 400 feet from the plate was installed to make the field more appropriate for amateur play.

Although Engel Stadium does not have a regular tenant to call it home these days, it does see use hosting baseball clinics and camps, and civic events. UTC currently has plans in the works to develop a track and field complex in the stadium's parking lot, and has pledged to keep the stadium intact. There has been talk of turning it into a local baseball museum, which sounds like a great idea.

Female sensation Jackie Mitchell with Joe Engel and strikeout victims Lou Gehrig (left) and Babe Ruth (right)

Decades before cities like San Francisco, Cincinnati, and Pittsburgh realized the aesthetic value of building their ballparks on the waterfront, the folks in St. Petersburg got it right. Yes, you read that correctly. Believe it or not, the Gulf Coast city that now hosts games in a catwalk-ridden dome was a trailblazer in maximizing the outdoor fan experience. The city was also a leading force in the evolution of spring training. In fact, if not for St. Petersburg and the vision of one of its former mayors—a gentleman named Al Lang—Florida's Grapefruit League might not exist.

Today, a trip to St. Petersburg's former spring training hub—Al Lang Stadium—allows you to learn about the city's proud baseball history by perusing dozens of bronze plaques mounted on its interior and exterior walls. You can also sit in the sun and watch an amateur game while enjoying breathtaking views of sailboats bobbing on the blue-green Gulf waters just beyond the left field line.

The story of how Al Lang brought spring baseball to Florida dates back to the early 1900s. In those days most big-league teams traveled to underdeveloped Southern states like Alabama, Arkansas, and Georgia in the weeks before each new season to get their players in shape. As far as the teams were concerned, the more remote a camp's location the better, as rural environments offered less temptation for the rambling players of the era. In those days the players worked second jobs in the off-season and didn't have the luxury of devoting much time to winter conditioning. Thus, weight loss and extended sobriety were the main spring goals, rather than skill refinement and player evaluation. Teams trained in isolation, and spring exhibitions between different big-league clubs were rare.

But then Lang imagined that spring training could be something more. He envisioned

59. Al Lang Stadium

230 First Street South
St. Petersburg, Florida 33701
(727) 551-3000
www.stpeteinternationalbaseball.com/index.php

a centralized location in Florida where teams could scrimmage one another before audiences of paying fans. Hoping to not only revolutionize the spring game but transform St. Petersburg from a small fishing village to a resort town, Lang traveled to St. Louis in December of 1913 to meet with St. Louis Browns president Robert Hedges and Browns manager Branch Rickey. Lang enchanted the two men, filling their heads with images of a spring filled with trophy fishing, sunshine, and baseball. He also made sure to mention that St. Petersburg was a dry town. Lang offered the Browns a 20-acre lot rent free for one year. Hedges and Rickey took the bait.

In February of 1914 the Browns arrived in St. Petersburg, and several other teams followed their lead, traveling farther south than they had ever been before to play exhibitions. On February 27, 1914, the Browns lost to the Cubs 3–2 at a field near St. Petersburg's Coffee Pot Bayou in the first professional baseball game ever played in Florida. More than 4,000 spectators turned out for the event, many arriving by boat at a special dock installed for the occasion.

Due to a financial dispute between Lang and the Browns, the team did not return in 1915. But Lang was undeterred in his quest to make

The onetime spring home of the Tampa Bay Rays, New York Yankees, and St. Louis Cardinals now serves Team Canada.

St. Petersburg a spring training hotbed. In 1922 Waterfront Park opened not far from where Al Lang Stadium stands today to serve as the spring home of the Boston Braves. The Braves made camp in the city through 1937. The Yankees also came to town each year beginning in 1925, after the Bronx Bombers had to leave their previous camp in New Orleans once heavy-drinking slugger Babe Ruth wore out his welcome. Almost immediately, Ruth was in trouble again, this time with an alligator that chased him off the outfield grass of St. Petersburg's Crescent Lake Park. In between games and 'gator racing, Ruth danced at the Coliseum and entertained guests on the tuba at the Jungle Country Club. By 1929 ten of

the sixteen major-league teams were training in Florida.

St. Petersburg built Al Lang Field in 1947. The facility was rebuilt in 1977 and renamed Al Lang Stadium at that time. Through the years the old and new versions of the park served as the spring home of the Giants, Mets, Orioles, Cardinals, and Rays. Finally, in 2008, when the Rays moved their spring camp to Port Charlotte, Al Lang Stadium was left without a big-league tenant. The stadium still sees plenty of use though, as both a minor league soccer venue, and as one of the sites the International Baseball Federation uses to prepare teams for competition. Since 2011, the Dutch and Canadian national teams have trained and played exhibition games against big-league and minor-league teams at Al Lang Stadium. During March of 2014, for example, the big-league Blue Jays, Orioles, Tigers, Braves, and Phillies all visited St. Petersburg to play against Team Canada. Tickets are cheap, and the big-league players are even more accessible than during regular preseason games.

When you visit, be sure to check out the dozens of bronze historic markers that once lined St. Petersburg's "Baseball Boulevard." For a time Baseball Boulevard was a charming, if underpublicized, baseball landmark. Taking the form of eighty-five home-plate-shaped plaques on the sidewalks between Al Lang Stadium and Tropicana Field, it was unveiled in 1998. Strolling along Central Avenue and First Street, you could learn that the Yankees and Cardinals met in the 1942 World Series after sharing the same spring training park in St. Petersburg; that Lou Gehrig collapsed during a 1939 exhibition game, foreshadowing the end of his streak of 2,130 consecutive games played and the onset of his terrible illness; that a trainer "parboiled" Joe DiMaggio's ankle during a spring treatment in 1936, causing the Yankee Clipper to miss the first month of the season; and that fans turned out at Waterfront Park for a game of Donkey Baseball in 1940. All of these moments and many more were captured on the monuments along Baseball Boulevard. In 2012, however, St. Petersburg made the decision to uproot most of the markers and to transplant them to Al Lang Stadium. Apparently, the salt air, tree roots, and skateboarders had done a number on the bronzes over the course of a decade and a half, and moving them was more cost-effective than refurbishing them. The good news is that you can now enjoy almost all of the plaques in one location.

Another highlight is the bronze bust of Lang, inscribed with the words:

> This stadium is dedicated March 12, 1977 in honor of Albert Fielding Lang (1870–1960), Florida's sunshine ambassador to major league baseball. It was through his dedication, vision and love of the game that the big leagues discovered Florida's excellence as a conditioning site and that St. Petersburg became baseball's spring training capital. This stadium is built on the site of Al Lang Field, erected in 1947.

Al Lang is often called the Father of the Grapefruit League.

60. The Back Porch Seats at Banner Island Ballpark

404 West Fremont Street
Stockton, California 95203
(209) 644-1900
www.stocktonports.com

When it comes to offering a special ballpark seating location that makes the game-day experience even more enjoyable than it already is, Stockton's Banner Island Ballpark really gets it right. The California League yard offers the inspired Jackson Rancheria Back Porch, where fifty lucky fans per game watch in style from right field home-run territory. Beneath the protected canopy of a wooden trestle that looks like it came straight from someone's lodge, you find two rows of comfortable Adirondack-style wooden rocking chairs aimed squarely at the field. Reclining in one of these as you indulge in the all-you-can-eat buffet that comes with Back Porch admission, you're closer to home plate than you would be sitting perched above the right field fence at most other minor-league parks. That's because after tracing an ordinary-enough course from center field into right-center, Banner Island Ballpark's outfield wall suddenly arcs dramatically toward the infield, before straightening out again and continuing toward the right field foul pole. Elevated above the fence on this "bubble," the Back Porch seats seem to hover beyond the infield.

In truth, the field dimensions in Stockton are rather odd all around. It's only 300 feet down the line in left, where a truncated version of Fenway Park's Green Monster can be found slanting back rather dramatically to a measurement of 350 feet in straightaway left. The oddities were created by necessity as the park sits on the banks of the Stockton Deepwater Ship Channel, a waterway dug in the 1930s to allow for big boat passage to the San Joaquin River. As a result, a long fly ball to right field that clears the fence and then either the right field seating lawn or Back Porch only has to travel about 390 feet to splash down.

Banner Island Ballpark was designed by the ballpark experts at HKS and built at a cost of $22 million. It opened in 2005 to replace Billy Hebert Field. As it is city owned, the facility's official name is "Stockton Ballpark," but local fans, sportswriters, and the Ports' front office all call it Banner Island Ballpark.

The Ports have been a fixture in these parts since 1946 with just a few interruptions in play along the way, but Stockton's baseball history goes back even further. Baseball has been played on the once muddy island where the Ports reside since the 1860s. By the 1880s, Stockton had a team in an early California League, and often the local field was flooded, earning the island the nickname Mudville. Then, in 1888 Ernest L. Thayer, writing under the pen name Phin, published the poem "Casey at the Bat" in the *San Francisco Daily Examiner*. The poem tells the story, as you will surely recall, of Mighty Casey and his Mudville Nine. Over the years, the poem has been canonized as one of American culture and baseball literature's great works, and Stockton has been happy to claim its place in that canon. However, Thayer never said that his Mudville was inspired by Stockton, and today Holliston, Massachusetts, also claims that *it* was the inspiration for the poem's setting, as you will find detailed elsewhere in this book.

Fans recline on comfortable Adirondack chairs as they watch the game from Stockton's Back Porch.

Whether Stockton's Mudville or Holliston's was the site of Casey's epic strikeout, you should make a point to visit Banner Island Ballpark before *you* strike out. There's only one small rub, though, when it comes to getting your fanny into one of the comfy wooden rocking chairs in right field: The Back Porch is a group party area only accessible to groups of twenty-five people or more. For less than $30 per person you get a ninety-minute pregame spread that includes tri-tip steak, barbecue chicken, hot dogs, baked beans, coleslaw, and more. Then you get to watch the game from one of the best seats in the house. But you can't buy just one or two seats to this special section. Now, you might well be the type that travels via one of the many ballpark coaches that have sprung up in the past two decades and you might have the chance to sit in a block of seats like this along with at least twenty-four new friends. But if you're the type that prefers to travel solo or in a smaller party, well, you will need to find a creative way to get into one of these excellent seats for at least one game.

61. The House of David Baseball Museum

1380 Napier Avenue
Benton Harbor, Michigan 49022
(269) 325-0039

Back in the days before television and mass transportation, we Americans depended on live entertainment to fill our leisure hours. Imagine, the horror! The good news was that rather than having to travel great distances to be entertained, you could usually sit back and wait for the entertainment to come to you. The live theater and vaudeville circuits both channeled steady streams of talent into small-town America in the first few decades of the 1900s, and baseball, above all other sports, did its part to fill the leisure hours too. While the big cities fielded major-league teams and the midsize cities had minor-league and Negro Leagues teams, the smaller cities cheered for various semi-pro teams. Mill towns and agricultural communities alike sported semi-pro clubs of young men who liked to play after work and on weekends. Those smaller communities also enjoyed watching barnstorming baseball teams, which were touring groups of major leaguers, former major leaguers, or Negro Leaguers who would visit small fields across the country where they could showcase their skills against the best squad of locals each community could muster. The most popular of these barnstorming outfits was the House of David Baseball Team.

Today, the House of David Baseball Museum does an amazingly comprehensive job of preserving the memory of this unusual bunch of

Members of the barnstorming House of David baseball team were prohibited from cutting their hair . . . but could play baseball.

Members of the House of David baseball team wore thick wool uniforms like this one.

bearded ballers that transcended the norms of sport, religion, and culture to chisel out a place in American society from the 1920s into the 1950s.

The team represented the House of David, which was a Christian commune founded in Benton Harbor, Michigan, in the early 1900s under the auspices of uniting the twelve lost tribes of Israel. Members of the colony agreed to refrain from sex, smoking, drinking, eating meat, cutting their hair, and shaving, while they awaited the millennium. Members also renounced their worldly possessions, handing them over to leader Benjamin Purnell. At its height, the House had nearly a thousand members, and owned more than 100,000 acres of pasture and timber land in the Midwest, as well as several factories, foundries, and mines.

Though they may have been fanatical in their beliefs, members of the House of David loved baseball and their religion had no restrictions on their playing it. With the blessing of Purnell, the House of David formed its first baseball team in 1913. And by the early 1920s, the commune's popular travel team had become its chief means of recruiting new members and making money. The players were known for their long beards, unruly hairdos, thick wool uniforms, and fun-loving attitudes. They were wizards on the diamond who entertained fans with a mixture of baseball and vaudeville skills. Of course, they also distributed promotional propaganda espousing their beliefs, and they sent the gate receipts from their games home to Purnell in Michigan.

Before long, the House of David was fielding several teams and employing mercenary players who would wear fake beards and long wigs while they waited for their own hair to grow into the expected costume. These shaggy globetrotters were an inclusive bunch that often barnstormed with travel partners from the Negro Leagues. They were particularly fond of the Kansas City Monarchs, and as they became nationally known, they used their popularity as leverage to ensure that their Negro Leagues brethren could eat in the same restaurants and sleep in the same hotels as they did when they visited each new town. The House of David baseball team also invented the baseball-practice game "pepper," which a group of players would perform at midfield between innings. The commune was an early innovator of night baseball too, as 1930s House teams traveled the country with trucks carrying lighting scaffolds that could be quickly erected at each venue along the way.

At the House of David Baseball Museum, you find a wealth of artifacts related to the old teams. Among the many hilarious photos of hairy-headed hardballers are ones of Babe Ruth, Grover Cleveland Alexander, and Satchel Paige, who all donned fake beards to play in exhibitions with the House of David. According to legend, pitcher Percy Walker once struck out the great Ruth in consecutive at-bats. Also on display are old uniforms, promotional posters, and some of the early ballpark lighting equipment.

More than just being a baseball landmark, the museum tells the whole story of the commune's history, which also included running a popular amusement park and zoo in Benton Harbor, owning a diamond mine in Australia, and sponsoring nationally known musical and vaudeville acts.

As for the museum, it was founded in Benton Harbor in 1997 by Chris Siriano, who grew up in town and carried into his adulthood fond memories of visiting the House of David amusement park as a child. Later, as a history major at Western Michigan University, Siriano laid the foundation for the museum he would one day open. Over the past few decades, the museum has accumulated thousands of artifacts. Additions to the collection in the past few years have included dozens of vintage photographs of different House of David players and teams, broadsides of several Negro Leagues teams that played against the House of David, team uniforms from the 1930s and 1940s, signed baseballs from several 1930s teams, original reel-to-reel film footage of the 1923 team in action, and handwritten letters between the House of David players and managers.

The museum is open Saturday and Sunday from 10:00 a.m. until 4:00 p.m., and weekdays by appointment. Acquiring, preserving, and exhibiting these unique mementos is a labor of love for Siriano, and he delights in guiding visitors through the museum. Admission costs $5.00 for adults, and $1.00 for children under age twelve; group rates are also available.

Lloyd Dalager, the last living member of the House of David baseball team, stopped by the museum in 2009. Well into his mid-nineties at the time, Dalager still sported the shaggy beard that had been part of his "uniform" back in his heyday, and still had clear memories of playing with and against baseball immortals like Ruth, Paige, Alexander, and Dizzy Dean.

As you've likely noticed, this book is devoted to detailing 101 places that you should make a point to visit, because as a baseball fan it would be pretty cool to see and experience them. In almost every case these are places you actually *can* visit, so long as you can fund the cost of transportation and, in some cases, an admission ticket. In other words, the book doesn't offer entries like "Bud Selig's private jet" or "Alex Rodriguez's personal art collection," which may be awe-invoking sites (then again, they may not), but are off-limits to the typical wanderer. This entry is a little bit different though. While technically you *can* visit the site where the mud that's used to "rub up" every minor-league and major-league ball is collected, chances are that if you did, you wouldn't know for sure that you had found it. That's because the exact location of the public riverbank where the Lena Blackburne Rubbing Mud Company gets its silky till has been a closely guarded baseball secret dating all the way back to before World War II. According to the Mud Company, the site is accessible via a narrow trail leading from a public road. The trail leads into the woods before suddenly opening up along the riverbank. We just don't know which road or which trail leads to this unique baseball pay dirt.

Here are the details we do know. When the official major-league baseball that's made by Rawlings comes out of its box, its rawhide surface is slick and shiny. In this condition the ball doesn't allow pitchers to get a good grip on it, nor does it allow hitters to get a good look at it, owing to the glare on its surface created by the sun or ballpark lights. Thus, before each game the home plate umpire is responsible for rubbing a smudge of mud that looks something like chocolate pudding onto several dozen game balls. This pregame ritual is nothing new. During

62. The Baseball Mud Site

The Delaware River
Burlington County, New Jersey
http://baseballrubbingmud.com

the early part of the twentieth century teams rubbed Dead Ball Era horsehide with tobacco spit and shoe polish, substances that tended to mark balls inconsistently, or they would make mud by mixing infield dirt with water, which made the ball soggy and too easy for pitchers to illegally scuff.

In 1938, ball rubbing took a huge evolutionary step forward when former Chicago White Sox infielder Lena Blackburne, who was coaching third base for the Philadelphia Athletics at the time, happened upon a special patch of mud while swimming in the Delaware River. The mud was dark but not too dark, and exceptionally smooth. On a whim, Blackburne tried rubbing some onto a baseball, and he liked the result: a sphere that was easy to grip and that had lost its shine.

Blackburne returned to the river's edge with a couple of buckets and the motivation to enter the mud-distribution business. Within a year, every team in the American League was pretreating its balls with Lena Blackburne mud. An American Leaguer through and through, Blackburne initially demurred when National League teams expressed their interest in purchasing some of his special sludge, but finally in the early 1950s he began supplying the Senior Circuit as well. Every major-league baseball since—including the one Don Larsen threw past Dale Mitchell to complete

Lena Blackburne founded the Lena Blackburne Rubbing Mud Company in the 1930s.

his perfect game in the 1956 World Series, the one Carlton Fisk clanked off Fenway Park's left field foul pole to win Game Six of the 1975 World Series, and even the one that Barry Bonds hit out of AT&T Park to controversially pass Babe Ruth on the all-time home-run list in 2006—has been rubbed with Lena Blackburne Rubbing Mud.

Mr. Blackburne died in 1968, but before he did he passed along the secret of the magical mud's location to his childhood friend John Haas. Haas managed the company for a time, then passed on the secret to his son-in-law, Burns Bintliff, who has since passed it on to his son, Jim Bintliff, the company's present owner. Though inquiring minds have often pressed him for details, Jim Bintliff has guarded the secret as well as his predecessors did. All he's revealed to date is that he visits his mud hole once a year

in July, at which time he collects hundreds of pounds of mud, which lasts through the entire next year.

The umpires of Major League Baseball rub approximately one million balls per year with Blackburne Mud, while minor-league and amateur teams across the country treat their own balls with the same product. If you would like to rub up your balls at home, you may visit the Blackburne Rubbing Mud Company website, where a "personal size" tub of mud sells for $24.00. A 2-pound "professional size" tub, meanwhile, sells for $75.00.

If you'd like to learn more about Blackburne Mud, you can check out the excellent children's book *Miracle Mud: Lena Blackburne and the Secret Mud that Changed Baseball* by David A. Kelly (2013).

The Yankees got a lot of things right when they designed and built their new $1.5 billion stadium in the Bronx, but the reincarnation of Monument Park was not one of them. The new stadium included ample space within its footprint for a classy Babe Ruth Plaza outside, a regal Great Hall just inside the entrance gates, a well-done Yankees Museum (which is treated with a chapter elsewhere in this book), and a Yankees timeline that encircles the entire first level concourse. But for some reason, when they designed Monument Park they made it about a third of the size they should have. Why they skimped when it came to allocating space for one of their franchise's signature features is anyone's guess. Let's hope it wasn't so they could squeeze a few more seats into the abutting MasterCard Batter's Eye Cafe. Whatever the reason, Monument Park occupies less space than the visitors' bullpen. It is cramped, crowded, and not so easy to explore on your own; rather, you must proceed in an orderly fashion through the labyrinth of monuments, so those behind you have a chance to see them too.

The original lot that had sprouted at the old Yankee Stadium from a single slab erected in 1932 to honor Yankee manager Miller Huggins was widely considered the most impressive open-air museum the game had ever known. Today, you walk down the normally bright and airy first level concourse at Yankee Stadium into the dark corridor behind left field home-run territory, and take your place in line with the other Yankee enthusiasts and ballpark pilgrims waiting to enter Monument Park. Then you file along with the rest of the procession past the monuments and plaques. At old Yankee Stadium, you could see Monument Park looming behind the left field fence from practically any seat in the house. It was one of the design elements that

63. Monument Park

Yankee Stadium
1 East 161st Street
Bronx, New York 10451
(646) 977-8687
http://newyork.yankees.mlb.com/nyy/ballpark/stadium_tours_details.jsp#classic

gave the place mystique and made visiting teams feel as if at any moment the ghosts of so many Yankee greats who'd donned pinstripes in years past might rise up and conspire to give the home team a lift. At new Yankee Stadium, you hardly notice Monument Park. Rather than existing behind a see-through fence in left field, it is tucked behind the solid blue fence in center. It is dwarfed by the restaurant and massive video screen directly above it.

Having said all that, Monument Park is worth visiting. In fact, you *should* visit to see the monuments, plaques, and retired numbers that were brought over from the old stadium in 2009. As long as you don't expect the experience to match your previous visits at the old stadium, you will likely find yourself moved.

Like many baseball landmarks, the original Monument Park arose organically, and developed over many years. After the installation of the aforementioned Huggins monument in 1932, a second monument was added in 1939, honoring Lou Gehrig. Then, a year later, a plaque was hung on the outfield wall honoring longtime Yankees owner Jacob Ruppert. In 1949 a third monument, honoring Ruth, was

Fans flow through the latest incarnation of Monument Park in a line that doesn't allow much room for independent exploration.

placed beside Huggins's. Together the three monuments stood in the field of play 450 feet from home plate and remained there until Yankee Stadium was renovated during the 1974 and 1975 seasons. As part of the remodeling, the left-center field fence was brought about 30 feet closer to home plate, relegating the monuments to the no-man's-land between the playing field and bleachers. Through the ensuing decades, the Yankees added plaques as well as a long line of pinstriped circular placards that faced the field honoring the team's many retired numbers: 1 for Billy Martin, 3 for Ruth, 4 for Gehrig, 5 for Joe DiMaggio, 7 for Mickey Mantle, 8 for Bill Dickey, another 8 for Yogi Berra, 9 for Roger Maris, 10 for Phil Rizzuto, 15 for Thurman Munson, 16 for Whitey Ford, 23 for Don Mattingly, 32 for Elston Howard, 37 for Casey Stengel, 44 for Reggie Jackson, and 49 for Ron Guidry. In 1997, the Yankees added a number 42 plaque for Jackie Robinson, whose number was universally retired at that time. However, Mariano Rivera was one of several players allowed to continue wearing number 42, as per the league's grandfather clause. Later, when Rivera was nearing the end of his long and storied career in 2013, the Yankees retired *his* number 42 too, making 42 the second number they have retired in honor of two different players.

Monument Park is dwarfed by the center field restaurant and massive video screen above it.

Today's Monument Park includes these pinstriped placards as well as biographical information about each retiree. It also hangs the bronze plaques that honor lesser stars in Yankees history like Lefty Gomez, Allie Reynolds, and Red Ruffing. The three original monuments are the highlight of a visit, as well as ones honoring Mantle and DiMaggio, which were added in 1996 and 1999, respectively. More recent monuments added by the Yankees include one that pays tribute to the victims and rescue workers of the September 11, 2001, terrorist attacks on New York City's World Trade Center, and one dedicated to late Yankees owner George Steinbrenner that was added shortly after his death in 2010. There is also a plaque honoring Robinson, which was added in 2007 on the sixtieth anniversary of his breaking baseball's color barrier.

Like its predecessor, this Monument Park also includes plaques honoring figures from outside the sports world whose paths crossed with the Yankees and their ballpark. These include three different popes who led masses at the old Yankee Stadium (Pope Paul VI in 1965, Pope John Paul II in 1979, and Pope Benedict XVI in 2008), and South African anti-apartheid-activist-turned-president Nelson Mandela, who donned a Yankees cap and jacket when he spoke at Yankee Stadium in 1990 just weeks removed from his twenty-seven-year incarceration as a political prisoner.

On game day, you may access Monument Park beginning when the stadium gates open two hours before the first pitch, and continuing until forty-five minutes before the start of the game. You should enter the stadium through Gate 8 on River Avenue, and then hurry to the

Monument Park entrance on the left-center field concourse. If you find the line already too long, you'll at least be able to see the retired numbers the Yankees have painted on the walls of the concourse. On weekdays throughout the season and during the off-season, you can also visit Monument Park by taking a Yankee Stadium Tour. The tour runs about an hour in length, with new groups departing daily beginning at noon and continuing every twenty minutes until 1:40 p.m. You can buy a tour pass through the phone or Internet by contacting TicketMaster, or you can purchase a pass at any of the Yankees Clubhouse Shops in Manhattan or at the Yankee Stadium ticket window on the day of your anticipated tour. The cost is $25.00 for adults, and $23.00 for senior citizens and children.

64. The Arizona Spring Training Experience and Cactus League Hall of Fame

Mesa Historical Museum
51 East Main Street
Mesa, Arizona 85201
(480) 835-2286
http://azspringtraining
experience.com

Born in 2008 as the brainchild of Mesa Historical Museum director Lisa Anderson, the Arizona Spring Training Experience museum tells the story of the Cactus League's inception, evolution, and culture. Currently, the museum offers more than 4,000 artifacts spread between its permanent location within the Mesa Historical Museum and exhibits at two of the Cactus League ballparks. The eventual plan is for the museum to build its own consolidated home in either Mesa or another Phoenix Valley city. Initially, Anderson expected to mount a one-room exhibit in the converted schoolhouse on Mesa's Main Street that serves as the Mesa Historical Museum, but as an ever-increasing number of people from Mesa and its surrounding communities stepped forward to donate old photos, signed balls, tickets, game programs, and newspaper clippings, and to offer their own personal stories about the March Game's arrival and emergence in Phoenix Valley, she realized her idea had much greater potential.

The initial exhibit that grew out of Anderson's efforts was called Spring Training Experience—Play Ball. After that first spring, it became a permanent part of the Mesa Historical Museum. The exhibit then spawned installations at Goodyear Ballpark and Tempe Diablo Stadium. A few years later, Anderson and her emerging spring training museum founded the Cactus League Hall of Fame. The hall inducted its inaugural class of seven members in 2014. The first group included Bill Veeck, who brought his Indians west to Arizona to make camp in Tucson in 1947, and Horace Stoneman, who brought his Giants to Phoenix that same year. Also inducted were Dwight Patterson, a Mesa rancher who helped lure the Cubs to Mesa in 1952, and Hi Corbett, an Arizona state senator who helped convince Veeck to leave the Grapefruit League. Rose Mofford was also enshrined; as governor of Arizona, she created a task force in 1988 that was instrumental in retaining several Cactus League teams that appeared on the verge of departing for the Grapefruit League. Finally,

Ted and Alice Sliger, a husband-and-wife team, rounded out the inaugural class of inductees; the Sligers owned Buckhorn Baths mineral springs in Mesa, where back in the Cactus League's early era players visited to bathe and talk shop. The plan for the Cactus League Hall of Fame is to let fans have a say in future elections through voting that will take place at least in part via social media.

Where the Arizona Spring Training Experience and Cactus League Hall of Fame ultimately puts down its roots was still an open question at the time of this book's writing. For a time it appeared destined to land at the Cubs' new complex in Mesa, but the expectations that the two entities would forge a partnership did not come to fruition. Dubbed "Cubs Park at Wrigleyville West," and modeled to also offer a bustling entertainment district something like the one on Chicago's North Side, the complex opened in March of 2014. The museum isn't a Cubs museum, though, so the fit would have been less than ideal.

Eventually, the expectation is that this museum will build a state-of-the-art new home, capable of becoming a heavily trafficked national tourist attraction. The museum has already amassed a hefty list of local and national partners. And more than that, some of the most ardent supporters of the idea of a museum dedicated to honoring the pioneering front office executives, local men and women, and players who brought the March Game west have been the former players themselves. Three-hundred-game-winner Gaylord Perry helped launch the initial exhibit at the Mesa Historical Museum back in 2008 by turning out to sign autographs for fans on the day the exhibit opened, and made a donation to support the museum's growth. Following Perry's lead, former players like Ferguson Jenkins, Ray Fosse, Jimmy Wynn, and Marty Pattin have visited the museum and helped in its fund-raising.

Old uniforms and equipment on display at the Mesa Historical Museum

Some of the highlights recently added to the museum include watercolor renderings of all of the Cactus League ballparks, past and present; never-before-seen photographs of some of baseball's biggest stars relaxing at Arizona destinations during spring training; film footage that has been integrated into several exhibits; and artifacts from Fitch Park and Hohokam Park, where the Cubs used to play in Mesa before opening their new home.

The Arizona Spring Training Experience exhibit at the Mesa Historical Museum is open year-round from Wednesday through Saturday from 10:00 a.m. to 4:00 p.m. Admission costs $5.00 for adults, $4.00 for senior citizens, and $3.00 for children. If your group includes ten or more members, you receive a discounted price of $3.00 per person.

65. The Nolan Ryan Center

Alvin Community College
2925 South Bypass 35
Alvin, Texas 77511
(281) 388-1134
www.nolanryanfoundation.org

If you'd like to learn more about the life and career of the best strikeout pitcher the game has ever known, you should head to Alvin, Texas, where the tributes to Nolan Ryan are as plentiful as his fastball was fast. Ryan, whose family moved to Alvin when he was a wee babe, grew up in a house on Dezso Drive. He played Little League baseball in town and made the local All-Star team as an eleven-year-old. He worked as a delivery boy for the *Houston Post* and dreamed of a career as a veterinarian. After a standout career at Alvin High School, though, it became apparent to just about everyone who had ever seen him pick up a baseball that Ryan was ticketed for a career in the big leagues, not an animal hospital.

Decades later, Alvin is obviously quite proud of its local son made good. Whether you approach Alvin on the Nolan Ryan Expressway (State Highway 288) or just about any other route leading into town, you will notice plenty of signage trumpeting Alvin as the "Home of Nolan Ryan." Some of these signs display the number 34, which Ryan wore while playing for the Houston Astros and Texas Rangers, and oversize renderings of the Hall of Famer's autograph. If you're having trouble picturing this, imagine a billboard-sized baseball card.

Upon arriving in Alvin, you should make your first stop the Nolan Ryan exhibit, located within the Nolan Ryan Center on the campus of Alvin Community College. As you arrive, you are greeted by a statue of Ryan in the parking lot. The piece depicts Ryan raising his hat to the crowd in appreciation, and is surrounded by flagpoles flying the Stars and Stripes, Texas state flag, City of Alvin flag, and the colors of the four big-league teams for which Ryan played.

Inside, about a third of the floor space within the Center is dedicated to honoring baseball's all-time strikeout king, while the rest of the space serves the college's Continuing Education Department. The $1.2 million facility, which opened in 1996, was funded by the Nolan Ryan Foundation, which donated it to Alvin Community College. In turn, the college leases the space used for the Nolan Ryan exhibit back to the foundation. This may sound a bit complicated, but the bottom line is that Alvin is home to a nice little museum that traces Ryan's exploits from his humble beginnings as a pitcher for the Alvin High School Yellow Jackets in the early 1960s, through his three years in the minor leagues, his epic twenty-seven-year big-league adventure, and into his post-playing career as a baseball executive.

This comprehensive museum includes the very first glove Ryan owned as a child, as well as the first million-dollar contract he signed. The exhibit also has an interactive area where you can feel the smack of a Ryan fastball popping into a catcher's mitt, a feature reminiscent of a similar exhibit that used to exist at the now defunct Legends of the Game Museum at the Texas Rangers' home ballpark in Arlington. There are also photos, videos, and audio broadcasts telling the story of each of Ryan's record seven no-hitters. The hard-throwing right-hander tossed his first no-no at age twenty-six, when he led the California Angels

The flag court outside the Nolan Ryan Center with the statue of Ryan

past the Kansas City Royals 3–0 on May 15, 1973, and tossed his last at age forty-four, when he pitched the Rangers past the Toronto Blue Jays 3–0 on May 1, 1991. In addition to those gems, he also pitched twelve one-hitters.

The museum also offers user-friendly computer kiosks loaded with stats pertaining to every one of Ryan's 807 big-league games. Want to see the box score from any of Ryan's 324 wins, or from any one of his record 215 ten-strikeout games? No problem. Meanwhile, a display of horsehide offers a ball for every one of Ryan's record 5,714 strikeouts. A Ryan timeline provides photos, pieces of equipment, and other mementos from Ryan's years with the Mets, Angels, Astros, and Rangers. If you're collecting souvenirs on your baseball odyssey,

you can purchase a replica strikeout ball, signed photos, and other pieces of Ryan memorabilia. The Nolan Ryan exhibit is open Monday through Saturday from 9:00 a.m. to 4:00 p.m. Admission costs $5.00 for adults and $2.50 for children and senior citizens.

Other Ryan landmarks in Alvin include another statue of Ryan—this one depicting him rearing back to deliver one of his trademark heaters—outside **Alvin City Hall** (216 West Sealy Street); Ryan's favorite local eatery, **Joe's Barbeque Company** (1400 East Highway 6), where the walls display Ryan memorabilia and a Ryan-used saddle sits by the cash register; and **Nolan Ryan Field** (802 South Johnson Street), where Ryan's old high school jersey is on display in a weatherproof case.

66. The Yankee Tavern

72 East 161st Street
Bronx, New York 10451
(718) 292-6130

When the Yankees unveiled their gleaming, new stadium in 2009, they introduced a third incarnation of Yankee Stadium that includes a downright silly number of inside-the-stadium restaurants and watering holes. Within the House that Steinbrenner Built you find the Hard Rock Cafe, New York Steak, the Mohegan Sun Sports Bar, the Jim Beam Suite, the Malibu Rooftop Deck Bar, the Legends Suite, the Delta 360 Sky Bar, and the list goes on and on. If you didn't know better, you'd think the stadium was built amid the asphalt wasteland of some isolated sports complex, or at the junction of two interstates far from downtown. In fact, the South Bronx provides more than ample dining and drinking options for fans. And none serves up a larger helping of nostalgia and history than the Yankee Tavern. This friendly neighborhood dive devoted to all-things-Yankees can be found just up the hill from Yankee Stadium, about a block from the stadium gates.

The Yankee Tavern has been a Bronx institution almost as long as the Yankees themselves have. To review our history of New York's Junior Circuit team: After the Yankees of Babe Ruth, Wally Pipp, and Bob Meusel departed the Polo Grounds—where they had spent ten seasons paying rent to the New York Giants—and moved to brand-new Yankee Stadium in 1923, they immediately cemented a unique franchise identity in that first season in the Bronx. In the first game

ever played at Yankee Stadium, Ruth swatted a three-run homer to lead the way in a victory over the team's rivals from Boston. Ninety-eight regular season and four World Series wins later, the Yankees capped Yankee Stadium's inaugural season by celebrating their first World Series championship, which they won, for good measure, against their old landlord the Giants and clinched on the Polo Grounds lawn.

Today, you can't visit *that* Yankee Stadium. It has receded into memory and into the colorful pages of the baseball history books, which is a poetic way of saying it was rebuilt in the 1970s, and then that successor was demolished in 2010 after the Yankees' first season at their new stadium. But you can still visit another Bronx landmark that debuted during that first decade of baseball in the Bronx.

The Bastone family, which has owned the Yankee Tavern since its opening, enjoyed quick success upon opening the doors at the corner of Gerard Avenue and 161st Street in 1928. Not only did Yankees fans stop in for a drink, but the players of the day made a habit of doing so too. Following Yankees victories, Ruth, Gehrig, and other players would often celebrate by tipping back a couple of frosty pints and buying a round for the Yankee Tavern's patrons on their way home from the ballpark.

Decades later, the Yankee Tavern is still the gathering place of choice for serious Yankees rooters. While the yuppies and college kids might prefer the drink-'em-quick watering holes closer to the stadium on River Avenue, hardcore fans don't mind walking the extra steps to the same venerable bar where their fathers and grandfathers used to sit. Once there, they drink their pregame beverages amid the glorious backdrop of only slightly faded murals that honor Ruth, Gehrig, Mickey Mantle, and other

Babe Ruth, Lou Gehrig, and other stars of the era used to buy drinks for patrons at the Yankee Tavern.

famous Yankees. A replica of the ornate white filigree or "frieze" that rimmed the upper deck of the original Yankee Stadium, spanned the outfield retaining wall behind the bleachers of the renovated Yankee Stadium that opened in 1975, and that now rims the rooftop of the new Yankees palace hangs down above the bar. As for the walls, they're absolutely plastered with Yankee memorabilia, ranging from a bat that once belonged to Yogi Berra to glossy photos of Derek Jeter and scores of other artifacts representing the favorite Yankees in between. Even the floor is laid with tiles spelling out the Yankees name and showing off the team logo. And the TVs are perpetually tuned to the YES Network, as you might expect.

The Yankee Tavern is more than simply a friendly bar and baseball museum though. It's also a pretty good place to eat. Since ownership bought the abutting storefront and added a dining room in the 2000s, the menu includes steaks, fried seafood, Italian dishes, deli sandwiches, soups, and pub fare, in addition to the traditional appetizers served at the bar. The potato croquettes are a house specialty, and if you can excuse the plastic plates, most of the menu items rate above average, and they're a heck of a lot cheaper than the grub you'll find at those restaurants and concession stands inside the stadium. The Yankee Tavern is open for lunch and dinner seven days a week and stays open late to accommodate the postgame crowd.

67. The Uecker Seats at Miller Park

◇◇

1 Brewers Way
Milwaukee, Wisconsin 53214
(414) 902-4400
http://milwaukee.brewers.mlb.com/
mil/ballpark

It's rare that a major-league team sees fit to erect a statue outside its home park to honor a man who batted a lowly .200 in an utterly forgettable playing career. It is more common, however, for a team to raise a bronze in honor of a beloved broadcaster. And Bob Uecker certainly is *that*: Through 2014 the man they lovingly call "Uke" in the land of brats and breweries had served forty-four years behind the Brewers' play-by-play mic. So the statue honoring Uecker outside Miller Park makes sense, in the way the Harry Caray one at Wrigley Field and Ernie Harwell one at Comerica Park do. The kicker in Milwaukee, though, is that Miller Park features not one but *two* Bob Uecker statues. And the second one captures the self-deprecating, affable persona of baseball's longtime funnyman just perfectly.

The first Uecker likeness stands outside Miller Park's home plate plaza, greeting fans on game day along with similar bronzes that depict Bud Selig, Robin Yount, and Hank Aaron. The second Uecker statue *sits* inside the park. No, not behind a microphone. And it's not in the press box either. It's in the seats, where the real fans sit. The good news is that the full-color bronze of the reclining Uecker has a ticket directly behind

home plate. The bad news, from a sight-line perspective, is that the statue is located in the very last row of the stadium's fourth level, directly behind a steel girder that supports Miller Park's retractable roof. To say that the statue enjoys an "obstructed view" of the field is actually being generous; the view isn't quite that good!

The statue sits among a whole section of so-called Uecker Seats, which have been a tongue-in-cheek Miller Park feature since the space-aged stadium opened in 2001 as an antidote to those chilly Aprils that had made early-season games at County Stadium more of a chore to attend than a delight. Since the park's debut, the Brewers have sold these obstructed view tickets, which are actually labeled "Uecker Seats," for $1.00. True, your view of the plate or of the pitcher's mound might be blocked by one of the roof supports, but for $1.00 how much can you complain? You can't even buy a pack of baseball cards for a buck these days.

Sitting in the Uecker Seats is a sort of badge of honor for Brewers fans; if you don't mind sitting up there for an otherwise sold-out game, you must *really* love baseball. Thankfully, since the Brewers added this second Uecker statue in 2014, now if you hold a Uecker ticket you can plop down in the empty seat beside it and pose for a picture with the man after whom the "cheap seats" are literally named.

You'll find the statue in the last row of Section 422 on the Terrace Level. Whether you hold a Uecker Seat ticket or ticket to any other seat in the park, you can stop by to pose for a picture in the unassigned seat next to it. Uke even sits with his right arm outstretched as if welcoming you to join him. The Brewers have a house photographer on hand during games to take fans' photos with Uke, in exchange for a small donation to the Brewers Community Foundation and

This statue of Bob Uecker sits in the last row of Uecker Seats at Miller Park, offering an ideal place to pose for a photo and yell, "He missed the tag!"

the Make-A-Wish Foundation. But you can also snap off your own photo for free if you want.

The punchline which the statue plays off, of course, is from a famous Miller Lite commercial in which Uecker starred. More than just being a witty, entertaining, and wonderfully descriptive broadcaster, Uecker enjoyed a highly successful acting career. He shined in a supporting role in the hit 1980s sitcom *Mr. Belvedere* and in the late-1980s/early-1990s *Major League* movie trilogy, in which he played hilarious play-by-play man Harry Doyle. But Uecker's claim to fame as an actor was earned in those hilarious Miller Lite commercials from the 1980s, when the joke always seemed to be on him.

On the wall behind the Uecker statue, a plaque describes how a backup-catcher-turned-broadcaster became a household name.

It begins, "Bob Uecker was cast in one of television's longest-running and most popular ad campaigns, the Miller Lite All Stars, and one spot created in 1984 has become iconic for the Brewers legend." The plaque goes on to describe how Uecker had originally plopped down in a primo ballpark viewing location, only to be informed by a none-too-amused usher that he was in the wrong seat. As Uecker is escorted from the field boxes, he utters the famous line, "I must be in the front row." When viewers next see Uecker he is in the very last row at the top of the bleachers.

Today, the Brewers have furnished Uecker with an even worse seat. But the statue depicts him, the eternal optimist, with a wide smile on his face. He's at the ballpark, in the cheap seats, where he belongs.

68. The Elysian Fields Site

11th Street and Washington Street
Hoboken, New Jersey 07030

As discussed earlier in the chapter devoted to Cooperstown's Doubleday Field, baseball mythology offers two conflicting accounts of baseball's origin—the one that credits Abner Doubleday with inventing baseball in 1839, and the other that credits Alexander Joy Cartwright with conjuring up the game at a park called Elysian Fields in Hoboken, New Jersey, in 1846. These are both myths, however. The truth is that neither man invented the game. Baseball historians agree that the game evolved more organically out of English precursors like cricket and rounders throughout the early 1800s, refining itself along the way and slowly incorporating many of the rules and subtleties by which it is today defined. Later in the 1800s, as the railways made the United States a smaller place, the different versions of the game that had grown popular in different regions slowly melded into one game with one set of commonly accepted rules.

Just as it is an oversimplification to attribute the creation of the game to one divinely inspired father, it misses the point to label any one place *the* primordial field from which it sprung. In fact, scores of playing fields, some pastoral and idyllic (as the hopeless romantic in us all would like to believe), others cramped and cluttered and squeezed into urban centers, played a role in the game's growth over several decades. While most

of these venues have long since faded out of memory and into history, the site of Elysian Fields, where Cartwright made his contributions—however large or small they might have been—to the game, has long been viewed by some as holy ground. The once-expansive baseball diamond has been reduced to a strip of lawn in the center median of Hoboken's 11th Street, a monument, and four bronze bases inlaid in concrete at the four corners of the intersection of 11th and Washington.

The monument is inscribed with the words: "Baseball: On June 19, 1846, the first match game of baseball was played here on the Elysian Fields between the Knickerbockers and the New Yorks. It is generally conceded that until this time the game was not seriously regarded."

You will note that the inscription stops short of proclaiming Hoboken the birthplace of baseball. But that doesn't mean this humble monument isn't worth your visit. Elysian Fields did play a role in the formalization of baseball's previously unwritten rules, even if the rules employed for the first baseball game on the site in 1846 bore only a shadowy resemblance to the ones that define the game we know and love today.

According to baseball lore, Mr. Cartwright, a local banker, spent the early 1840s playing regular afternoon games of "base ball" at a vacant lot in Manhattan with other professionals who had spare time after work. Then in 1845 the lot the group had been using was marked for redevelopment, causing Cartwright and his chums to look elsewhere for a yard. Enter Elysian Fields, a tree-lined park just across the Hudson River that Cartwright's newly formed club of "Knickerbockers" began traveling to via ferry. At the time of the move, in the winter of 1845–1846, Cartwright put pen to paper and outlined a set of fourteen rules that characterized the game he and his friends

This wood engraving from 1859 depicts a game played at Hoboken's Elysian Fields.

had already been playing for several years. He was not inventing the rules of baseball, merely recording the parameters of the game he and his friends had been playing. Most notably, the Cartwright Rules stipulated that baseball be played on a diamond, not a square; that the distance between home plate and second base should measure 42 paces (which makes for approximately 75 feet between each base); that balls struck outside the baselines be declared foul; and that runners must be tagged out, as opposed to being pegged by thrown balls. The rules Cartwright recorded did not stipulate a distance between the pitcher's box and home plate, nor did they specify that there should be 90 feet between bases, nine players per team, or nine innings per game, although Cartwright's plaque at the National Baseball Hall of Fame—hung in 1938—credits him with establishing these modern conventions.

In any case, on June 19, 1846, a game closely resembling baseball was played following the rules Cartwright had outlined. Cartwright's Knickerbockers faced a group of pals from Manhattan who called themselves the New York Nine, and lost 23–1 in four innings. Was it the only game involving four bases, a bat, and a ball played in the United States on that spring day? Surely not. Was it *the* evolutionary link between rounders and the modern game that would come to be known as baseball? No, probably not. But it was *one* of the early games played that day, and it was *one* of the sport's evolutionary links, and in the absence of other memorable early games to celebrate it therefore qualifies Elysian Fields as someplace special.

After visiting the monument on the median and finding the bases on the sidewalks, you can treat yourself to a stroll in scenic Elysian Park about a block away. Although there is no baseball historic marker here, this is the last remaining parcel of the riverside park to which Elysian Fields once belonged.

69. Hi Corbett Field

◇◇◇◇◇◇◇◇◇◇◇◇◇◇◇◇◇◇◇◇◇◇◇◇◇◇◇◇◇◇◇◇◇◇◇◇◇◇◇

3400 East Camino Campestre
Tucson, Arizona 85707
www.arizonawildcats.com/
ViewArticle.dbml?&DB_OEM_
ID=30700&ATCLID=208232653

Tucson was a hotbed of spring hardball activity for more than fifty years, as Cactus League teams set up camp in its dry welcoming climes to prepare for the upcoming baseball season. Unfortunately, spring training gradually deserted the "Old Pueblo" over the first decade of the 2000s. When the new century began, the southern Arizona city had three teams—the Colorado Rockies, Arizona Diamondbacks, and Chicago White Sox—training within its limits. By 2010, the Cactus League's fifteen teams had consolidated their camps in the Phoenix Valley. While it sure is convenient to have all of the Cactus League teams within an hour's drive of one another, the Cactus League just isn't the same without historic Hi Corbett Field.

After hosting the very first Cactus League game—a 3-1 Cleveland Indians victory over the New York Giants on March 8, 1947—Hi Corbett Field was a consistent presence in the upstart circuit that would eventually grow to encompass fully half of the game's thirty teams. Though Hi Corbett is a relic today, fortunately it is a functional relic. Since 2012 the municipally owned park has been home to the University of Arizona Wildcats. When visiting the modern Cactus League, you should make the two-hour drive south to Tucson to catch at least one Pac-12 game at the old gem in the Old Pueblo.

The life of this delightfully Southwestern baseball grounds dates back to long before the big leaguers arrived in the state. It debuted as a professional facility in 1928 when the Arizona State League was founded. The Tucson Cowboys joined the Bisbee Bees, Miami Miners, and Phoenix Senators to compose the first Arizona league recognized by the National Association of Baseball Leagues. In those early days Tucson's Randolph Municipal Baseball Park, as Hi Corbett was called, was the finest diamond in Arizona. It was the only one that offered a grass infield; the other clubs played on sunbaked "scratch" diamonds consisting of gravel and hard-packed sand. After just three seasons, the ASL merged with the Texas League to form the Arizona-Texas League (also known as the Border Conference). Tucson placed a team in the new alliance throughout the next three decades.

Major League Baseball arrived in 1947 when Indians owner Bill Veeck and Giants owner Horace Stoneham brought their clubs west. Bob Feller was a member of those trailblazing Indians, and as the team prepared to head to the Grand Canyon State for the first time, he was full of excitement. Feller said he "looked forward to training among the cowboys and the cactuses," but later summed up the experience of training in Arizona in less romantic terms, saying Tucson was "nothing but cottontails and rattlesnakes." Nonetheless, led by Feller and player-manager Mel Ott, the Indians won that first big-league game in Arizona before 4,934 fans. In total, the Tribe and Giants drew 15,600 spectators to seven games that spring. The Indians returned to Tucson for spring training every year after until 1993, when they moved to Winter Haven, Florida. Sixteen years later the Indians would

Pictured here in its final season as the spring training home of the Colorado Rockies, Hi Corbett Field now serves as the home field of the University of Arizona Wildcats.

return to Arizona to open a new Cactus League park in the Phoenix suburb of Goodyear.

Although the Indians didn't bring any African Americans west in 1947, historians often cite Veeck's desire to integrate his team as a factor in his decision to train in Arizona. The Southwest was considered a more tolerant racial environment than Florida's Deep South. Larry Doby joined the Indians during the 1947 regular season and Satchel Paige followed in 1948, and while they were later treated better in Arizona than they would have been in Florida, they still were not treated as equals among their white teammates. Each spring, Doby and Paige had to find lodging with host families in Tucson's African-American community, while their teammates stayed at the Santa Rita Hotel.

In 1951 Randolph Park was renamed Hi Corbett Field in honor of a ninth-generation Tucsonan named Hiram Steven Corbett (1886–1967). Corbett, who served five terms in the Arizona State Senate, was an avid sportsman who did much to promote the state's athletic interests.

In its later years as a Rockies outpost (1993–2010), Hi Corbett Field stood out due to its distinctive Southwestern facade, the beige stucco of which is complemented by a clock tower above the ticket office. Where once the Rockies logo hung, today the words "Arizona Baseball" appear. Inside, the patchwork seating bowl places nearly all of the seats above the interior concourse. The majority of these are found around the infield in high-rising bleachers. Only the seats directly behind home plate are shaded by a small sunroof atop the press box. The stadium configuration looks very much like the type you would expect to find at a facility that had been enlarged gradually over a period of decades.

If the field looks familiar upon your arrival, you may be having a flashback to your viewing of the 1989 movie *Major League*, in which a group of upstart Cleveland Indians goes from worst to first and wins the AL pennant. All of the spring training scenes from the movie were filmed at Hi Corbett, including the one in which Willie Mays Hayes's cot is carried out of camp, into the parking lot, while he sleeps, after he crashes camp without an invitation.

70. The St. Louis Walk of Fame

Delmar Boulevard
St. Louis, Missouri 63130
http://stlouiswalkoffame.org/inductees

On the West Coast, the most renowned American walk of fame of all, the one in Hollywood, honors just a handful of former baseball players and personalities, and even then the individuals memorialized are famous for reasons other than their associations with the game. Yes, Chuck Connors played first base for the Dodgers and Cubs, but he earned his place in America's heart and his star on the Hollywood Walk of Fame as TV's *Rifleman*. And yes, Gene Autry owned the Angels for nearly four decades, but in our memories he will always be the "Singing Cowboy." And Ronald Reagan? Well, he's remembered more often as "the Gipper," or as our president, than for his having used telegraph accounts to create play-by-play accounts of those Cubs games he wasn't even watching.

Fortunately, there are some other walks of fame across this great land of ours that offer a heavier baseball focus. In addition to the aforementioned one in Louisville, Kentucky, you also find a star-studded path in the city that bills itself as the "Gateway to the West." Here, St. Louis goes above and beyond the call of duty to celebrate a whole bunch of former baseball players and baseball personalities that earned their way into our hearts through their exploits in the game. A stroll through the St. Louis Loop Neighborhood is as interesting as it is educational and should rank high on your personal bucket list.

The St. Louis Walk of Fame was founded in the late 1980s by Joe Edwards, the owner of popular Loop restaurant and live music venue **Blueberry Hill** (6504 Delmar Boulevard, University City). The project's mission in embedding stars and accompanying informational plaques in the sidewalks along Delmar is to celebrate "St. Louisans past and present who have made significant contributions to life in America." Consequently, the more than 120 stars along the walk honor people who have made all sorts of professional and cultural contributions to American life. Strolling along, you find stars celebrating the contributions of actors Redd Foxx and Kevin Kline; writers

Maya Angelou, T. S. Eliot, and Tennessee Williams; musicians Tina Turner, Chuck Berry, and Miles Davis; civil rights activists Dred and Harriet Scott; journalists Elijah Lovejoy and Joseph Pulitzer; and Charles Lindbergh and Ulysses S. Grant. But most important of all, for our purposes, you find stars honoring baseball players, executives, and broadcasters who left their mark on the game.

Along the walk, you find stars honoring Yogi Berra, who grew up with fellow honoree Joe Garagiola in southwest St. Louis, in the Italian-American neighborhood known as The Hill; Negro Leagues star Cool Papa Bell; and Cardinals immortals Lou Brock, Dizzy Dean, Bob Gibson, Rogers Hornsby, Stan Musial, Red Schoendienst, and Ozzie Smith. Former St. Louis Browns star George Sisler is also represented, as is former Browns manager and front-office pioneer Branch Rickey. Famous broadcasters Jack Buck, Harry Caray, and Bob Costas have stars too. All of the stars are located between 6200 and 6600 Delmar Boulevard on either side of the street. While the walk's official website lists the exact location of each star, part of the fun in taking the walk lies in discovering each one for yourself, so don't over-prepare. Let the thrill of discovery light your footsteps.

To be eligible for a star, you must have been born in St. Louis or lived a significant portion of your life in the city, and you must have made a far-reaching contribution to American culture.

Stan Musial's star on the St. Louis Walk of Fame

Each summer an induction ceremony is held outside Blueberry Hill to honor the individuals for whom new stars are being added. But you needn't arrange your travel plans to visit during this special time of year. The great thing about this unique civic attraction is that it is not only absolutely free, but it's always open, twenty-four hours a day, seven days a week. You just might want to think twice about visiting though if there's freshly fallen snow on the sidewalks!

71. The Tiger Stadium Site

2121 Trumbull Avenue
Detroit, Michigan 48216

Usually when a big-league city builds a new ballpark for its team, it simultaneously demolishes its old park. This is especially true with cities that have older stadiums in downtown locations that equate to prime space for redevelopment. Well, in Motown the wheels of change turn a bit more slowly than in most places. And the developers aren't quite as willing to gamble on the sort of urban renewal projects that have turned out to be gold mines in other cities. Although the Tigers played their final game at the corner of Michigan and Trumbull on September 27, 1999, Detroit didn't start razing Tiger Stadium until the summer of 2008, and the city didn't finish the project until September of 2009.

In the decade Motown waited, local taxpayers footed the bill for basic maintenance of the facility. And in all that time, Detroit officials couldn't assemble the various public and private entities necessary to redevelop the ballpark site. As a result, the 9-acre parcel that once housed Tiger Stadium remains a city-owned greenspace in Detroit's Corktown neighborhood that you can actually visit. And get this, you'll find the baseball diamond still intact, complete with a pitcher's rubber and home plate in the ground. Even the demarcation between the infield dirt and infield grass looks pretty much like it did when this century-old field was actually hosting big-league games. Or, if you show up in the

winter months, you might find a team of snowmen standing in the familiar fielders' positions on the diamond.

In a city that filed for bankruptcy in 2013, it should come as no surprise that it has been left to local volunteers from the neighborhood to maintain the infield and cut the grass. These lawn-mowing, rake-pushing Tigers fans call themselves the Navin Field Grounds Crew, and their Facebook page has racked up several thousand "Likes."

The Tigers won the final game at their long-time home, beating the Royals 8–2 in their last home game of the 1999 season. The finale even included one of those classic Tiger Stadium home runs, the type that—as readers of a certain age will recall—ricocheted off the facing of the roof in right field and then dropped back onto the field. That last homer was a grand slam, no less, struck by Robert Fick in the bottom of the eighth inning. It was a fitting way for the Tigers to bid their longtime yard adieu.

After beloved Tigers broadcaster Ernie Harwell said his final farewell to the Tiger Stadium press box and the players cleaned out their lockers, the grounds crew mowed the infield one last time. Then the Tigers headed northeast to Comerica Park. And the ballpark known as Navin Field from 1912 to 1938, Briggs Stadium from 1939 to 1960, and Tiger Stadium from 1960 to 1999 was forced to suffer the indignity of waiting a decade to be put down. With each year, it lost more and more of its luster and came less to resemble the gleaming monument to the game it had once been. But in the early period of its limbo, it managed to make a fairly important contribution to baseball's pop culture, serving as the primary film site for the 2001 movie *61**, which chronicled Mickey Mantle and Roger Maris's epic pursuit of Babe Ruth's single-season home-run record in 1961. The

As plans to redevelop the Tiger Stadium site stalled, the old field became a neighborhood park.

ballpark interior was dressed up and reconfig- ured slightly to make it resemble Yankee Sta- dium, then computer-generated images took care of the rest. In the end, HBO viewers had to agree that Tiger Stadium was a dead ringer for the House that Ruth Built. A short while later, in 2002, the Tigers hosted a fantasy camp at Tiger Stadium, but that was the last time the field was put to any real use.

By 2006, it seemed likely the stadium would be replaced by a mixed-use retail and residential center. Detroit mayor Kwame Kil- patrick announced that would be the case. But the plan never came to fruition, and Kilpatrick is now serving a twenty-eight-year prison sen- tence after being found guilty in 2013 of twenty- four federal felonies. With no new plans having gained traction since then, it seems possible that this unique field of dreams that came about

seemingly by accident just might have some staying power.

When you visit the site, be sure to also seek out **Nemo's Bar and Grill** (1384 Michigan Ave- nue), a classic Tigers joint that has managed to survive despite the team moving from the "Cor- ner" to greener baseball pastures. All these years after Tiger Stadium closed, Nemo's still sees loyal customers return to its doors on game days. They come for the frosty beverages, cheeseburg- ers, and shuttle buses that ferry back and forth between Nemo's and Comerica Park. They also come for the friendly atmosphere and walls laden with framed newspaper headlines remembering great Detroit moments like the 1968 World Series win that prompted the *Detroit Free Press* to run a giant "We Win" headline, and the 1984 World Series win, and Cecil Fielder rounding the bases after blasting his fiftieth homer in 1990.

72. Centennial Field

XXXXXXXXXXXXXXXXXXXXXXXXXXXXXXXXXXXX

Vermont Lake Monsters
287 Colchester Avenue
Burlington, Vermont 05401
(802) 655-4200
www.vermontlakemonsters.com

Depending upon whom you ask, you're apt to get a different answer to the question, which is America's oldest minor-league ballpark? The topic inevitably engenders a debate concerning what qualifications should make a park eligible for consideration. How extensive a renovation can a stadium undergo before it becomes a "new" stadium? Does a stadium's "life" date back to its first minor-league game or to its first use as a baseball field at any level? Is it enough for an old yard to host just one or two ceremonial throwback games a year, or does it have to be the local team's primary field?

Rather than wading into the treacherous waters of ordaining one minor-league park the oldest in the land, let's simply say that Burlington's Centennial Field offers as charming an old-time ballpark environment as you'll find anywhere, one that seems better suited for the 1930s than the modern day. The grandstand's Fenway-style wooden seats pack you tightly together with other fans behind home plate, while steel pillars rise up to support the low roof. A press box barely big enough to hold the public-address announcer and local radio broadcaster sits atop the last row. On either side of the aged grandstand, a bank of more comfortable stadium chairs provides views along the baselines. In left field home-run territory, a small video board appears on the back of the adjacent football field's bleachers, while the rest of the outfield is left to showcase lush green trees.

On summer nights, a refreshing breeze blows through the park off nearby Lake Champlain. The environment is pristine, the crack of the bat is audible, and the focus is where it ought to be—on the game. This is bush-league baseball at its best.

Centennial Field opened as a college field on April 17, 1906, as the University of Vermont beat the University of Maine 10–4. The field was named at that time in honor of the one hundredth anniversary of UVM's first graduating class. Seven years later the wooden grandstand burned to the ground, prompting the installation of "temporary" wooden bleachers that stood for more than a decade. Finally, in 1922 UVM constructed a new concrete-and-steel grandstand. Today this structure appears much as it did then, save for some new field-level seats that were added as part of the 2012 renovation that brought the aforementioned video board and seats along the baselines. The $2 million project also expanded the dugouts, renovated the clubhouses, re-graded the infield, brought the outfield fence closer to home plate, replaced the aging light towers, and relocated the bullpens from along the foul lines to behind the right field fence. To their credit, the local New York–Penn League franchise, the Vermont Lake Monsters, who coordinated the project, modernized the facility without compromising its old-time charm.

During its first three decades, Centennial Field was used almost exclusively as a college field, excepting the occasional exhibitions that brought to Burlington big leaguers like Smokey Joe Wood, Harry Hooper, Tris Speaker, Larry

The tree-lined outfield of Centennial Field provides a gorgeous backdrop for a game.

Gardner, and Ray Collins. From 1936 through 1950, the ballpark hosted a semi-pro Northern League team. During that time, Burlington native Birdie Tebbetts, who played for the Detroit Tigers, visited with barnstorming big leaguers too. Among Tebbetts's guests who played at the field were Jimmy Piersall, Vern Stephens, and Vic Wertz.

In 1955 Burlington joined the affiliated minor leagues for the first time when the Kansas City A's sent their Class C prospects to Burlington to play in the Provincial League. When that league folded after one season, Burlington returned to being solely a college-baseball town; and Centennial Field lost that distinction too when UVM discontinued its varsity program in the 1960s.

Baseball bounced back in Burlington though. UVM reinstated baseball in the 1970s, then in 1984 minor-league baseball returned to the Green Mountain State when the Cincinnati Reds sent their Eastern League prospects to Burlington. After future stars like Barry Larkin, Rob Dibble, and Chris Sabo spent time in Burlington playing Double-A ball, the local franchise switched allegiances to the Seattle Mariners in 1988. Among the M's very first crop of players to explore Burlington were Ken Griffey Jr. and Omar Vizquel. The eighteen-year-old Griffey batted .279 with two home runs and ten RBI in seventeen games, while the twenty-one-year-old Vizquel wowed fans with his flashy defense and swiped thirty bases.

The Mariners' affiliation with Burlington lasted just that one season, though, and from 1989 through 1993 the city was left without a minor-league team again. Burlington's fortunes turned again in 1994, though, when the short-season New York–Penn League dispatched a Montreal Expos affiliate to Centennial Field.

From the cozy grandstand at Centennial Field, Vermont rooters have cheered on Barry Larkin, Omar Vizquel, Ken Griffey Jr., and others on their way to the majors.

Eventually that franchise became a Washington Nationals affiliate. Then, in 2011 the Lake Monsters became a rung in the Oakland A's minor-league ladder. Today, the Vermont Lake Monsters draw enthusiastic crowds all summer long. They begin play in mid-June and continue through the first week of September.

During the month of September, you might also have a chance to see the UVM club baseball team play at Centennial Field. Unfortunately, UVM's varsity team was eliminated again in 2009—along with the softball team—in the name of cost-cutting.

Whether or not you're old enough to remember what the minor leagues used to be like, you should make a point to visit Burlington to experience the pastoral beauty of Centennial Field. Upon arriving at this hidden gem, you can check out the historic marker behind the grandstand, which reads:

Named to commemorate the 100th anniversary of the University of Vermont's first graduating class, Centennial Field has been the home of UVM athletics since 1906. The three ballparks that have stood on this site have hosted semi-professional and minor league baseball, as well as exhibitions by visiting Major League and Negro League ball clubs. The current grandstand, constructed in 1922, is one of the oldest still in use. Among the outstanding players who have graced Centennial's diamond are Larry Gardner, Ray Collins, Tris Speaker, Jesse Hubbard, Robin Roberts, Kirk McCaskill, Barry Larkin, and Ken Griffey, Jr.

It didn't take long for Bob Feller to become a household name. The farm boy from Van Meter, Iowa, made his major-league debut as a seventeen-year-old in 1936. After skipping the minor leagues entirely, Feller struck out fifteen St. Louis Browns in his very first big-league start. Later that season, he set an American League record by striking out seventeen Philadelphia Athletics in a nine-inning game. In 1938 he broke his own record when he whiffed eighteen Detroit Tigers. In 1939 he began a string of three straight seasons in which he would lead the American League in wins—or five straight if you discount the 1942 through 1945 campaigns when Feller missed all but nine games to serve as an antiaircraft gunner on a World War II battleship.

Feller had already won 109 games for the Cleveland Indians by the time he enlisted in the Navy at the age of twenty-two. By then he was known throughout the game as "Rapid Robert." Alliterative though it may have been, this nickname was not the first that had been crafted to pay tribute to Feller's blazing fastball. Back in his early days, when he was playing American Legion and semi-pro ball and was not yet a national phenomenon, he was known as "the Heater from Van Meter."

Feller actually grew up a couple miles northeast of Van Meter, doing chores on his family farm and throwing baseballs on a diamond that his father built for him. During the colder months, he would pitch to his father inside the big red barn that is today listed on the National Register of Historic Places. You can visit the **Robert William Andrew Feller Farmstead** (340th Trail, Dallas County) and see the plot just southwest of the barn, where Feller spent so much time honing his windmill delivery as a youth.

Van Meter also celebrates the accomplishments of its most famous son at the Bob Feller

73. The Bob Feller Museum

310 Mill Street
Van Meter, Iowa 50261
(515) 996-2806
http://bobfellermuseum.org/the-museum

Museum. Steve Feller, a local architect who just happens to be the Hall of Fame pitcher's son, designed the museum's stately brick building, which opened on June 10, 1995. More than 800 townsfolk visited on the day of the grand opening, and ever since a steady stream of baseball pilgrims and luminaries has flowed to this landmark 12 miles west of Des Moines.

The museum displays old uniforms bearing Feller's number 19; collectible pennants, plates, and posters dedicated to Feller; trophies that Feller won during his playing days; signed bats and balls from Feller; photographs of Feller from his time in the game; and vintage newspapers marking Feller's greatest accomplishments—like his three no-hitters, his 1946 season when he returned from war to whiff a then-record 348 batters and lead the Indians to the World Series, and his induction into the Hall of Fame in 1962.

The museum also showcases visiting baseball exhibits from Cooperstown and the Negro Leagues Baseball Museum. The National Baseball Hall of Fame, for example, loaned the Bob Feller Museum all three balls that Feller threw to clinch his three no-hitters, as well as the bat that Babe Ruth famously leaned on during his retirement ceremony at Yankee Stadium in 1948, which he just so happened to have borrowed

Mr. Feller was a frequent visitor to his namesake museum prior to his passing in 2010.

from Feller whose Indians were in town to play the Yankees that day.

Another highlight of the museum is its collection of Feller-inspired paintings. A piece by artist Gregory Perillo depicts Feller delivering a pitch to Joe DiMaggio, while another by artist Graig Kreindler portrays Feller pitching to the White Sox' Joe Kuhel in the eighth inning of his Opening Day no-hitter in 1940.

Although Mr. Feller passed away in 2010, his memory lives on at this fine museum in Van Meter. Through the years, it has welcomed fellow stars of the game like Ted Williams, Don Larsen, Bruce Sutter, Tony La Russa, Yogi Berra, Ozzie Smith, and Brooks Robinson as guests. An on-site gift shop sells autographed memorabilia from Feller and also from some of those stars who have visited. The museum is open Tuesday through Saturday from 10:00 a.m. to 4:00 p.m., and Sunday from noon to 5:00 p.m. during the baseball season, but typically closes during the winter months. Admission costs $5.00 for adults and $3.00 for school-age children and senior citizens.

If you seek out the location of Cincinnati's fabled Crosley Field at the corner of Findlay Street and Western Avenue, you'll find only a small plaque and a few aged stadium chairs marking the site at what is now an industrial park. Outside the Reds' Great American Ballpark, you'll find a nice tribute to the historic stadium, as Crosley Terrace includes statues of Reds greats Frank Robinson, Joe Nuxhall, Ernie Lombardi, and Ted Kluszewski frozen in time as they play an imaginary game of baseball. But the most unique tribute of all to the ballpark Queen City fans enjoyed for generations can be found 12 miles northeast of Cincinnati in the town of Blue Ash. Here, you can explore a classy tribute to the ballpark that served as Cincinnati's baseball grounds from 1912 until the middle of the 1970 season.

The Crosley Field replica in Blue Ash was built in 1988. It mirrors the old field's dimensions right down to the famous 4-foot-high incline that gently rose between medium-depth left field and the home-run fence. It also features a five-story-high replica of the old park's scoreboard above the fence in left. This re-creation of the distinctive Crosley board previously stood at a private farm in Union, Kentucky. The owner, Larry Luebbers, had an impressive personal collection of Reds memorabilia and tried to convert his pasture into a Reds museum and ballpark in the mid-1970s. When the initiative fell flat, Luebbers sold the scoreboard to the City of Blue Ash. Except for the line score, which is left blank so the board can serve a useful purpose when the field hosts amateur games, the board looks exactly the same as it did when the last big-league pitch was thrown at the old yard in June of 1970. The uniform numbers and fielding positions of the home team and visiting San Francisco Giants appear in the order of each team's lineup that

74. The Crosley Field Replica

The Blue Ash Sports Center
11540 Grooms Road
Blue Ash, Ohio 45242
(513) 686-1270
www.blueash.com/
content/87/195/2639/303/
default.aspx

day, while the out-of-town scores of the day are also displayed. The square-faced Longines clock mounted atop the scoreboard looks just like the one that existed for so many years at Crosley. To complete the old-time effect, some of the original ticket booths and more than 400 stadium chairs from Crosley are set around the infield. No, the old stadium facade and grandstands have not been reproduced. This is a community rec field, mind you, not a movie set.

In addition to this fine Crosley Field replica, the 37-acre Blue Ash Sports Center includes swimming pools, an amphitheater, soccer fields, tennis and basketball courts, and ten other baseball fields, including one that replicates the cookie-cutter field dimensions of Crosley's successor, Riverfront Stadium. At the time of this book's publication, Blue Ash was working to reconstruct some of Riverfront's design aspects. The city had already purchased stadium seats from the stadium, which was demolished following the 2002 season to make way for Great American Ballpark.

Clearly, the Crosley Field replica will remain the most compelling reason to visit this complex in Blue Ash. While the field sees

This replica of the scoreboard from Crosley Field has drawn visits from Pete Rose, Joe Nuxhall, and other former Reds stars.

"In the heart of the West End, nestled amongst the hills that surround Cincinnati, was a place where for years people young and old periodically congregated by the thousands . . . Crosley Field."

Indeed, Crosley struck an iconic presence in the Queen City during its long reign. Baseball had been played at the corner of Findlay and Western dating back to 1884. After a fire destroyed "League Park" in 1902, the stadium was rebuilt and renamed "The Palace of the Fans." After another fire ten years later, the stadium was rebuilt again, this time using concrete and steel. Cincinnati opened that third incarnation of the park the same month Boston unveiled Fenway Park and Detroit inaugurated Tiger Stadium. Of the three additions to the big-league landscape, Crosley, which would be called Redland Field until being renamed in honor of Reds owner Powel Crosley in 1933, was the smallest, offering just 20,000 seats in its cozy double-decked grandstand.

Those cozy confines provided the backdrop for many historic moments in the life of the national game—including eight no-hitters, two All-Star games, four of the games played during the controversial 1919 World Series, and parts of three other World Series. Crosley is also remembered as the place where night baseball made its major-league debut on May 24, 1935. Seeking to increase attendance in the midst of the Great Depression, the Reds installed light towers and invited President Franklin Delano Roosevelt to throw the ceremonial "first switch" to light up the Cincinnati sky. After the lights flickered on, the Reds posted a 2–1 win over the Philadelphia Phillies.

its most regular use as the home park of the Moeller High School junior varsity and freshman baseball teams, it also hosts occasional Reds old-timers' games. Autographed plaques hang behind the home dugout honoring such Cincinnati legends as Johnny Bench, Dave Concepción, George Foster, Dave Parker, and Pete Rose, all of whom have stopped by Blue Ash at one point or another. A larger plaque remembers the original Crosley Field, reading,

When it comes to standing the test of time, Ernest L. Thayer's baseball poem "Casey at the Bat" certainly knocks the ball out of the park. If you want to talk best baseball songs, "Take Me Out to the Ballgame" is the hands-down winner, and if you want to talk best baseball poems, Thayer's ballad detailing Mighty Casey's at-bat for the Mudville Nine remains the gold standard.

You probably already know the narrative arc of the poem. The outlook appears bleak for the home team as the game enters the ninth inning. But then two light-hitting batters in front of Mudville's best hitter, Casey, miraculously work their way onto base, setting up a chance for Mudville's big bopper to send the 5,000 fans in attendance home happy with one glorious swing of the bat. But things do not go well for Casey. He watches the first two pitches sail past for called strikes, then whiffs on the third offering. The final lines lament:

> And now the pitcher holds the ball, and now he lets it go
> And now the air is shattered by the force of Casey's blow.
> Oh, somewhere in this favored land the sun is shining bright,
> The band is playing somewhere, and somewhere hearts are light,
> And somewhere men are laughing, and somewhere children shout
> But there is no joy in Mudville—mighty Casey has struck out.

Since its initial publication in the *San Francisco Daily Examiner* in 1888 and its later recitation on the vaudeville circuit by DeWolf Hopper and others, "Casey at the Bat" has remained a part of American popular culture. But you

75. Mudville

Exchange Street and Mechanic Street neighborhood
Holliston, Massachusetts 01746

already know that. What you may not know is that an actual real-life community that calls itself "Mudville" happily stakes the claim to being *the* Mudville that inspired Thayer to write about Casey's tragic strikeout. Actually, *two* communities make the claim, but more on their friendly rivalry in a moment.

First, the Mudville neighborhood of Holliston, Massachusetts, honors its real or imagined connection to Thayer's nifty work of baseball verse with a **Mighty Casey statue** (School Street). After an initial statue was installed in the early 2000s, a commemorative plaque was added in 2008, offering the final six lines of the poem, and a lengthy narrative describing Holliston's first use of the Mudville name in 1856, Mudville's incorporation on St. Patrick's Day in 1858, and Thayer's connection to the neighborhood. The initial oak statue has since been replaced with a colorful new Casey that looks something like a cartoon come to life. The kid-friendly rendering was handcrafted by Holliston native Jesse Green and installed in 2011 at the conclusion of a neighborhood parade. The statue stands in a garden in the side yard of unofficial "mayor of Mudville" Bobby Blair, right near the sidewalk, so you can easily hop out of your car and pose for a few photos. In fact, the affable Blair sometimes sits on his porch to watch visitors pulling up, and has been known to recite "Casey at the Bat" from

The Mudville Base Ball Club at the entrance to Mudville

memory. As for the original statue, it has been refurbished and now resides inside **Casey's Pub** (81 Railroad Street) along with a host of other local sports memorabilia.

So, was Thayer really thinking of a game he had witnessed here, about 20 miles southwest of Boston, when he wrote his famous poem? Of course the folks in Holliston think so and will happily recount that Thayer grew up in nearby Worcester and attended Harvard University, and that his family owned a woolen mill less than a mile from where the statue of Casey now stands. But the people who live in another historic Mudville, 70 miles east of San Francisco, California, also make the claim. The baseball team in Stockton played in a precursor

to the California League in the 1880s and used a field on the oft-flooded island known as Mudville, where Thayer sometimes covered games. The folks in Stockton will tell you that some of those games Thayer witnessed included barnstorming Boston Beaneaters star Mike "King" Kelly as a participant. Some believe that Kelly was the inspiration for Thayer's Casey. Kelly himself, much to Thayer's annoyance, was known to recite "*Kelly* at the Bat" when he moonlighted as a vaudeville performer, and liked to say that the poem was written for him. But Thayer publicly disputed this, and always insisted the poem was entirely a work of poetic fancy.

In 2010, the Mudville Base Ball Club of the Vintage Base Ball Association traveled to

Peter "Casey" Geurtsen bears an uncanny resemblance to Mudville's Mighty Casey statue.

Stockton to take on Northern California's Amador County Crushers who represented the "other" Mudville in a game that followed 1861 town rules (no gloves, underhanded pitching, players are out on balls that only bounce once before being fielded) for the first three innings, and 1886 National League rules (overhanded pitching, small gloves) for the final four innings. Despite the best efforts of Mudville's John "Choo Choo" Shannahan, Jimmy "Pipes" Cormier, Mare "Go-Go" Golding, and Allen "Rooster" Goldberg, in the end the much younger team playing under Stockton's banner won 10–4. Little was settled that day though. After all, Casey's team loses at the end of Thayer's poem, so in losing perhaps the Mudville team from Holliston further burnished its credentials as true descendant of *the* Mudville team.

There is a rivalry between the two Mudvilles, but it is a tongue-in-cheek one. People from both communities will tell you theirs was the field Thayer was evoking when he sat down to write, but they'll do so with a smile on their face and with fondness in their voice for their sister city a continent away. In any case, if you love baseball and those delightful moments when it crosses over into our other forms of popular entertainment, you should make a point to visit Holliston's Mudville and its two Casey statues.

As for the Mudville Base Ball Club, you may find it practicing or hosting opponents at Holliston's **Goodwill Park** (416 Green Street) where baseball has been played in some form dating back to the 1850s. And you might well find them far afield. Since its founding in 2003 with an assist from local baseball historian Joanne Hulbert, who explained the intricacies of the Massachusetts Game of 1858 to team members, the Mudville team has traveled North America in search of opponents who share its love of the game and culture.

76. The Baseball Reliquary

Exhibits at Several Locations
Los Angeles County, California
(626) 791-7647
www.baseballreliquary.org

As most fans living in Southern California already know, the most eclectic collection of artifacts you'll find in the baseball universe resides not in one single location but spread across several locations in Los Angeles County. With a stated mission of displaying objects that "more conservative, timid, or uninformed baseball museums have failed to bring to the public's attention," the Baseball Reliquary is truly a one-of-a-kind outfit that since its establishment in 1996 has amassed and displayed an amazing collection of baseball art and pop artifacts. The items in the Reliquary's collection range from the sublime to the surreal to the just plain silly.

Among the Reliquary's most prized possessions are a half-smoked stogie that Babe Ruth left on the nightstand of a Philadelphia brothel in 1924; the sacristy box that a priest from New York's St. Patrick's Cathedral used to administer the Bambino's last rites on the evening of July 21, 1948 (Ruth felt better by the next morning and lived nearly another month); a trophy presented to "Humanitarian of the Year" Ty Cobb after he made a donation toward the building of a hospital in his hometown of Royston, Georgia, in 1950; the jockstrap worn by Bill Veeck's 3-foot, 7-inch-tall pinch hitter Eddie Gaedel during his lone at-bat for the St. Louis Browns in 1951; a pair of skimpy thong panties worn by Wade Boggs's mistress, Margo Adams, during the 1986 season; a singed vinyl record from Bill and Mike Veeck's infamous "Disco Demolition Night" at Comiskey Park in 1979; a soil sample from the batter's box of Hoboken, New Jersey's Elysian Fields; a collection of provocative baseball-themed orange-crate paintings created by Southern California artist Ben Sakoguchi; and a collection of "Blue Bum" paintings from Los Angeles artist Stephen Seemayer, who resurrected through the series the untidy, uncouth, cigar-chomping Dodgers fan who was the original creation of sports cartoonist Willard Mullin, who offered regular installments of the Bum's exploits in the pages of the *New York World-Telegram* back in the 1930s.

True to form, the Baseball Reliquary does not offer a traditional hall of fame that celebrates members' statistical achievements but rather a "Shrine of the Eternals" that honors individuals for "the distinctiveness of play (good or bad); the uniqueness of character and personality; and the imprint that the individual made on the baseball landscape." On the third Sunday in July each year, members of the Reliquary hold an induction ceremony at the **Pasadena Central Library** (285 East Walnut Street).

Among the baseball luminaries who have been enshrined by the Reliquary are Jim Abbott, who pitched in the big leagues despite having been born with only one functional hand; Lefty O'Doul, the San Francisco icon who had a short-lived but prolific big-league career and then as a minor-league manager led barnstorming tours to Japan that broadened baseball's horizons; catcher Moe Berg, who served overseas as a spy for the United States during World War II; Buck O'Neil, the Negro Leagues star made famous by his role in Ken Burns's acclaimed PBS

Contemporary artist Stephen Seemayer breathed new life into the cigar-chomping "Blue Bum" from Willard Mullin's 1930s cartoon series.

documentary *Baseball*; Ila Borders, who became the first woman to play in a men's professional game when she toed the pitcher's rubber for the St. Paul Saints in 1997; Jim Bouton, who authored the controversial baseball book *Ball Four*; "Dummy" Hoy, the turn-of-the-nineteenth-century player whose hearing impairment catalyzed the invention of baseball's hand signals; Minnie Minoso, who played professional baseball in six different decades and even collected a hit for the White Sox at the age of fifty-three in 1976; Jimmy Piersall, who endured mental illness to succeed in the big leagues during the 1950s and 1960s; Jackie Robinson, who broke baseball's color barrier, and his wife, Rachel Robinson; Veeck, whose promotional antics made the game eminently more interesting; the ever-colorful Dizzy Dean; Dr. Frank Jobe, the orthopedic surgeon who invented "Tommy John" surgery in 1974 when he transplanted a tendon from

John's right forearm to his left elbow to reinvigorate John's pitching arm and pave the way for countless pitchers since to prolong their careers; Luis Tiant, who was a pretty good pitcher for the Red Sox in the 1970s and perhaps an even better practical joker; Ted Giannoulas, aka the original San Diego Chicken; Jim Eisenreich, who overcame Tourette syndrome to play in the bigs and later founded the Jim Eisenreich Foundation for Children with Tourette syndrome; and Bill Buckner, who had an exceptional big-league career only to be stigmatized as one of the game's great goats when he allowed Mookie Wilson's ground ball to trickle through his legs in Game Six of the 1986 World Series.

The Reliquary also hands out two other awards at its annual event. The Hilda Award, named for legendary Brooklyn Dodgers fan Hilda Chester, is presented to a fan that has gone above and beyond the ordinary call of rooting duty to contribute to the game. And the Tony Salin Memorial Award, named for a

Southern California artist Ben Sakoguchi created this work in his series of provocative baseball-themed orange-crate paintings.

noted baseball historian and researcher who passed away in 2001, is presented to a baseball researcher that has made a special contribution to preserving the game's past.

Pasadena resident Terry Cannon founded and still runs the nonprofit Reliquary, which derives a portion of its funding from the Los Angeles County Arts Commission. Throughout the year, the Reliquary sponsors an ever-changing slate of exhibits you may visit for free at various locations in Southern California, including the Burbank Public Library, Los Angeles Archives Bazaar, Pasadena Central Library, and Pasadena's Jackie Robinson Center. For information about upcoming displays, consult the Reliquary's website.

77. The Cy Young Exhibit

Temperance Tavern
221 West Canal Street
Newcomerstown, Ohio 43832
(740) 498-7735
www.newcomerstownmuseums
.com/Our-Museums.html

During an illustrious playing career that spanned twenty-two seasons on either side of the turn of the nineteenth century, Cy Young was known as the most effective, efficient, and durable pitcher the game had yet seen. Young began his career with the Cleveland Spiders in 1890 at a time when pitchers stood just 55 feet from home plate at the back of the pitcher's box. Then in 1893 organized baseball took an evolutionary step forward when it moved the pitching rubber back 5 feet to its present location 60 feet, 6 inches from home plate. While the change bothered some veteran hurlers, it didn't faze Young all that much. Sure, his ERA rose from 1.93 in 1892 to 3.36 in 1893, but his record slipped only slightly, from 36-12 to 34-16. Young eventually adjusted further, and finished with a sub-3.00 ERA in most of his remaining seasons. By the time he hung up his spikes, he had won twenty or more games in fifteen different seasons, and thirty or more in five seasons, while compiling a 2.63 ERA.

Since Young's death and the establishment of the pitching award in his name, when we fans invoke the name of the man who established "unbreakable" records in categories like wins (511), losses (313), complete games (749), and innings pitched (7,357), we speak in the reverent tones reserved for only a handful of individuals among the upper echelon of baseball royalty. Young, Cobb, Ruth, and later Robinson—these are the men who transformed the game.

The Cy Young Award, established by Commissioner Ford Frick in 1956 and presented to the best pitcher in each league ever since, has appropriated the Young name to a degree though, so that when we refer to *the* Cy Young or to a *Cy Young–caliber season* we usually do so without really giving the man, Cy Young, much thought. This is not the case in the community where Denton True Young spent his life before, during, and after his baseball career, however.

In Newcomerstown, Ohio, where Young picked rocks from his father's pasture in his

The Cy Young exhibit is located within Newcomerstown's ancient Temperance Tavern.

childhood and threw them against the side of a barn until the structure looked as if a cyclone had pummeled it, where Young farmed in the off-season during his playing days, and where he hunted and fished with his friends in his retirement, he is still remembered first as a man and only then as a legend.

Three Young landmarks in and around Newcomerstown speak volumes to the affection Young's contemporaries and their descendants have felt for the humble farmer among them who just happened to also be the greatest pitcher to ever set foot onto a baseball diamond.

The Cy Young exhibit is located within Newcomerstown's ancient Temperance Tavern, which served as a stopover for travelers on stagecoach routes as early as the 1840s, but has since become the home of the local Historical Society. Among the items on display are Young's favorite rocking chair, his fedora hat, a replica of the plaque that hangs to honor him at the National Baseball Hall of Fame, a life-size cardboard cutout of him, and his complete 1908 Boston Red Sox uniform, which a local woman reportedly found years after his death when she was cleaning out a trunk in her deceased father's closet. Temperance Tavern is open from Memorial Day through the end of October, Tuesday through Saturday, from 10:00 a.m. to 4:00 p.m., and Sunday from 1:00 p.m. to 4:00 p.m.

Meanwhile, **Cy Young Memorial Park** (591 North College Street) offers year-round access to the Young Monument behind the bleachers of a community field that was dedicated in the pitcher's honor in 1950. The eighty-three-year-old Young was on hand for the ceremony and was deeply touched by the town's gesture. He frequently visited the park in his later years, before passing away in 1955. The cement monument features an engraved image of Young;

The Cy Young exhibit is located within Temperance Tavern, which was once a stopover for travelers on stagecoach routes.

nearby there is also a State of Ohio historical marker praising Young.

The third Young destination is his gravesite at the **Peoli United Methodist Cemetery** (State Route 258) in the nearby town of Peoli, where Young lived in his later years. Young's headstone is adorned with a baseball sprouting angel's wings. His epitaph reads, "From 1890 to 1911, Cy Young pitched 874 major league baseball games. He won 511 games, three no-hitters, and one perfect game in which no man reached first base." It is a local tradition to decorate the grave with flowers and baseballs each Memorial Day, and local superstition holds that any youngster who places a ball on Young's grave will soon see his or her baseball skills improve.

78. McKechnie Field

1611 Ninth Street West
Bradenton, Florida 34205
(941) 747-3031

Should you find yourself pining for the quintessential Grapefruit League experience, you should look no further than Bradenton's McKechnie Field. Spring training has blossomed into big business in recent decades, reinventing itself with gleaming new stadiums across Florida and the Phoenix Valley. We fans imbibe readily in the specialty foods, premium seating, and other creature comforts the new parks provide, but the downside of this revolution has

At various times, McKechnie Field has seen home-run kings Hank Aaron, Babe Ruth, and Barry Bonds play spring games on its grounds.

been the shedding of some of spring training's intimacy. Gone, for the most part, are the cozy ballparks staffed by local retirees. In their place, you now find state-of-the-art stadiums that provide only-slightly scaled-down versions of the big-league experience. The friendly, casual atmosphere of the spring game's yesteryear has faded into memory in most towns. But through it all, McKechnie Field has stayed true to its idyllic roots.

But that's not to say the ballpark hasn't changed with the times since hosting its first Grapefruit League games back in 1923, when the St. Louis Cardinals arrived in this Gulf Coast town. In fact, the stands around the near-century-old field have been rebuilt several times. Wisely, though, city officials have preserved the

park's vintage look through each renovation and expansion.

McKechnie offers a cream-colored facade behind the home plate grandstand that reflects the Spanish Mission architecture common to the area. The structure rises in several arches to a rounded top. At street level, green iron gates separate the sidewalk from the concourse behind the seating bowl. The decorative green sunroof provides a distinctive finishing touch. Instead of a unified "seating bowl" inside, you find three freestanding grandstands around the infield—one behind home plate, one along the first base line, and one along the third base line. These covered stands mimic the wooden bandboxes that stood at ballparks across the country before the concrete-and-steel construction era

McKechnie Field didn't add stadium lights to its grounds until 2008.

dawned in the 1910s, and look like something right out of a Ken Burns documentary.

Practically any seat within these cozy boxes positions you close enough to the action to hear the home plate ump barking out each strike call, and to see which players are chewing tobacco, which ones are spitting sunflower seeds, and which ones are blowing bubbles. You can't say that about too many of the other spring parks.

Since debuting in the 1920s when the Cardinals, Red Sox, and Phillies made camp in Bradenton, this park has seen such giants of the game as Babe Ruth, Hank Aaron, Jimmie Foxx, Eddie Mathews, Roberto Clemente, Willie Stargell, and Barry Bonds grace its lawn. During the 1930s the Cardinals would send Dizzy Dean to Bradenton a few weeks ahead of his teammates, since he tended to get himself into trouble if he had too much idle time during the off-season.

Much to his teammates' surprise, Ole Diz fell in love with sleepy little Bradenton, so much so that he bought a service station on the Tamiami Trail and spent his every waking hour away from the ballpark pumping gas. And you probably thought those Red Bird clubs of the era earned their "Gashouse Gang" nickname due to some gassy train rides their beat reporters endured as they rode the rails together from St. Louis to points elsewhere in the National League!

After the Cardinals sought a new March roost following the 1936 Grapefruit League season, McKechnie Field provided a spring home to the Boston and Milwaukee Braves, and then to the Kansas City and Oakland Athletics. In 1969, the Pirates landed in Bradenton, and they haven't left since.

Cut from much the same cloth as working class Pittsburgh, Bradenton has supported the

Pirates through good times and bad. The locals remember fondly the days when Pirates managers like Danny Murtaugh and Chuck Tanner predicted great things for their clubs during the springs of 1971 and 1979, respectively, and then returned as world champions the next years to see their faces plastered on the billboard above the DeSoto Bridge, which spans the Manatee River. Today, the men and women of the Bradenton Pirate Boosters club serve as volunteer ushers and concessionaires at McKechnie during spring training. In return for their service, they are treated to a complimentary picnic hosted by the Pirates each spring, and are invited to be the Pirates' guests in one of PNC Park's luxury suites each summer. These friendly folks—most of whom are local retirees—are committed to ensuring your ballpark experience is a special one.

The park is named for Hall of Fame manager Bill McKechnie, who distinguished himself during a managerial career that spanned from 1922 through 1946. McKechnie piloted the National League clubs in Pittsburgh, Boston, and Cincinnati, racking up World Series titles with the Pirates in 1925 and Reds in 1940. Upon his retirement, McKechnie settled in Bradenton and made himself a fixture at the tiny ballpark on the corner of Ninth Street and 17th Avenue, until his passing in 1965.

Amazingly, McKechnie Field didn't have stadium lights until a set was installed in 2008, meaning the folks in Brandenton held out nearly two decades longer than the folks on the North Side of Chicago before ceding that night games were a necessity of the modern era. The park also underwent a $10 million renovation in 2013; the work added outfield seating and group areas, an outfield boardwalk, and new concession space. The project also reseated the grandstand, outfitting the bandboxes with 4,600 comfortable new stadium chairs. The work was well received by ballpark purists, as the aesthetically in-tune folks at *Ballpark Digest* named the project the "Best Ballpark Renovation of 2013."

In addition to serving as the spring home of the Pirates, McKechnie Field hosts about sixty Florida State League games between April and August each year. The High-A Pirates—known as the Bradenton Marauders—have drawn very well at the park since debuting in 2010.

· ·

Given the popularity youth soccer and hockey enjoy in America's suburbs, and the stranglehold basketball has on the inner-city sports scene, and the amount of time today's kids and teens spend playing video games and using social media, it's little wonder old-timers often lament that "kids nowadays just don't play baseball." The truth is, however, that we adults don't play baseball like our forebears did either. In the America of the early 1900s, people from all walks of life turned out at the village green or on vacant city lots to play and watch the game. But

79. Big League Dreams

33700 Date Palm Drive
Cathedral City, California 92234
(760) 324-5600
www.bigleaguedreams.com

today our busy lives preclude such active adult participation in the game. And when we do make time for recreational activities we typically play a round of golf or turn out at the local rec club for competition in basketball or soccer. Too few of us make time to play baseball. We play fantasy baseball instead, or watch the local big-league or minor-league team, or cheer for our children's teams, and that's as close as we come to satisfying the itch we developed as kids.

Well, as the 1990s drew to a close, forward-thinking brothers Rick and Jeff Odekirk weren't ready to give up on the idea that baseball could still be the national game. With a *Field of Dreams*–like faith, the brothers founded Big League Dreams, USA. If they built the right kind of baseball fields, the Odekirks believed, the players would materialize. They set out to build diamonds that, like the one Ray Kinsella chiseled into his Iowa cornfield, would be magical. At their initial Cathedral City location, the Odekirks built replicas of the big leagues' most iconic existent facilities: Yankee Stadium, Fenway Park, and Wrigley Field. The trio became the template for similar parks Big League Dreams would soon build across the American Southwest.

The model of Yankee Stadium features decorative white arches and filigree across the outfield, just like the ornate metalwork that existed at the old Yankee Stadium in the Bronx. The scoreboard reflects the line score from Don Larsen's perfect game in the 1956 World Series. The bleachers in center are blacked out to serve as a batter's eye, and a crowd of New Yorkers is painted onto the bleachers above the fence in left and right.

The Fenway Park replica features a facsimile of the Green Monster in left, of course, with its black-slate scoreboard frozen in time at the moment Carlton Fisk hit his dramatic walk-off home run in Game Six of the 1975 World Series. Atop the wall is a long screen just like the one that spanned the wall atop Boston's famous edifice prior to the Red Sox' installation of the Green Monster Seats in 2003.

At the faux Wrigley Field, the brick outfield wall is covered with ivy, the bleachers are packed with fans, the manual scoreboard rises among the center field seats, and the rooftops of a fake Waveland Avenue hover beyond the outfield, providing free views to cutouts of beer-drinking Chicagoans. All of the fields have sunken dug-outs, are surrounded by stadium-style seating, and have quality stadium lighting systems to allow for evening play.

To top off the physical infrastructure of this baseball playground, the complex offers a Stadium Club restaurant and sports bar where you can buy lunch or dinner and have a few drinks while watching different MLB games on the TVs overhead, or watching the games taking place on the surrounding replica fields.

More than just coming up with the idea for these special fields, Big League Dreams also perfected the social infrastructure necessary to ensure the complexes are populated. Leagues are formed, tournaments are scheduled, and the games take place guided by their expert handling.

As you might imagine, the residents surrounding the original complex just east of Palm Springs were transfixed by the idea of playing baseball, fast or slow pitch softball, or even coed kickball in leagues that would utilize these funky retro fields. They showed up at the Cathedral City complex to play, and a new type of recreational sports complex was born. In the years ahead, Big League Dreams brokered development agreements with towns and cities across California and even ventured into other states where you can now find Big League Dreams fields. Each complex offers anywhere from three to six replica fields that draw from a Big League Dreams portfolio that has grown to include old-time yards Forbes Field, Crosley Field, Ebbets Field, Tiger Stadium, the Polo Grounds, and Sportsman's Park, as well as replicas of the current home parks of the Los Angeles Angels of Anaheim, the Texas Rangers, the Arizona Diamondbacks, and the Los Angeles Dodgers. Many of the complexes also include batting cages, playgrounds, arcades, and soccer fields, as well as their own versions of the aforementioned Stadium Club.

Owing in part to the fine attention to detail with which the parks are crafted, and in part to the fact that we Americans really do love baseball—and not just watching it, but playing it—the Big League Dreams complexes have been hugely successful. When the Northern California city of Redding opened its complex featuring replicas of Wrigley Field, Fenway Park, and Yankee Stadium, for example, it hoped to attract 125,000 players in its first year. But in the first twelve months, the Redding complex drew more than 350,000 ballplayers to its grounds.

Adult and youth baseball and softball leagues account for most of the action at the Big League Dreams sites, while regional tournaments sometimes draw as many as seventy teams at a time. The complexes are also highly accessible to you as a road-tripping fan. During normal daylight hours, whichever fields are not in use are open for non-scheduled public practices. So bring your glove, a bat, and a bucket of balls, and take a few swings at one of your favorite parks. Then you can grab a bite to eat in the Stadium Club while you overlook the fields.

In addition to the Cathedral City complex where this vision first came to life, you will find Big League Dreams fields in **Chino Hills** (16333 Fairfield Ranch), where the championship game scenes for the movie *The Benchwarmers* were filmed; **Manteca** (1077 Milo Candini Drive); **Redding** (20155 Viking Way); **Perris** (2155 Trumble Road); **Riverside** (10550 Cantu-Galleano Ranch Road); **West Covina** (2100 South Azusa Avenue); **Gilbert, Arizona** (4536 East Elliot Road); **Mansfield, Texas** (500 Heritage Parkway South); **League City, Texas** (1150 Big League Dreams Parkway); and **Las Vegas, Nevada** (3151 East Washington Avenue).

• •

In twenty-one seasons as a Major League Baseball park, Metropolitan Stadium attracted about twenty-two million fans to its suburban plot between Minneapolis and St. Paul. Today, the Mall of America, which sits on the old ballpark site, draws more than forty million visitors per year. Most of the tourists and local shoppers don't take time to seek out the subtle nods to Minnesota's baseball past within this gargantuan mall that boasts more than 4 miles of retail frontage, an amusement park, movie theater,

80. The Mall of America/Metropolitan Stadium Site

60 East Broadway
Bloomington, Minnesota 55425
www.mallofamerica.com

wedding chapel, the Sea Life Minnesota Aquarium, and more than twenty restaurants. As a

This plaque marks the spot where home plate once lay at Metropolitan Stadium.

baseball pilgrim, though, you can make a fun little scavenger hunt out of a trip to the mall . . . then you can get your Orange Julius, buy that new pair of pants you've been meaning to pick up, and watch a movie.

Metropolitan Stadium opened in 1956 to serve as the home of the brand-new American Association Minneapolis Millers. Although the stadium was built in Bloomington, the City of Minneapolis picked up the $8.5 million construction tab. From the outset, Minneapolis was thinking big, as in *big leagues*. The Met was built to major-league specs and was promptly proclaimed the finest bush-league ballpark in the country when it opened. With a triple-deck grandstand that could seat nearly 20,000 fans and massive light banks, it was almost too

impressive, some said, to languish in the minors. Indeed, it didn't languish long. After the 1960 season, Minnesota struck a deal with the woebegone Washington Senators, and a stadium-expansion project began to increase the Met's seating capacity to more than 30,000.

And so, the hapless Washingtonians relocated to the Land of Ten Thousand Lakes after their seventh straight losing season. It would still be five years before the franchise broke its losing skein, but when it did, it broke it in a big way: The 1965 Twins took home the American League pennant with a 102-60 record. Although that team fell to the Dodgers in a tightly contested seven-game World Series, it managed to put Minnesota on the national baseball map, and led by the face of the franchise, Harmon

Killebrew, the Twins remained perennial contenders throughout the next decade.

Killebrew belted 573 home runs in a career that began in 1954, when he got his first cup of coffee in the big leagues with Washington, and lasted until 1975, when he hit fourteen homers for the Kansas City Royals in the only season he spent outside the Senators/Twins organization. Today, there is a statue of Killebrew outside Target Field in Minneapolis, while the Mall of America offers its own tribute to him. You will find this unique baseball attraction within the mall's sprawling indoor amusement park known as Nickelodeon Universe. High above the rocky terrain of a theme roller coaster, a red stadium chair from Metropolitan Stadium is bolted to the wall. While the seat may not sound like such an impressive baseball memento in its own right, when viewed in its proper context, it is.

The seat was the landing spot of a 534-foot home run that Killebrew drove into the Met's left-center field upper deck against the Angels in 1967. The shot was the longest dinger of Killebrew's career and the longest in stadium history. To appreciate the magnitude of this epic long ball, you can actually stand beside a bronze home plate, laid into the amusement park floor 534 feet away, and squint to make out the distant chair. You'll find the home plate right outside the entrance to the SpongeBob SquarePants Rock Bottom Plunge. From there, the distant chair looks like it would be reachable with a three wood and Titleist perhaps; with a Louisville Slugger and a hardball though . . . well, not for most mortals.

The Mall of America opened in 1992, eleven years after the Twins left Metropolitan Stadium to play indoor baseball at the Metrodome, and seven years after the Met's demolition. The mall cost $650 million to build, or about seventy-five times what it took to erect Metropolitan Stadium. Aside from offering the Killebrew seat and the home plate, which bears the words "Metropolitan Stadium: Home Plate, 1956-1981," the Mall of America is also bounded on its south side by a road named Killebrew Drive.

• •

After a day spent at San Francisco's ballpark by the bay or, better yet, bobbing in a kayak on the bay, you can retire to nearby McCovey's Restaurant for a postgame dinner that comes with a side order of memorabilia. The restaurant, which opened in 2003, honors former San Francisco Giants first baseman and 500-home-run club member Willie McCovey. A frequent dinner guest, Mr. McCovey usually eats in the private McCovey Room but makes time to mingle with patrons on his way in and out.

Inside and out this casual restaurant and sports bar bleeds Giants' orange and black. Outside, the facade mimics the brick-and-steel

81. McCovey's Restaurant

◇◇

1444 North California Boulevard
Walnut Creek, California 94596
(925) 944-9444
www.facebook.com/McCoveys

exterior of AT&T Park. Inside, the dining area is laid out in the shape of a baseball diamond, and every nook and cranny of the field is filled with

The exterior of McCovey's Restaurant mimics the facade of the Giants' home park, which sits on the shores of McCovey Cove.

jerseys of famous players—ranging from Jackie Robinson, Ernie Banks, and Willie Mays, to Pete Rose, Ken Griffey Jr., and Barry Bonds—baseball equipment, photographs, and other memorabilia. High above, the jerseys belonging to the members of the Giants' current roster are also on display. Some of the other impressive items include a ball signed by Satchel Paige, the trophy McCovey was awarded for winning the National League home-run title in 1963, the trophy McCovey received for winning the National League Most Valuable Player Award in 1969, and an autographed photo of McCovey posing alongside Johnny Carson. There are also displays showing how Louisville Slugger bats are made and how Rawlings makes the official major-league ball. Overhead, in the middle of the "infield," a circular display traces Mr. McCovey's remarkable career with an illustrated timeline. There are also more than forty high-definition TVs, and as you might expect when the Giants are playing, the game is on.

The menu offers some ballpark treats as well as more imaginative entrees. The highlights include the signature "521 Burger," which consists of 44 ounces of ground Angus beef and is big enough to feed a family of four; the pulled-pork sandwich, which consists of slow-roasted pork shoulder on a French roll with coleslaw and crispy onions piled right on top of the meat; and the Southern-style fried chicken with garlic mashed potatoes and gravy.

The man known as "Stretch" burst onto the big-league scene in 1959, when he went four-for-four against future Hall of Famer Robin Roberts in his debut. McCovey went on to bat .354 over that first season and to hit 521 home runs over a twenty-two-year career. He played his first fifteen years and his final four in San Francisco. He played the 1974 and 1975 seasons in San Diego after an unpopular trade and then split the 1976 season between San Diego and Oakland, but those are years that most McCovey fans choose to forget. Today, Mr. McCovey is back home in the suburbs of the city where he amassed his Hall of Fame credentials, and his restaurant offers a wonderful tribute to the game he still loves.

McCovey's is open daily from 11:00 a.m. until 10:00 p.m. It is run by longtime McCovey friend Rocky Dudum, who has known McCovey since the late 1950s. The Giants had just moved from New York to San Francisco in 1958, and in 1959 McCovey was a twenty-one-year-old rookie. Before he would go on to win the National League Rookie of the Year award, McCovey received some help from Dudum in locating and setting up the furnishings for his first big-league apartment. A friendship was born, and through the years the two kept in touch. Years later, they launched this business together, and judging from the crowds that turn out at McCovey's for the good eats and great atmosphere, they hit the ball out of the park!

Some of the places profiled in this book are landmarks that have helped shape baseball's identity over the course of decades, while others are landmarks that are still evolving. The National College Baseball Hall of Fame belongs to the latter category, as an emerging baseball site that appears well on its way to becoming a must-visit stop on the American baseball landscape. Since shortly after its founding in 2004, the Hall has offered a small display in a library on the campus of Texas Tech University, but efforts are well under way to construct a breathtaking new building for the Hall that is scheduled to open in 2017.

The new museum will trace the confines of an actual regulation baseball field that is also being constructed. The field will host youth tournaments and offer seating for nearly a thousand people. As such, the Hall will have a first base side and a third base side. The first base side will house a function hall, catering kitchen, and storage area for artifacts. The third base side will house the gallery and exhibit portions of the Hall, in addition to a theater, an interactive area for kids, and a gift shop. The product of an $18 million capital campaign, the new facility

82. The National College Baseball Hall of Fame

Fourth Street and Avenue O
Lubbock, Texas 79401
http://web.collegebaseballhall.org

will be named for former US president George H. W. Bush, who played for Yale in the first two College World Series. The entire complex will be named for the Moody Foundation, which was a leading force in the fund-raising for the museum and field, which are being built on a 4.9-acre site just north of the Lubbock Memorial Civic Center.

The rapidly growing National College Baseball Hall of Fame fills a void that had existed on the baseball landscape. Although college baseball has been played in the United States for more than a century, until the Hall inducted its first class of five former players and five former coaches in 2006, no comparable effort had been made to honor the legends of the collegiate ranks. To make up for lost time,

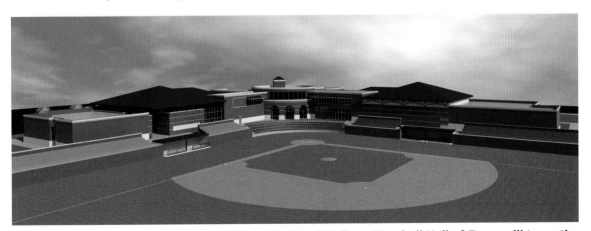

The new building being constructed for the National College Baseball Hall of Fame will trace the perimeter of a regulation baseball field.

San Diego State pitcher Stephen Strasburg interviews with Dave Shore following the presentation of the 2009 National Pitcher of the Year Award.

each year the Hall inducts a class of recently retired players and coaches and also a class of "veterans."

The Hall welcomes each new group over a three-day event in late June or early July, and as it does its impressive collection of portraits and memorabilia grows. The inaugural class of 2006 included players Will Clark, Bob Horner, Brooks Kieschnick, Robin Ventura, and Dave Winfield, and coaches Skip Bertman, Rod Dedeaux, Ron Fraser, Cliff Gustafson, and Bobby Winkles. The portrait of Winfield captures the future big-league slugger in his Minnesota Golden Gophers uniform. Rather than showing him in the batter's box, it depicts him on the pitcher's mound, where he excelled as a collegian. The portrait of Clark shows a softer side of the player who would come to be known throughout the bigs for his fiery intensity.

Wearing his crimson Mississippi State Bulldogs cap and plenty of eye black, the 1984 and 1985 All-American smiles broadly. As for Ventura, who racked up a remarkable fifty-eight-game hitting streak while at Oklahoma State, he is captured in the midst of a picture-perfect left-handed swing.

The second class of inductees included Pete Incaviglia of Oklahoma State, Fred Lynn of Southern California, John Olerud of Washington State, Phil Stephenson of Wichita State, and Derek Tatsuno of Hawaii.

In the years since, the inductees have included such familiar baseball names as Jackie Robinson, Branch Rickey, Dick Howser, Lou Brock, Sal Bando, Roy Smalley, Joe Carter, Barry Larkin, George Sisler, Terry Francona, Nomar Garciaparra, Tino Martinez, and others who enjoyed big-league fame. But the Hall also includes players who were excellent collegians but never made good in the bigs.

The annual summer festivities also include the presentation of the Dick Howser Award, which honors the nation's top collegiate player, its Pitcher of the Year Award, its Stopper of the Year Award, its John Olerud Award, given to the best two-way player, and its Brooks Wallace Award, given to the best shortstop.

While it continues to offer a display in the Texas Tech **Southwest Collection/Special Collections Library** (15th Street and Detroit Avenue), you may peruse the National College Baseball Hall of Fame exhibit Monday through Friday from 9:00 a.m. to 5:00 p.m., and Saturday from 9:00 a.m. to 1:00 p.m. When the Hall opens its own museum in 2017, these particulars will change, so be sure to consult the website before planning your trip to Lubbock.

• •

While baseball lore provides abundant examples of players and coaches who have made profound contributions to the sport's evolution, only a select few baseball personalities have transcended the bounds of the playing field to make further-reaching cultural contributions to our American way of life. And Bobby Valentine is one such individual.

A once-coveted prospect whose path to superstardom was impeded by injury, "Bobby V." toiled for five teams during a mediocre ten-year career in the big leagues. He managed the Texas Rangers from 1985 through 1992, spent 1995 managing in Japan, and skippered the New York Mets from 1996 through 2002. Then, Valentine returned to Japan to manage the Chiba Lotte Marines of the Nippon Professional Baseball League. From 2004 to 2009, Valentine made his mark in Japan as the most successful "gaijin" (as Japanese fans call foreigners) to ever guide a Japanese league team. His success and widespread popularity in the baseball-crazed Land of the Rising Sun helped bridge the gap between Major League Baseball and the Japanese league, making it easier for players and coaches to migrate across the Pacific in either direction. It also landed Valentine's smiling mug on a wide range of "Bubby"-endorsed products

83. Bobby Valentine's Sports Gallery Cafe

225 Main Street
Stamford, Connecticut 06901
(203) 348-0010
www.bobbyv.com/index.html

in Japan, including beer bottles, packs of chewing gum, and lunch boxes. And Valentine was the subject of several documentary films in the United States and Japan during the first decade of the 2000s. Just how successful was Valentine in Japan? Well, he took over a team that hadn't won a Pacific League pennant since 1974 and led it in 2005 not only to a pennant, but a four-game sweep in the Japanese World Series too.

Of course, Valentine returned to the United States in 2010, and after a colorful stint as a member of ESPN's *Sunday Night Baseball* broadcast team decided to give managing in the American bigs another go-round. Although his one season in Boston did not end well, that gloomy 2012 campaign should not overshadow Valentine's body of work in the game.

The walls, tables, and ceiling are adorned with baseball memorabilia at Bobby Valentine's.

And yet, Valentine's contribution to US and Japanese baseball relations may not be his most significant cultural achievement. For that, you must look to Stamford, Connecticut, where in 1980, shortly after retiring as a player, Valentine opened a baseball-themed restaurant in his hometown. There, in his first year as a restaurateur, Valentine had a culinary stroke of genius that would soon transform our nation . . . or at least the lunch menus at our nation's sandwich shops.

Just before closing time one night, a hungry traveler bellied up to Valentine's counter and ordered a sandwich. Valentine suddenly flushed. Only a few minutes earlier he had used his last hoagie roll. But Bobby didn't want to turn away a paying customer. So he thought fast and improvised. He cut a pita pocket in half the flat way, laid some meat and cheese on it, and added some leafy greens and condiments. Then, he rolled it up to make it approximately the length

and width of a sub. Bobby Valentine had just invented the sandwich wrap, an offering that over the next several decades would become standard lunchtime fare at restaurants across the country.

Today, Bobby Valentine's Sports Gallery Cafe keeps plenty of hoagie rolls in stock and also an ample supply of the flat breads with which it makes its trademark wraps. The wrap menu includes six selections: Cajun chicken, beer-battered fish, chicken Caesar salad, buffalo chicken, Asian, and Cobb salad. Other menu favorites include "Mexican League Specials" and baseball-themed munchies like the Rollie (chicken) Fingers, and the World Series tower of appetizers. The seven juicy half-pound burgers are named and topped in honor of the teams for which Valentine suited up as a player, coach, and manager. Each burger listing on the menu provides a colorful fact about Valentine's time spent with the club. For example, the Padres Burger's heading notes, "Bobby [was] traded from here to the Mets for Dave Kingman."

A popular hangout for Stamford sports fans whenever the Mets or NHL's New York Rangers are playing, Bobby V's features plenty of baseball memorabilia, collected during Valentine's years in the game. The dinner tables and bar top are covered with baseball cards and ticket stubs laid beneath glass. You'll also find lots of autographed photos, *Sports Illustrated* covers, game-worn uniforms, and flat-screen TVs tuned into games being played around the country. Bobby

V's is open Monday through Friday from 11:30 a.m. to 1:00 a.m. and Saturday and Sunday from noon to 1:30 a.m.

Also worth visiting in Stamford is the **Jackie Robinson Park of Fame** (860 Canal Street), where you find a life-size statue of Robinson. The baseball icon moved to Stamford in 1955 while still a member of the Brooklyn Dodgers and spent his final two decades in the city before passing away in 1972 at the age of fifty-three. The statue, which was unveiled in 1999, is emblazoned with the words "Courage," "Confidence," and "Perseverance."

● ●

A year before he broke the major-league color barrier and became the first African American to play in a regular season big-league game since Moses Fleetwood Walker was released by the Toledo Blue Stockings in 1884, Jackie Robinson reported to his first spring training camp in March of 1946. The Dodgers trained in Jacksonville in those days, but that city wouldn't let Robinson take the field with white players. And so Robinson's first exhibition game as a member of the Montreal Royals took place in Daytona Beach, which had been handpicked by Branch Rickey due to its progressive attitude toward race. At a time when blacks were treated like second-class citizens throughout the Jim Crow South, Daytona matriarch Mary McLeod Bethune had fought to ensure civil rights and educational opportunities for the blacks in her community, and by 1946 there was a thriving black middle class in the coastal city.

Unfortunately, Daytona Beach was an island of tolerance amid a sea of ignorance and hatred Robinson had to navigate during his first spring in Florida. At points elsewhere in the state, he

84. Jackie Robinson Ballpark and Museum

105 East Orange Avenue
Daytona Beach, Florida 32114
(386) 257-3172
http://daytona.cubs.milb.com

was prevented from taking the field by racist threats and by laws prohibiting blacks from participating in sporting events with whites. In Sanford, for example, a police chief threatened to stop a game if Robinson didn't leave the field. In Jacksonville, the stadium was padlocked an hour before a game to ensure the Dodgers didn't try anything forward thinking. But at Daytona Beach's City Island Ballpark, Robinson was allowed to play. His first game as a member of the Dodgers' International League affiliate occurred on March 17, 1946, when he trotted out to second base for a Sunday afternoon

Jackie Robinson played his first professional game in Florida at the ballpark now named in his honor.

exhibition against Brooklyn's big leaguers. More than 4,000 people were on hand to witness the occasion, including about a thousand members of Daytona's African-American community, who were relegated to a segregated seating area along the right field line. Robinson went 0-for-3 but reached on a fielder's choice, stole a base, and scored a run. Most importantly, he was cheered by the crowd, white and black, every time he came to the plate.

Two years later, after he had won the 1946 International League Most Valuable Player award and the 1947 Major League Rookie of the Year award, Robinson acknowledged the importance of that first game at Daytona Beach, saying, "When I got home, I felt as though I had won some kind of victory. I had a new opinion of the

people in the town. I knew, of course, that everyone wasn't pulling for me to make good, but I was sure that the whole world wasn't lined up against me. When I went to sleep, the applause was still ringing in my ears."

City Island Ballpark was renamed Jackie Robinson Ballpark in 1990, and entered into the National Register of Historic Places in 1998. Today it is home to the Daytona Cubs, who perennially vie for the distinction of being the best-drawing club in the Florida State League. Outside "The Jack," you find a scenic River Walk that traces the banks of the Halifax River. The River Walk serves as an extension of the **Jackie Robinson Museum,** which is open daily from 9:00 a.m. to 5:00 p.m. and is free of charge to visit. There are exhibits and activities that pay tribute to Robinson, and also to other "Barrier Breakers," or social trailblazers who overcame the narrow-minded thinking of others to redefine the possibilities for minorities.

The Robinson highlights include a bronze statue that depicts the baseball great in his earlier days wearing a Montreal Royals uniform and standing with two young children. A timeline traces Robinson's life accomplishments along the exterior wall of the home clubhouse. And plaques offer black-and-white photos along with text that tells the story of how Robinson integrated the game. The Picnic Porch along the ballpark's right field line, meanwhile, sits approximately where the segregated "black seating area" was at City Island Ballpark when Robinson made his debut; a historic display recalls the occasion.

The interactive attractions along the river include a regulation-length base line that allows you to make like Jackie Robinson—who stole home nineteen times in his big-league career—and race for the plate. Basketball hoops and a long-jumping pit show you firsthand just how hard it is to excel at the sports Robinson mastered as a collegian. Robinson, who lettered in baseball, basketball, football, and track at UCLA, was the nation's first four-sport letterman. He twice led the Pacific Coast Conference in scoring on the basketball court, was an All-American in football, and posted an NCAA-best broad jump of 25 feet, 6½ inches in 1940.

The Barrier Breaker displays near the Orange Avenue entrance to the ballpark pay tribute to Robinson and to four other individuals who followed his lead in expanding the opportunities available to minorities in the United States. One display tells the story of Althea Gibson, a professional golfer and tennis player, who broke international tennis's color barrier when she played at Wimbledon in 1951. She won eleven Grand Slam titles, competing in singles, doubles, and mixed-doubles tournaments. Then she retired from tennis to focus on golf and in 1964 became the first African-American woman to play in the LPGA.

Willie O'Ree, the first African-American hockey player to suit up for an NHL team, is also honored here. He broke hockey's color line with the Boston Bruins in 1958. Roberto Clemente, who was the first Latino to win a Most Valuable Player Award, a World Series Most Valuable Player Award, and to be enshrined in the National Baseball Hall of Fame, is also honored. And finally, the fifth Barrier Breaker marker pays tribute to Shirley Chisholm, who became the first African-American woman elected to the US Congress in 1968, representing New York's 12th District.

2003 North 19th Street
Tampa, Florida 33605
(813) 247-1434
http://tampabaseballmuseum.org

Situated in the very house where future Hall of Famer Al Lopez grew up as the son of Cuban immigrants in the 1910s and early 1920s, and continued living for most of his adult life, the Tampa Baseball Museum at the Al Lopez House opened in late 2014 after various entities in the Tampa community worked together to make it a reality.

The project represents an excellent example of a city capitalizing on an opportunity created, at least in part, by necessity. The story goes something like this. . . . The ancient house on 12th Avenue where the former big-league catcher and longtime major-league manager had spent most of his life stood in the direct path of a Florida Department of Transportation project to widen Interstate 4 and was slated for demolition. When one of the construction workers realized the house's ties to Tampa's first big-league baseball player and first Cooperstown inductee, however, a plan was developed to relocate it to a stretch of other historic homes in Ybor City, Tampa's historic cigar-manufacturing district and hub of Cuban culture. After a slow mile-and-a-half ride, on May 15, 2013, the Lopez House was deposited on a vacant lot that Hillsborough County had leased to the Ybor City Museum Society at virtually no cost for thirty years, with an option to extend the lease for an additional thirty.

Rather than just moving the house and leaving it to sit idly, the Museum Society built a coalition of civic leaders and organizations who collectively envisioned turning it into a place where Tampa could celebrate its proud tradition of turning out major leaguers. The Lopez House would be a living monument, where visitors would drop in to learn more about Tampa's baseball heritage within the very walls that had once housed Lopez and his eight siblings. Joining the Museum Society in the pursuit were the Florida Department of Transportation, which moved the house (a fourteen-hour ordeal), and Hillsborough County, which not only furnished the land but awarded a $250,000 challenge grant to fund the remodeling of the interior so that it could serve as a museum. The City of Tampa also chipped in a grant to fund exterior restoration of the house and landscape its grounds.

Work began on the interior on November 13, 2013, as Al Lopez Jr. and Miami Marlins pitcher Sam Dyson—who played his schoolboy ball at Jesuit High School of Tampa, just like Lopez—joined Museum Society staff and local civic leaders to take turns swinging ceremonial golden sledgehammers. In the months to follow, other local MLB alums including Lou Piniella, Luis Gonzalez, and Tino Martinez visited the house.

The next step involved collecting artifacts suitable for display. The call went out that the Museum Society was seeking old pieces of baseball gear, uniforms, photos, ticket stubs, newspaper and magazine clippings, trophies, pennants, and signed balls related to the early years of the city's love affair with the game. One unique item that turned up was a ball signed by not only Lopez but the entire 1959 Chicago White Sox team. The White Sox won

The Al Lopez house at its original location, preparing for its move to its permanent site to become the Tampa Baseball Museum at the Al Lopez House

the American League pennant that year, claiming their first pennant since the fateful season of 1919 when eight of their players had allegedly thrown the World Series. Other highlights include a set of three signed seats from the historic Grapefruit League park that was named after Lopez; a set of 1946 Tampa Smokers baseball cards; and one of Piniella's game-used gloves.

In addition to Lopez—who after signing with the Class-D Smokers as a sixteen-year-old, made his big-league debut with the Brooklyn Dodgers three years later in 1928 and played nineteen seasons before retiring with the most career games played at catcher—the group of players hailing from this baseball hotbed includes fellow Hall of Famer Wade Boggs, as well as the aforementioned Piniella, Martinez, and Gonzalez, and also Fred McGriff, Gary Sheffield, Tony La Russa, Dwight Gooden, and Dave Magadan.

The museum's permanent and rotating displays celebrate more than 125 years of local baseball history, beginning with the details of baseball's origins and evolution in Tampa, West Tampa, and Ybor City. Tampa's youth leagues (Little League, high school, and American

Baseball signed by Al Lopez and the entire 1959 Chicago White Sox team

the Tampa Black Smokers and Tampa Rockets are also remembered, as are the fields that have hosted big-league spring training games in the area through the years, including Al Lopez Field, where the White Sox (1955–1959) and Reds (1960–1987) once played their March games.

Admission to the museum costs $8.95 for adults, $6.95 for adults over the age of sixty, and $4.95 for children and teens ages six to eighteen. Admission is always free for any current or former major leaguer who should happen to stop by. Consult the museum's website for updated information on its hours of operation.

While in town, you may also enjoy visiting **Al Lopez Park** (4810 North Himes Avenue), which sits across the street from Jesuit High School. A statue on the grounds depicts Lopez ripping his catcher's mask from his face as he stands up to pursue a foul pop.

Legion) receive treatment, as do historic men's leagues like Tampa's Inter-Social League and the old Cigar City League. Negro Leagues teams like

86. The Ripken Complex

873 Long Drive
Aberdeen, Maryland 21001
(410) 297-9292
www.ripkenstadium.com

Along Interstate 95, in the hometown of Hall of Famer Cal Ripken Jr., you find a hardball destination that offers several different ways to celebrate the game we love. If your playing days are through, you can watch a minor-league game. If you're still lacing up your spikes and

dreaming big-league dreams, you can visit with your youth team to compete against other top teams at the complex's five replica fields that mimic Ripken's favorite big-league stadiums. If you're still learning the game, you can participate in youth camps run on-site throughout the summer.

The story of how Ripken Stadium, the replica diamonds, and the Ripken Experience youth academy came to exist in this small town 25 miles northeast of Baltimore began on the very night when Ripken became baseball's "Iron Man," playing in his 2,131st consecutive game to surpass Lou Gehrig's longstanding record. That night, in September of 1995, Ripken's fellow players gave him a gift of $75,000 through the Major League Baseball Players Association, with the suggestion that he use the money to

Cal Senior's Yard features a brick hotel in right field similar to the B&O Warehouse at Orioles Park at Camden Yards.

build or restore a baseball field in his hometown. Ripken talked with his brother Billy and father, Cal Sr.—both of whom also left their mark on the Orioles as second baseman and coach/manager respectively—and the trio decided to think much bigger than just building one field.

After honing their vision to create a minor-league and youth baseball complex in their hometown, the Ripkens bought the short-season Utica Blue Sox and moved the team to Aberdeen in 2002. As of this book's writing, the Aberdeen IronBirds have sold out every home game in their history, a streak spanning more than twelve seasons. The fans pass through the regal brick entryway to Ripken Stadium to size up the latest crop of Orioles draft picks. Aside from the game on the field, the delicious blue shell crabs provide a compelling reason for fans to keep turning out at the ballpark to the tune of 6,300 strong all summer long. Fans sit at picnic tables down the right field line and smash open their crabs with wooden hammers. Then they clean themselves up at the stadium restrooms before settling down to watch the rest of the game.

In addition to this state-of-the-art minor-league park, the 110-acre complex also features five fields that serve the Ripken Experience camps, clinics, and tournaments, welcoming campers and teams from across the country and around the world. The highlight is the Cal Ripken World Series each August, the final games of which are played at **Cal Sr.'s Yard,** which recreates the brick facade of Oriole Park and the outfield flag court, and even offers its very own B&O Warehouse looming behind the right field fence. The building beyond the fence in Aberdeen is not an old railroad facility, as in Baltimore, but a Courtyard Marriott, which is booked full each August when the twelve-year-old-and-under division of Babe Ruth League baseball (recently renamed the "Cal Ripken Baseball" division) plays its two-week championship tournament at the Ripken Complex.

More than 700,000 children play on nearly 70,000 teams worldwide in this division of the Babe Ruth League, but only the top fifteen teams each year—ten from the United States and five from overseas—earn tickets to Aberdeen to compete in the World Series. While the tournament has yet to reach the stature of the Little League World Series, it has grown quite a bit since its inception in 1999.

In addition to Cal Sr.'s Yard, the youth academy offers fields that mimic Baltimore's Memorial Stadium, the converted football field that was the home of the Orioles from 1954 to 1991; Fenway Park, with a miniature Green Monster in left field; Wrigley Field, with ivy on the outfield walls; and Yankee Stadium, complete with a Death Valley in left-center field and a looming home-run porch in right field.

One final attraction at the complex is a life-size **statue of Ripken,** holding his hand high as if waving in appreciation to the fans that cheered for him on the night when he broke the consecutive games played record. The statue previously stood on Route 40 in Aberdeen, welcoming visitors to town, but was relocated to the Ripken Complex in 2012. The inscription on its base reads in part:

> I've been asked this question, a lot, "How do you want to be remembered?" And my response to that question has been, "To be remembered at all is pretty special."
> —Cal Ripken, Jr., on September 6th, 1995.

87. Scottsdale Stadium

7408 East Osborn Road
Scottsdale, Arizona 85251
(480) 312-2586
www.scottsdaleaz.gov/stadium.asp

If ever there were a baseball park for all seasons, it is Scottsdale Stadium. Here, you can enjoy a professional baseball game under the warm March sun, in the twilight of a scorcher in mid-July, or in the long shadows of a November afternoon. Whether you're visiting Scottsdale to watch the San Francisco Giants take on a Cactus League foe during spring training, the Class-A Giants during the Arizona League season, or the Scottsdale Scorpions during the Arizona Fall League, one thing's almost certain: You'll fall in love with the charm of this old Western city and the ballpark at its center.

Chances are you're already familiar with the Cactus League, and have also been to your fair share of minor-league games. But you may not know much about the Arizona Fall League. If you ever find yourself unable to let go of baseball season as the World Series draws to an end, you should really consider getting to know it. You can head to Greater Phoenix to prolong the baseball calendar by an extra month before you accept winter's grim reality. Major League Baseball founded the developmental league in 1992 to provide top prospects a place to further develop their skills under the watchful eyes of their parent organizations.

The league begins play in the second week of October and finishes in the third week of November, fielding six teams that each draw rookie and minor-league players from five major-league clubs. It utilizes six ballparks—Mesa's Hohokam Stadium, Glendale's Camelback Ranch, Surprise Stadium, Peoria Stadium,

Scottsdale Stadium, and Scottsdale's Salt River Field at Talking Stick—all of which double as Cactus League parks in March. These facilities offer relaxed environments where you can plop down beside a radar-gun-toting scout and enjoy an up-close look at the game's best prospects. But clearly, Scottsdale Stadium is the league's signature facility. In addition to serving as league headquarters, and housing the Arizona Fall League Hall of Fame, it is where the league championship game is played each November.

Originally built in 1956 to serve as the spring home of the Baltimore Orioles, Scottsdale Stadium has been the Cactus League outpost of the San Francisco Giants since 1984. Well, not this Scottsdale Stadium. The Giants' arrival actually predates this incarnation of the park, which was built prior to the 1992 spring season. The complete tear down and rebuild project was drawn up by the architects at HOK, whose Oriole Park at Camden Yards would be unveiled just a month after the new Scottsdale Stadium opened.

Scottsdale Stadium showcases the stunning peaks of the four Camelback Mountains rising beyond its third base line. The park's charming old-time effects include antique light fixtures, and a facade of redbrick pillars and green iron gates that meshes well with the surrounding neighborhood. A grass seating berm extends across the outfield. Misters built into the grandstand roof spray cool water down onto the fans on hot days. Cacti, desert flowers, jacaranda trees, paloverdes, red gum eucalyptus, and Chinese elms adorn the ballpark interior, as well as the sidewalks outside.

The Arizona Fall League Hall of Fame is beneath the grandstand. The Hall provides bronze plaques to honor inductees. Although more than 1,300 Fall League alumni have reached the majors, the Hall included only

The grounds of Scottsdale Stadium are adorned with cacti and desert trees.

twenty-three members through 2013. The Hall charter says that for a player to be considered, he must have won a Rookie of the Year award, league MVP award, Gold Glove award, or Silver Slugger award, or have been named to an All-Star team at the big-league level. And that's just to get on the ballot.

As of this book's writing the inductees (including the managers enshrined) were Garret Anderson, Dusty Baker, Chris Carpenter, Jermaine Dye, Darin Erstad, Terry Francona, Nomar Garciaparra, Jason Giambi, Brian Giles, Shawn Green, Roy Halladay, Todd Helton, Ryan Howard, Torii Hunter, Derek Jeter, Paul Konerko, Derrek Lee, Grady Little, Derek Lowe, Ken Macha, Jerry Manuel, Bob Melvin, Dustin Pedroia, Tony Pena, Troy Percival, Mike Piazza, Albert Pujols, Jimmy Rollins, Mike Scioscia, Alfonso Soriano, Mark Teixeira, Ron Washington, Eric Wedge, and Michael Young. But you've enjoyed the big-league contributions of far more Arizona Fall League alums that that; some thirty-six Fall League alums appeared in the 2013 All-Star Game!

The Hall also provides a wall of plaques displaying the names of the annual Joe Black

Most Valuable Player Award winners. Black, the 1952 National League Rookie of the Year and first African-American pitcher to win a World Series game, spent his final three decades in Phoenix. He is also honored with a statue outside the regular season home of the Arizona Diamondbacks.

Finally, not far from where the Hall of Fame is located, you can peruse the Scottsdale Sports Hall of Fame, which honors more than thirty local athletes, including baseball great Jim Palmer.

While these two shrines are interesting places to visit, undoubtedly the crack of the bat and pop of rawhide smacking into leather are what will really entrance you when you visit Scottsdale Stadium or any of the Arizona Fall League parks in late October or November when the rest of the baseball world has suddenly gone silent.

88. The Cincinnati Reds Hall of Fame and Museum

Great American Ballpark
100 Joe Nuxhall Way
Cincinnati, Ohio 45202
(513) 765-7000
http://cincinnati.reds.mlb.com/cin/hof/hof/index.jsp

On the west side of Cincinnati's Great American Ballpark, you find an excellent baseball museum. Although the Reds have been inducting retired stars into their Hall of Fame since 1958, when Ernie Lombardi, Johnny Vander Meer, Paul Derringer, Bucky Walters, and Frank McCormick composed the first class, the team didn't have an expansive museum like this one until it opened beautiful Great American in 2003. Decades earlier at Crosley Field, the team had hung plaques to honor its Hall of Famers on the beams above the concession concourse, but throughout the Reds' tenure at Riverfront Stadium, the plaques had remained tucked away in a storage closet.

During the Riverfront era, the Reds even stopped inducting players into their hall, since they didn't really have a physical space to honor legends. Thankfully, the extra space offered by Great American breathed new life into this proud team's celebration of its past. Today, the Reds Hall of Fame honors more than eighty former players, managers, and front-office executives. Yes, the Reds honor more of their old-time faves than any other team does—and some of the players they've enshrined fall a bit short of what we usually think of when we think of baseball royalty (Chris Sabo, Jose Rijo, Sean Casey, and Tom Browning come to mind as hall of famers that might cause us to raise an eyebrow)—but it's their club, so they're entitled to be more inclusive, rather than less, if they so choose. Despite honoring the occasional good but not great player, as the game's oldest team, the Reds have undeniably had a great many standouts through the years, whose credentials for a team hall are unimpeachable (Johnny Bench, Tom Seaver, Tony Perez, Joe Morgan, Barry Larkin, Dave Concepcion, etc.). No, Pete Rose doesn't have a plaque in this hall either, but from 2007 to 2008, the Reds museum offered a nice exhibit honoring the blacklisted Hit King.

Outside the Reds Hall of Fame and Museum, Joe Nuxhall delivers a pitch to Frank Robinson at Crosley Terrace.

Other past exhibits include ones that have celebrated the memories of the 1919 World Series team that beat Chicago's infamous Black Sox; the 1990 World Series winners; Joe Nuxhall, who reached the majors with the Reds as a fifteen-year-old, then after a long playing career became a beloved Reds' radio broadcaster; and Cincinnati's Negro Leagues history.

The continuing exhibits, which you'll find when you visit, include the Palace of the Fans Theatre, where you can sit in an old-style grandstand and watch footage from the team's historic games on a screen modeled to look like the old scoreboard at Crosley; an 1869 display that remembers the earliest days of the Reds with life-size statues of brothers Harry and George Wright; a Crosley Field retrospective spanning the park's history from 1912 until

1970; an interactive area where you can step into a batter's box and watch a 95-mile-per-hour fastball whiz past you; a gallery dedicated to the Reds' World Series–winning teams; an interactive radio broadcast booth where you can take a turn calling a game; a front office gallery that displays historic team documents like the paperwork associated with the Reds' acquisition of Morgan in a trade with the Astros in 1971; a Bench Statue; and a Hall of Records that displays the team's statistical leaders in a variety of categories. From the Hall of Records, you can look out large windows and see the rose garden that marks the spot where Rose's record-breaking 4,192th hit landed in the Riverfront Stadium outfield on September 11, 1985, as he moved past Ty Cobb to become baseball's all-time hits leader.

During baseball's off-season, the Reds Hall of Fame and Museum is open Tuesday through Sunday from 10:00 a.m. until 5:00 p.m. During the season, it is open daily, welcoming non-ticket-holders from 10:00 a.m. until the ballpark gates open, at which time it becomes accessible only to ticket holders. On nongame days, admission costs $10.00 for adults and $8.00 for children and senior citizens.

Outside Great American's main gate meanwhile, you find a tastefully landscaped plot poetically called **Crosley Terrace.** Here, baseball's most creatively composed statue collection is on full display. Rather than just depicting four beloved players from the Crosley Field era in isolation, the Reds offer these bronzes posed in the midst of a simulated game—a team scrimmage, perhaps—on a faux infield. Catcher Ernie Lombardi squats behind the plate awaiting a pitch from Nuxhall, who's just delivered from a mound 60 feet and 6 inches away, while Frank Robinson takes a mighty swing, and Ted Kluszewski stoically awaits his turn in the on-deck circle.

89. The Pink Pony

3831 North Scottsdale Road
Scottsdale, Arizona 85251
(480) 945-6697
http://pinkponyscottsdale.com

For decades the most popular postgame hangout for visiting players and traveling fans during the Cactus League season was the Pink Pony Steakhouse in Old Town Scottsdale. The city began its long life as a spring training hub in 1956 when the Baltimore Orioles became the first team to set up camp in Scottsdale, and since then the Red Sox, Cubs, A's, and most recently (and currently) the Giants have made Scottsdale their March home. As the Cactus League evolved, the Pink Pony—which predated big-league baseball's arrival in Scottsdale, having opened in 1949—embraced the game and its fans and quickly became the eating and drinking establishment of choice for players, coaches, executives, scouts, writers, broadcasters, and just about anyone else connected to the game.

Hall of Fame pitcher and good old boy Dizzy Dean played a leading role in catapulting the Pink Pony to prominence. One spring Ole Diz, who by the 1950s was working as a national play-by-play announcer for NBC, struck up a conversation with Pink Pony owner Charlie Briley. The retired pitcher discovered that the friendly barkeep really knew his baseball, and the two men became hunting buddies. As Diz talked up the Pony to his many friends in the game, word spread. Soon the bar was welcoming current and retired players like Ty Cobb, Joe DiMaggio, Jimmie Foxx, Rogers Hornsby, Willie Mays, and Ted Williams on a nightly basis. On one memorable evening, five Hall of Famers—Ernie Banks, Lou Boudreau, Bob Lemon, Mickey Mantle, and Eddie Mathews—all sat at the same table talking baseball. Another time, Billy Martin showed up with a stripper to celebrate Briley's birthday, and Briley's wife, Gwen, who comanaged the place, read the Yankees second baseman the riot act,

Although the Brileys no longer own and operate the Pink Pony, much of the baseball memorabilia they collected through the decades remains.

then said the woman could stay but couldn't take off her clothes until all of the families with children had departed for the night.

The neat thing about the Pony back in its golden era was that the players and fans would sit side-by-side at the bar or at abutting tables in the dining room and go about the business of eating and drinking and talking in an atmosphere that just oozed baseball enthusiasm. The Brileys never let the fans harangue the players for autographs and photos, and by the same token, they never gave the players special treatment. The big leaguers waited in line for tables or waited their turn to be served at the bar, just like everyone else.

As one generation of players gave way to the next, baseball royalty like Gene Autry, Don Sutton, and Reggie Jackson did their best to keep the Pony on baseball's "it" list; then Ferguson Jenkins, Bob Uecker, Dusty Baker, and Will Clark kept the Pony chic for the next generation.

By 2009, though, with Charlie Briley having passed away and Gwen working long hours to keep it running as she approached eighty years of age, the Pony had become something of a relic. Sure, the hard-core history buffs among baseball's traveling fandom still showed up to bask in the unique baseball memorabilia adorning the walls, and front office types and umpires turned out for postgame drinks or meals, but the game's players and rank-and-file rooters were no longer frequenting it to the degree they had. And so, Gwen Briley said goodbye to the final table of patrons who visited for the 2009 Cactus League season, then closed the Pony's doors for what looked to be the final time. After sixty years of running the place, she had decided it was time to call it quits.

Fortunately, though, in 2014 the Pink Pony reopened under new ownership. A lot has changed, thanks to a million-dollar renovation, but a lot has also stayed the same. The renovation brought a new kitchen with wood-fired ovens, a new menu that still offers the trademark steaks that were the Pony's hallmark in its glory years, but also includes gourmet entrees for more refined palates, a brighter atmosphere, outdoor seating, and a larger indoor dining space. A baseball-inspired mural was also painted on the building's exterior.

Despite the changes, you still find a collection of autographed jerseys and photos adorning the walls. A series of colorful caricatures mounted above the bar pays tribute in a funny way to some of the Pony's more notable visitors through the years. Initially, these were the creation of Walt Disney animator Don Barclay, and then when Barclay passed away, Charlie Briley's wife, Gwen, continued the tradition. Johnny Pesky is portrayed with his Red Sox hat inexplicably askew, and Williams with his nose seeming about three sizes larger than it was in life. Other nice touches include the home plate from the original Scottsdale Stadium that stood from 1956 until 1991, and a bat-rack stocked with vintage lumber left for the Brileys by their big-league friends.

90. Recreation Ballpark

440 North Giddings Street
Visalia, California 93291
(559) 732-4433
www.milb.com/index.jsp?sid=t516

The home field of the California League's Visalia Rawhide presents as intimate a setting for a game as any yard you'll encounter in baseball's bushes. With only 1,888 fixed seats, Recreation Ballpark has the smallest seating capacity of any park in the affiliated minor leagues. The park's total capacity tops out at 2,800 fans, after you factor in the "Pasture" seating area in the right field corner and several group and party areas. Amazingly, there are just twelve rows of seats in the uncovered grandstand behind home plate, and the effect of sitting right on top of the action is amplified further by the field's minimal foul territory. If you sit in the front row, you are only 28 feet from home plate, or less than half the distance from the plate as the pitcher.

Called Recreation *Ballpark* to distinguish it from Recreation Park, in which it sits along with basketball hoops, volleyball courts, a skate park, picnic tables, and other community facilities, this little field at the corner of Goshen and Giddings has been hosting minor-league ball since 1946. The ballpark was heavily renovated in 1967 and then again in 2009, but it hasn't lost its small-town charm. The most recent makeover was more an enhancement of preexisting facilities than a complete rebuild, and thankfully so.

The fans in the first few rows behind the plate are closer to the batter than the pitcher is at Recreation Ballpark.

Aside from retrofitting the grandstand with comfortable new plastic seats, the work also built a new structure down the third base line to house the team offices. The work also moved the main entrance of the park from behind the grandstand out to right field, added standard-size dugouts, moved the bullpens out of foul territory into actual pens, and added new lawn and party areas. The Hall of Fame Club was another new addition to honor the all-time greats who have passed through Visalia in its seven decades as a minor-league outpost. Nearly 250 Visalia alumni have reached the major leagues, including the team's representative in the National Baseball Hall of Fame: Kirby Puckett, who scored 105 runs while batting .314 with nine home runs and ninety-seven runs batted in for the Visalia Oaks in 1983. More recently, Barry Zito (2000), Justin Upton (2007), and Paul Goldschmidt (2010) have starred in Visalia on their way to the Show.

Previous to the 2009 renovation, the Visalia club had been known as the Oaks, but it took up the name Rawhide at that time to better hitch its wagon to Visalia's frontier roots. As such, many of the new ballpark features reflect the Old West theme. There's the Saloon party deck on the third base side, the Pasture lawn seating area in right field, and the Kids Corral play area in deep right. The Cowbell Section is an actual cowbell-shaped seating area that offers a complimentary cowbell to each ticketholder. The Bullpen

The grandstand is supported by a mound of dirt covered with shotcrete at Visalia's Recreation Ballpark.

Family Deck positions you a few feet behind the bullpen catcher, creating the effect that the ball is being thrown right at you as pitchers warm up. The Red Barn is a groundskeeping shed incorporated into the right-center field fence. The Barn is not just a nod to the Central Valley's agricultural heritage but also a target for heavy hitters who take aim at its 40-foot side that serves as the home-run fence.

The most inspired feature of all from the 2009 renovation though is the third dugout Visalia constructed just past third base. The players on both teams have a dugout, as usual,

and in Visalia the fans have one too. The dugout can be rented out by groups of up to twenty-five on a game-by-game basis. It is a true replica of a players' dugout, sunken and concrete, with a wooden bench and protective screen running along its front.

And yet, despite all these bells and whistles, Recreation Ballpark's most intriguing design feature might just be its aged grandstand, which is a holdover from the 1960s. Rather than using wood or steel to build the structure between the dugouts, Visalia's public works department used excess soil that had been excavated from trenches dug to lay the stretches of US Highways 198 and 63 that pass through town. The workers built a big mound behind home plate, then after piling the dirt as high as possible, encased the soil with shotcrete (a kind of spray-on concrete sometimes referred to as gunite that is applied by high-pressure hoses). The result is a sloping concrete berm that takes the ballpark-inside-a-hill design you might recall from historic Grapefruit League venues like Holman Stadium in Vero Beach or Chain O' Lakes Park in Winter Haven to entirely new heights.

● ●

"It ain't bragging if you can back it up." So said Dizzy Dean on many occasions. The colorful Cardinals pitcher of the 1930s was prone to boasting about his accomplishments, and also to making predictions about his accomplishments yet to come. Prior to the 1934 season, he forecast that he and his brother, Paul "Daffy" Dean, would combine to win forty-five games. The St. Louis stable mates did even better, as Dizzy won thirty and Daffy won nineteen to lead the Cardinals to the World Series, where they combined to win four more games in a seven-game series win against the Tigers. Another time, Dean predicted that he would strike out Vince DiMaggio four times in an upcoming game, and he did it, with a little help from his catcher, who intentionally dropped a foul pop by DiMaggio in his fourth at-bat so Dean could have another crack at him.

Heading into the 1937 All-Star Game, the twenty-six-year-old Dean had already won 134 games, a National League MVP award, and a World Series ring in his five and a half big-league seasons. He was the game's most dominant pitcher and one of its most beloved figures. His seemingly endless reserve of "Ole Diz" stories and his playful country persona made him a media darling. But then his career was cut short by an injury suffered in that fateful Mid-Summer Classic.

Dean was pitching during the third inning at Washington's Griffith Stadium when Cleveland

91. The Dizzy Dean Exhibit

The Mississippi Sports Hall of Fame and Museum
1152 Lakeland Drive
Jackson, Mississippi 39216
(601) 982-8264
http://msfame.com

Indians outfielder Earl Averill scorched a line drive up the middle. The ball struck Dean's right foot and broke his big toe. In the second half of the 1937 season, Dean rushed back to the mound before allowing his foot time to fully heal, and in overcompensating for the original injury he changed his pitching delivery, which in turn caused irreparable damage to his right shoulder. Dean won just sixteen games over his final five seasons, and then hung up his spikes. But he didn't disappear from the game in the way some star-crossed players do. Instead, he transitioned into a new role as a baseball broadcaster, sitting beside Pee Wee Reese to call the CBS *Game of the Week*. Dean's creative misuse of the English language during broadcasts heightened his legend further. Schoolteachers across the country no doubt shuddered to hear him talk, but most

This 3-D sculpture is just one of many Dizzy Dean attractions at the Mississippi Sports Hall of Fame and Museum.

fans could relate to the retired player who peppered his speech with words like "ain't" and sentences like "He weren't neither."

Today, you can learn more about this likable legend at the Mississippi Sports Hall of Fame and Museum, which includes an expansive Dizzy Dean exhibit. For years, many of the items housed in this collection were on display at a separate Dizzy Dean Museum in Jackson, then in 1996 the Mississippi Sports Hall of Fame and Museum opened and made the Dean collection one of its trademark exhibits. Thanks to the generosity of Dean's widow, there are many photos of Dean, including ones of him posing alongside friends like President Dwight D. Eisenhower and Satchel Paige, and with his brother, Paul. Dean's

World Series ring is on display, as is his National Baseball Hall of Fame ring, old pieces of equipment, and one of his game-worn Cardinals jerseys. There are balls signed by Babe Ruth, Ty Cobb, and Cy Young. Perhaps best of all, the exhibit offers video footage of Dean, including an episode of the *Mel Tillis Variety Show* from the 1970s that features Ole Diz in a rocking chair singing "Wabash Cannonball" and a Falstaff Beer commercial in which Dean and Reese wrap up the 1961 season.

The museum also honors another Magnolia State diamond king, Cool Papa Bell. The fleet-footed star of the Negro Leagues, for whom a nearby street in Jackson is named, became the first Mississippi-born player enshrined in the National Baseball Hall of Fame in 1974. (Although Dean considered Wiggins, Mississippi, his home, he was born in Lucas, Arkansas.) The museum includes a life-size photo of Bell and video footage of him playing alongside several other Negro Leagues stars. Among the more than thirty other baseball players enshrined in the Mississippi Hall of Fame are Bill Foster, the half-brother of Negro Leagues pioneer Rube Foster, who was himself one of the finest pitchers in Negro Leagues history; Boo Ferriss, who helped pitch the Red Sox to the 1946 pennant with a 25-6 record; Joe Gibson, who starred on the baseball field and basketball court at Ole Miss and then won a World Series ring with the Pirates in 1960; George Scott, who slugged 271 homers for the Red Sox, Brewers, Yankees, and Royals, while winning three Gold Gloves at first base in the 1960s and 1970s;

and more recent stars Will Clark and Rafael Palmeiro. The museum also showcases a collection of old-time equipment, including turn-of-the-twentieth-century uniforms, spikes, caps, gloves, bats, balls, belts, leggings, chest protectors, and jockstraps.

Legends from other sports who receive their due in the Hall of Fame include inductees Jake Gibbs, Bailey Howell, Archie Manning, Jerry Rice, and Walter Payton. A Wall of Fame depicts historic moments in Mississippi sports history, while a theater provides video highlights of Mississippi sports. There is also an interactive area where you can try your hand at baseball, golf, football, and soccer activities. The museum is open Monday through Saturday from 10:00 a.m. to 4:00 p.m. Admission costs $5.00 for adults and $3.50 for students between the ages of six and seventeen and seniors over the age of sixty.

• •

You won't find any part of the San Francisco Giants' original home, Seals Stadium, still standing to mark the site of the first big-league game ever played on the West Coast. Today a shopping center smothers the hallowed grounds where San Franciscans enjoyed nearly three decades of minor-league ball, and then celebrated the arrival of the Giants on April 15, 1958. The home team defeated the Los Angeles Dodgers 8–0 that day to officially announce the arrival of the major leagues in California. The Giants used Seals Stadium for two seasons before opening Candlestick Park in 1960.

Though Seals Stadium may be gone, it has not been entirely forgotten in its old neighborhood. At the Double Play Bar and Grill, across the street from where the old ballpark stood, you find a shrine to the old yard. The Double

92. The Double Play Bar and Grill

2401 16th Street
San Francisco, California 94103
(415) 621-9859
www.doubleplaysf.com/home.html

Play's relics and mementos honor the park's three resident teams—the Pacific Coast League Seals (1931–1958); the Pacific Coast League Missions (1931–1937), who played at the park as joint-tenants with the Seals; and the National League Giants (1958–1959). If you are interested in learning more about the dawning of

West Coast baseball, this is a site you will surely enjoy.

Perhaps the most unusual piece of memorabilia on the Double Play's artifact-laden walls is an original copy of the letter Giants owner Horace Stoneman sent to Giants season ticket holders prior to the start of the 1960 season, trumpeting the arrival of Seals Stadium's successor, Candlestick Park. It reads, "The new stadium is a beautiful structure. I believe it is the finest sports arena anywhere. . . . All San Franciscans have reason to be proud of it as one more expression of civic enterprise and progress. . . ."

You'll also find a slew of old ballpark photographs, baseball mitts, old-time jerseys and caps, seats from Seals Stadium, and the rounded top of the flagpole that once rose high above Seals Stadium's center field fence. Unfortunately, though, if you are just learning of the Double Play as you read this book, you've missed your chance to see the beautiful wraparound mural that once adorned the walls in the back banquet room. The mural, which portrayed Seals Stadium during a game between the Seals and the Oakland Oaks, was removed in 2013 when the room was demolished to make way for a twelve-unit apartment complex next door to the now slightly smaller Double Play. Don't blame Double Play management for the loss; the decision was made by their landlord.

A favorite corner bar since 1909, the Double Play was well positioned to chronicle the rise and fall of baseball in San Francisco's Mission district. Its patrons watched with anticipation as Seals Stadium was constructed in the early 1930s, then helped fill its 23,000 seats when the Seals and Missions arrived in the spring of 1931. In 1933 the locals watched in amazement as an eighteen-year-old San Franciscan named Joe DiMaggio hit safely in sixty-one straight games to establish a professional record that still stands.

At other cherished moments in time, Seals fans watched the home team post a remarkable 115-68 record in 1946, en route to a fourth straight Pacific Coast League crown, and in 1957 they watched the Seals bid the Pacific Coast League adieu by claiming their fourteenth and final title. During those halcyon days of Seals baseball, the team's players could often be spotted bellying up to the bar at the Double Play before, after, and sometimes even *during* games across the street. According to Double Play lore, it was not uncommon for a starting pitcher to wander across the street for a drink after he'd been removed from a game.

In 1958 and 1959, the Double Play became a major-league hangout as the Giants and their big-league opponents attracted 2.7 million fans to the neighborhood. The euphoria in the Mission was short-lived though, because the opening of Candlestick rendered Seals Stadium obsolete. The old ballpark was promptly demolished but not before Double Play patrons raised one last pint to the old yard and not before the joint's ownership scarfed up as much memorabilia from the park as it could, memorabilia that today keeps the memory of Seals Stadium alive for a new generation of fans to enjoy.

The Double Play serves breakfast and lunch seven days a week, opening at 7:00 a.m. on Monday through Friday, and at 8:00 a.m. on the weekend. In 2014 it began also serving dinner on Thursday and Friday nights, beginning at 5:00 p.m. It stays open until 9:00 p.m., or a little later if the Giants game is on TV. On any given day, you're apt to find local police officers congregating at the breakfast counter talking baseball or about their just-completed night's work. The breakfast burritos are a house specialty. Later in the day, you'll find a friendly crowd of hardball fans watching the Giants game—and if someone requests it, the A's game. It's a welcoming place with cheap beer, surprisingly good food, and a unique collection of baseball relics.

• •

In the wake of Oriole Park at Camden Yards opening in Baltimore in 1992, and attracting throngs of traveling fans to its turnstiles, other major-league teams began replacing their aged and nondescript stadiums with fan-friendly models designed to replicate the magical cathedrals of baseball's Golden Era. And before long, the teams of baseball's minor leagues caught the retro bug too. Among the first throwback parks to open in the bush leagues was Oklahoma City's Bricktown Ballpark, and upon its unveiling in 1998 it was hailed as one of the finest minor-league yards in the land. Many other cities have since followed suit, building their own old-timey minor-league gems, but all these years later a strong case can still be made that this park in Oklahoma City is the best bush-league park of the bunch. Because it reflects the essence of its downtown neighborhood so well, and because it offers top-notch historic nods to its region's hardball past, "the Brick" is a park you should add to your minor-league bucket list.

Similar to its big-league cousins in cities like Houston, Colorado, and, of course, Baltimore, the home of the Pacific Coast League Oklahoma City RedHawks was designed to reflect the aesthetics of the downtown neighborhood in which it resides. And like those big-league parks, it was designed to be the centerpiece of an urban revitalization effort that would turn a once struggling neighborhood into a vibrant entertainment district. By the time the $34 million publicly funded park opened, what was once a sagging warehouse district east of downtown Oklahoma

93. Chickasaw Bricktown Ballpark

2 South Mickey Mantle Drive
Oklahoma City, Oklahoma 73104
(405) 218-1000
www.milb.com/index.jsp?sid=t238

City was already well on its way to becoming a hopping spot for dining and nightlife.

As you near the ballpark, your GPS guides you along streets with names like Joe Carter Avenue, Johnny Bench Drive, and Mickey Mantle Drive. You pass sports bars, steakhouses, authentic Mexican eateries, and microbreweries. And just as you enter the shadows of the beautiful brick-and-steel ballpark, right across from the park on Mantle Drive you come upon **Mickey Mantle's Steakhouse** (7 Mickey Mantle Drive). Nestled in the heart of the pre- and postgame hub, this upscale restaurant/bar houses memorabilia dedicated to the most famous Sooner State slugger of them all. There are childhood photos of "The Mick," old Yankees caps and jerseys, trophies he won as a youth, and a plethora of framed 8x10 photos from his days with the Yankees. Mantle, who was also known as "the Commerce Comet," grew up the son of a miner in the northwest Oklahoma town of Commerce.

Throughout the streets of Bricktown, you find ornate mosaic murals rendering uniquely

Mickey Mantle takes a mighty cut outside Chickasaw Bricktown Ballpark.

Oklahoman scenes dating back to the early 1900s. It is fitting, therefore, that the exterior of the local ballpark is decorated in similar style, with colorful mosaics portraying baseball scenes and other aspects of Oklahoma City cultural life. The stadium is also rife with the sort of statues and busts you see at practically all of the big-league parks these days, but at few minor-league ones. These depict former Sooner State legends like Bench, Warren Spahn, and Mantle. There are also busts of former Yankees Allie Reynolds and Bobby Murcer, both of whom grew up in Oklahoma City and then returned to live in the city after their playing days were through. The Bench statue stands outside the home plate entrance on Johnny Bench Plaza. It depicts the legendary Reds backstop, who was

born in Oklahoma City and grew up in Binger, wearing his catching gear. The Mantle statue, which stands outside the third base entrance, catches The Mick in the midst of a mighty swing from the left-handed batter's box. Inlaid in its base are a set of Mantle's handprints and autographs from some of his friends and family members. The Spahn statue, which sits beyond the right field fence, honors the winningest lefty ever, the pride of Broken Arrow, Oklahoma, who is depicted in the midst of one of his famously high leg kicks.

As for the ballpark itself, as its name suggests, it offers an attractive redbrick facade. Inside, the Brick is large by minor-league standards—with slightly more than 13,000 seats—but it maintains a cozy atmosphere thanks to its low first level

The "Brick," as it is affectionately known to locals, offers an appropriately redbrick facade.

and minimal foul territory. The upper deck offers excellent sightlines too, thanks to seats that hang down over the wraparound concourse below. This excellent design, combined with the festive neighborhood around the park and the local interest fans have in seeing the Houston Astros' top prospects, makes the Brick a popular destination during the summer months. The RedHawks draw more than 400,000 fans per season, which usually places them among the top twenty-five or so minor-league teams in the country.

The Brick hosts one or two of the three-game Bedlam Series played each May between the Oklahoma State Cowboys and the University of Oklahoma Sooners. And the Big 12 Conference Championship is also played at the Brick in May.

Whether you're passing through the Sooner State when a college or minor-league game is taking place, the Brick and festive neighborhood surrounding it combine to make for an enjoyable evening of baseball entertainment.

94. Bernie Brewer's Original Chalet

◇◇

Lakefront Brewery
1872 North Commercial Street
Milwaukee, Wisconsin 53212
(414) 372-8800
www.lakefrontbrewery.com

If this were a book dedicated not to the most interesting baseball landmarks in America but the best breweries, the old brick building on the banks of the Milwaukee River that houses Lakefront Brewery would deserve inclusion on the merits of its exceptional microbrews, which beer aficionados enjoy across the Midwest. But this is not a book for beer lovers; it is a book for baseball lovers, and Lakefront Brewery earns its place within these pages by housing Bernie Brewer's original chalet and slide from the 1970s. The brewery tour offers you the chance to see many other items of Brew City historic import as well.

Bernie Brewer, you may recall, has enjoyed several distinct incarnations as the Milwaukee Brewers' mascot. The original Bernie was a sixty-nine-year-old man named Milt Mason, who famously mounted the County Stadium scoreboard in June of 1970 and refused to descend until the locals started supporting the Brewers in greater numbers. The team had arrived via Seattle—where it had played just one season under the Pilots banner—just that spring, and with attendance flagging, speculation was that the Brewers' stay in Milwaukee might be short. Enter Mason, who helped galvanize an entire community of rooters with his stunt. He set his benchmark at a crowd of 40,000 and, true to his word, didn't come down until nearly a month and a half later, when on August 16, more than 44,000 fans turned out at County Stadium to watch the Brewers play the Indians. The Brewers went on to finish with a dismal 65-97 record, thirty-three games behind the first-place Minnesota Twins, but they placed a respectable seventh out of twelve American League clubs in home attendance, and found a mascot their fans loved.

Sadly, Mason died in June of 1973. But his memory lived on. To honor him, the Brewers built a chalet atop a three-story-high tower behind the center field fence at County Stadium and introduced a mascot that had been created in his likeness. Whenever a Milwaukee batter hit a home run, the handlebar-mustached Bernie, who wore German lederhosen, would hop onto a slide and plummet into a big stein of foaming beer. It was quite a sight to behold and one that local fans loved. In the mid-1980s, however, a renovation to County Stadium necessitated the removal of Bernie's chalet, slide, and tower, putting the mascot out of work for the better part of a decade.

Finally, in the early 1990s, Bernie returned with a new chalet and slide not far from their original location. It was at this time that Bernie became a more family-friendly and politically correct mascot. The sanitized Bernie wore a colorful costume rather than a greasy mustache and five o'clock shadow. And locals noted that the pleasant aroma of fermented hops no longer filled the ballpark concourses whenever Bernie strolled past.

Later still, when the Brewers moved to Miller Park, they created a new perch and bright yellow slide for Bernie in the outfield rafters, but rather than having Bernie slide into a mug of beer, they built him a dry landing pad. As for the old slide, Lakefront Brewery moved quickly to purchase it from the team when it became available and happily installed it along its extremely popular brewery tour. You will observe that many former members of the Brewers have autographed the apparatus, none more famous than the team's famous sausage racers. Their signatures, along with the others, appear beneath a Plexiglas cover.

The Lakefront tour is offered several times daily and costs $7.00. You may order tickets ahead of time or buy them at the brewery.

Through the years, Bernie has never been the most famous baseball mascot—that distinction has been passed back and forth between the likes of the San Diego Chicken, the Phillie Phanatic, and other Johnny-come-latelies. He hasn't been the hardest working either, or the most lovable, or kid-friendly. But he embodies the unique personality of his home city in a way that few mascots do. Milwaukee is the land of brats and beer, and its residents—Bernie included—know how to enjoy both of these delicacies and aren't ashamed to admit it. Bernie's slide—the one the rough-and-tumble Bernie of the 1970s and 1980s used to mount so nobly—is a fitting tribute to his legacy.

Located within historic Camden Station just outside Oriole Park at Camden Yards, the Sports Legends Museum is a treasure trove of Baltimore sports memorabilia. The museum exhibits cover all three incarnations of the Orioles, the two Negro Leagues teams that once played in Baltimore, the early life of Babe Ruth, and the remarkable career of "Iron Man" Cal Ripken Jr. Other sports are also treated in displays related to the NFL's Baltimore Colts and Ravens, the University of Maryland Terrapins, the Preakness Stakes, and duckpin bowling. The life of Johnny Unitas is also especially celebrated thanks to the former Colt's generous donations.

But the highlight—as you might expect at a museum located just outside Oriole Park—is the extensive collection of baseball artifacts. Many of the items within the 22,000-square-foot museum were originally displayed at the Babe Ruth Birthplace and Museum, 2 blocks away. Having outgrown that small facility, in 2005 the Ruth museum refocused on Ruth's life and times and sent the rest of its collection up the street.

95. The Sports Legends Museum at Camden Yards

301 West Camden Street
Baltimore, Maryland 21201
(410) 727-1539
http://baberuthmuseum.org/sports-legends-museum

Today, the same nonprofit group runs both facilities.

Camden Station is a curiosity in its own right; the historic train depot dates all the way back to 1855. The building was abandoned in the 1970s and by the 1980s had fallen into disrepair. But the construction of Oriole Park presented an opportunity to restore it—along with the adjacent B&O Warehouse. The $16 million renovation was funded by the state of Maryland, the city of Baltimore, and the Orioles. Now the sprawling

The Sports Legends Museum is located just a long fly ball from Oriole Park.

sports emporium occupies the first two stories of the station, while Geppi's Entertainment Museum occupies the third floor.

A visit to the Sports Legends Museum enables you to learn the colorful history of the original Baltimore Orioles, a National League team that departed the city in 1903 to become the New York Highlanders. The Highlanders later became the Yankees. You also find artifacts related to the minor-league Orioles, who played in the International League from 1903 until the St. Louis Browns moved to Baltimore in 1954. Ruth made his pro debut for these early Birds of Baltimore, back in 1914. The "Babe Ruth, American Icon" exhibit traces the great slugger's cultural impact on the United States and globally.

You learn about Ruth's depiction in theater and film, and about his sojourns to foreign lands. One of the museum's most interesting artifacts is a kimono Ruth wore during a barnstorming tour of Japan in 1934. And yes, it is bigger than the typical kimono!

"Nine Innings of Orioles Baseball" tells the story of the current Orioles franchise, beginning in 1954 and continuing to the present day. Artifacts related to the team's three world championships and to Ripken's amazing record of 2,632 consecutive games played take center stage.

The Black Sox and Elite Giants of the Negro Leagues are remembered, most notably by a replica of a bus modeled after the vehicles that

Negro Leagues teams of the 1940s used to travel from city to city. Another interesting exhibit is a faux hotel room designed to look like the one Jackie Robinson and his roommate, Sam Lacy, an African-American and Native American sports reporter, lived in during Robinson's rookie year in Brooklyn.

During the baseball season the Sports Legends Museum is open seven days a week from 10:00 a.m. until 5:00 p.m., except on game days, when it stays open until 7:00 p.m. to accommodate the pregame crowd. During the off-season, it is open Tuesday through Sunday from 10:00 a.m. to 5:00 p.m. Admission costs $8.00 for adults, $6.00 for senior citizens, and $4.00 for children ages three through twelve.

As for the **Geppi's Entertainment Museum** upstairs, the 16,000-square-foot pop culture repository traces the history of American entertainment from the 1700s to the present day, devoting exhibits to the best actors, cartoon characters, comic book heroes, and zombies of all time. From Popeye to James Bond to Jack Sparrow, all the icons get their due.

Afterward, a stroll along **Eutaw Street** takes you to stores and restaurants that happily embrace the neighborhood's baseball theme. While you walk, you can check out the baseball-shaped bronze markers on the ground and on the facade of the B&O Warehouse, commemorating the landing spots of some of the longest homers in Oriole Park history. There are more than eighty bronze balls, and each tells the story of a memorable "big fly."

At the corner of South Eutaw Street and West Camden Street, you find the *Babe's Dream* statue, which depicts a young Ruth posing with his glove in his hand as he leans casually on a bat. Curiously, the bronze depicts the Bambino holding a right-handed fielder's glove. The Babe was a lefty, of course.

On game days, this stretch of Eutaw Street is barricaded and incorporated into the ticketed ballpark footprint. This becomes a festive place to shag incoming batting practice homers, or to meet former Orioles star Boog Powell at his famous Eutaw Street barbecue pit.

· ·

Some baseball players use the money and goodwill they amass during their years in the game to open baseball-themed restaurants. Others build minor-league ballparks and get into the management side of the game. Still others go into broadcasting, or serve as talking heads on the pre- and postgame shows that can be found on various regional sports networks carrying big-league games on a nightly basis. Then there's Red Sox slugger Mike Greenwell, who four years before he finished his twelve-year playing career with the Red Sox had already begun laying the groundwork

for his second career. In February of 1992, the former North Fort Myers High School star

Mike Greenwell's amusement park is just a short ride from Fort Myers, where the Red Sox play their spring training games.

opened Mike Greenwell's Bat-a-Ball and Family Fun Park.

In the years since, the friendly amusement park has thrived, to the point where it is now one of Lee County's most popular outdoor entertainment destinations. In addition to welcoming people of all ages who visit to play, the park hosts an annual October walk through its haunted forest, a safe trick-or-treat party, an annual spring Easter Egg Hunt, and other civic events that bring families from the area together.

Not surprisingly, an outdoor batting cage is one of the 10-acre park's most popular attractions. Greenwell's also showcases some baseball

memorabilia—mostly autographed bats—in its main building. The more than fifty pieces of game-used lumber combine to represent a veritable 1990s All-Star roster. As Greenwell played his entire career with the Red Sox, the bats demonstrate an extreme American League bias. The game-used models include ones from Hall of Famers Wade Boggs, Cal Ripken Jr., and Carlton Fisk, as well as ones from Ellis Burks, Wally Joyner, Harold Baines, Sandy Alomar Jr., Tim Raines, and Juan Gonzalez. One bat is signed by every member of the 1991 Red Sox, and another is marked as the one Greenwell used when he hit for the cycle against the Orioles on September 14, 1988.

If you remember the colorful slugger from his playing days, you won't be surprised to learn that the park also reflects one of his other passions. No, there isn't an alligator-wrestling pit, but Greenwell's does have four different go-kart tracks. As Red Sox rooters will recall, midway through the 1991 season Red Sox general manager Lou Gorman scolded Greenwell—who'd been advised by the team earlier in his career to curtail his barehanded alligator hunting—after a picture of the left fielder sitting behind the wheel of a race car wound up splashed across the pages of the *Boston Herald*. Greenwell insisted that he had only participated in a promotional lap around the track before a race in Seekonk, Massachusetts, and said he drove *to* the track faster than he did *on* the track. Nonetheless, the Red Sox put the kibosh on any future racing for the slugger, adding a clause to his contract to prohibit it. After his retirement, Greenwell got a chance to do some real stock-car racing, participating in the Limited Late Model series at a speedway in Punta Gorda, Florida. Today, he can race all he wants at his own facility's Junior track, Slick track, Grand National track, or Figure-Eight track. And appropriately, the main sign to Greenwell's features a hanging red, white, and blue go-kart.

In addition to the racetracks and batting cages, Greenwell's also has a miniature-golf course, a video arcade, a paintball field, and a dock overlooking a murky pond from which you can feed bass, catfish, turtles, and whatever other creatures happen to surface once you start unloading the fistful of pellets you can buy for twenty-five cents. Greenwell's also serves food and drinks at its Dugout Sports Bar and Grill. This casual, covered-deck setting is a nice place to tip back a few frosty beverages and have a snack after you're done playing.

Greenwell batted .303 in his career and finished second to a juiced Jose Canseco in the 1988 American League Most Valuable Player vote. He visits his amusement park regularly to take batting practice in the fast-pitch cage, zip around the go-kart tracks, or make the rounds with his staff. The park is open daily from 10:00 a.m. to 10:00 p.m. It's a favorite destination of fans and families during spring training, when the Red Sox and Twins play their Grapefruit League games just a few miles up the road in Fort Myers.

Phoenix Municipal Stadium, or the "Muni" as locals call it, is well worth visiting on your epic baseball adventure for at least two reasons. First, because it provides you with a chance to explore one of the seminal fields from which the Cactus League arose. There is history here, and plenty of it at Phoenix Valley's oldest baseball stadium. Second, because the Muni provides a surreal backdrop for a game that showcases the beauty of the Southwest desert landscape. The red rock formations beyond the outfield fence are an aesthetic delight that add to your sense of ballpark bliss. You know how you just feel as though all is right with the world as you glance up between pitches at AT&T Park in San Francisco and see those sparkling blue waves in the distance? Well, the effect is similar when you look up from the game and see the stunning rocks beyond the field at this park in Phoenix.

The Muni was a hotbed of spring training activity from 1964 through 2014, but when the Oakland A's relocated to Mesa's Hohokam Stadium in 2015, the spring game finally bid adieu to the old ballpark. Fortunately, the Arizona

97. Phoenix Municipal Stadium

5999 East Van Buren Street
Phoenix, Arizona 85008
(602) 392-0074
www.thesundevils.com/SportSelect
.dbml?SPID=126725

State Sun Devils—who previously played at the Muni from 1964 to 1974—happily pounced at the opportunity to return, signing a twenty-five-year lease agreement with the city of Phoenix in 2013 that ensures the Muni will have a tenant for a good long time.

Although the physical face of the Muni is unremarkable, the experience inside is magical. After parking in the stadium lot, you cross a pedestrian bridge to reach the main entrance on the third base side. The stadium hardly rises above street level and its facade is little more

The red rock formations of Papago Park rise beyond the outfield fences at "Phoenix Muni."

than a series of canvas sunscreens separating the parking lot from the concourse that runs behind the seating bowl. Inside, the grandstand offers a wavy concrete roof that resembles the one at Dodger Stadium. The grandstand structure itself consists of large rocks pressed into concrete. The steel press box looks like a 1950s-style diner.

Behind the left field fence, paloverdes and other desert plants grow on a sandy embankment. Looming slightly farther away, the red rocks of Papago Park seem to glow in the sun. These iron-rich sedimentary formations date back six to fifteen million years. One is particularly distinctive because of a circular hole in its middle that has earned it the nickname "Hole in the Rock." The hole has eroded over the course of millennia but looks pretty much the same as it

did when the Hohokam Indians used the ray of sunlight that passes through it to mark the changing seasons.

As for the chances the park presents for you to bone up on your Cactus League history, the concourse's timeline serves as a walking history book. The entries are engraved in the concrete slabs on the walkway. They read:

• March 26, 1929: The first spring training game in Phoenix, Arizona, was hosted by the Detroit Tigers. Immediately after the Ty Cobb era, the Tigers looked for inspiration and change for rebuilding, so therefore chose Phoenix for a portion of their spring training schedule. The Tigers hosted the Pittsburgh Pirates on an ideal Arizona baseball afternoon.

- 1930s and World War II: During the 1930s, spring training was played in California and Florida. At the onset of World War II, Commissioner Kenesaw Mountain Landis, in cooperation with the Department of Defense, barred teams from traveling west of the Mississippi and south of the Potomac in order to save the railway lines for troops and supplies. These four years of cold springs created a desire to reestablish spring training in warmer climates.

- 1946: A league of two is formed when the Cleveland Indians persuaded the New York Giants to join them in Arizona for spring training. The Giants chose Phoenix to train for the spring while the Indians adopted Tucson.

- Spring of 1948: The relaxed sociopolitical climate of Arizona helped to further the integration of African Americans into the major leagues after Jackie Robinson broke the color barrier playing for the Brooklyn Dodgers. The Giants and Indians each acquired two African American players to their rosters.

- Spring 1951: New York Yankees co-owner and Phoenix resident/developer Del Webb trades spring training sites with the New York Giants in order to show off his talented team to Phoenix family and friends. This brought the Yankees to Phoenix for one year with a talented 19-year-old rookie named Mickey Mantle.

- Spring of 1952: New York Yankees owner and Phoenix resident/developer Del Webb convinced the Chicago Cubs to make the "Valley of the Sun" home for spring training. They ultimately settled in Mesa, Arizona.

- 1954: The "Cactus League" officially began, comprising four teams, after the arrival of the Baltimore Orioles and the Chicago Cubs to the state. Both teams joined the New York Giants in the Phoenix Valley, playing at Scottsdale and Mesa, while the Cleveland Indians remained in Tucson.

- 1964: Phoenix Municipal Stadium, often referred to as the "Muni," opened for its first spring training season as the home of the Giants who brought with them the lights from the Polo Grounds which illuminated the night skies of New York until September 18, 1963.

- March 8, 1964: Willie Mays hit the first home run at Phoenix Municipal Stadium, 420 feet to left-center field, in the stadium's inaugural game. The Giants defeated the Cleveland Indians 6–2 in front of an opening crowd of 8,502 people.

- Spring of 1972: The Oakland A's return to spring training as the defending World Series champions and the first Cactus League team to bring a World Series championship to the Valley.

- Spring of 1984: The Oakland A's make Phoenix Municipal Stadium their home.

- 1986: A study deemed Phoenix Muni as a viable temporary solution in attracting an MLB team to the Valley. The plans included expanding the stadium by more than four times its original size. This plan was not implemented, as instead Bank One Ballpark [later renamed Chase Field] was constructed prior to the Diamondbacks' first season in 1998.

The wavy roof above the grandstand bears a resemblance to the outfield roof at Dodger Stadium.

- Fall of 1989: As a result of the devastating earthquake in the San Francisco/Oakland Bay area during the World Series, the A's returned to Phoenix Municipal Stadium for practice. Before resuming the series, the A's played against their minor league players in an exhibition game at Phoenix Muni, with all proceeds going to the earthquake relief fund.

- 1994: The Oakland A's make Phoenix their home for all operations with renovations at Phoenix Municipal Stadium and construction of a training complex atop a former World War II German prisoner of war camp in Papago Park.

- Summer of 1996: The Arizona Diamondbacks called Phoenix Muni home with their first ever professional team which competed in the Arizona Rookie League. The Rookie League is a player development league, which plays in June through August of each year.

- 2004: The Cactus League celebrates its 50th year and new Phoenix Municipal Stadium renovations are completed.

Aside from having served as the spring home of the Giants and A's, the Muni also was home to the Dodgers during the latter half of the 2008 spring schedule. After departing their legendary Dodgertown camp in Vero Beach, Florida, midway through spring training, the Dodgers played five Cactus League games before continuing on to Los Angeles for the regular season. At the time, the A's were in Japan, playing two exhibition games and two regular season games against the Red Sox. With the A's away, the Dodgers moved into the Muni. The next spring, they completed their relocation from the Grapefruit League to the Cactus League, opening brand-new Camelback Ranch on the Phoenix/ Glendale line.

Although you can no longer watch the pros play at the Muni, you can watch ASU and its Pacific-12 Conference opponents from mid-February through May each year. The Sun Devils are perennially ranked among the Top-25 NCAA Division I baseball teams in the country and have sent plenty of players on to big-league stardom through the years, including Reggie Jackson, Barry Bonds, Dustin Pedroia, and Jason Kipnis.

• •

A s new stadium construction projects took place across America in the 1990s, gaining momentum with the swiftness and conviction of 40,000 fans rising from their seats to partake in a ballpark wave on a summer's day, many teams adorned their new yards with historic touches to allow fans to connect with the home team's history. From the South Side of Chicago, to Milwaukee, New York, and Kansas City, you'll find statues, World Series trophies, facsimiles of National Baseball Hall of Fame plaques, and other relics of proud years past. Many of the current parks also offer in-house museums where for no additional cost or a nominal charge you can learn more about the home team's history. Perhaps the most interesting of these is the Braves Museum—currently located at Turner Field, but slated to move to the new stadium the Braves will open in Cobb County, Georgia, in 2017. The museum pays homage to all three eras of Braves history: Boston (1871–1952), Milwaukee (1953–1965), and Atlanta (1966–present).

The Boston section is highlighted by a beautiful mural of the South End Grounds, which from 1871 through 1915 served as the home field

98. The Braves Museum

Turner Field
755 Hank Aaron Drive
Atlanta, Georgia 30312
(404) 614-2310
http://atlanta.braves.mlb.com/atl/
ballpark/information/index
.jsp?content=museum#educational

of the team that would eventually come to be known as the Braves. In those early days of National League hardball, the Boston club went by a variety of monikers, including the Beaneaters, Bees, Doves, Red Stockings, and Rustlers, as illustrated by the museum's "What's in a Name?" exhibit. This part of the museum also includes photographs and artifacts related to the Braves' involvement in the 1914 and 1948 World Series, which they won and lost, respectively. Another exhibit details Babe Ruth's final twenty-eight major-league games, which he spent with the

The Braves Museum and Hall of Fame honors all three incarnations of the Braves franchise.

Boston Braves in 1935. Although the Bambino batted just .181 with the Braves, he did manage to hit three home runs in a game against the Pirates at Forbes Field before retiring on June 1.

Another exhibit honors Braves players who served in the different branches of the US military, displaying, among other items, the Purple Heart earned by Warren Spahn after he suffered a foot injury in Germany during World War II.

As for the Milwaukee section, the highlight is a 26-foot-long car from an actual B&O railroad train, just like the ones the big leaguers used to ride from city to city. You can walk through the restored car to get a better sense of what a player's life was like before the advent of the luxury charter and stretch limo, while listening to audio of Hank Aaron discussing what it was like to ride baseball's rails at the

beginning of his career. (In case you're wondering, the game made the transition to air travel in the late 1950s and early 1960s.) The Milwaukee section also highlights the Braves' 1957 World Series win over the Yankees, providing photographs of key team members like Lew Burdette, Spahn, and Aaron.

The Atlanta section displays a dugout bench from Atlanta–Fulton County Stadium, aka "The Launching Pad," as well as the ball Hank Aaron lined over Dodgers left fielder Bill Buckner's head and into the Braves bullpen on the night of April 8, 1975, for homer No. 715, to become baseball's all-time home-run king. Other displays from this period include Dale Murphy's 1982 and 1983 National League MVP trophies, the Braves' 1995 World Series trophy, and a locker of mementos related to each of the seasons—between 1991 and 2005—during which the Braves won a record fourteen straight division titles.

The museum also houses a "Braves in Cooperstown" exhibit with photos of every National Baseball Hall of Fame inductee that suited up for the Braves in his career. As of 2015, this surprisingly expansive club included forty-six members. The "Braves Hall of Fame," meanwhile, honors many of the same players, coaches, and executives who have earned enshrinement at Cooperstown, but also the likes of Murphy, David Justice, and others who fell short of Cooperstown but still left a mark on the Braves. From Eddie Matthews to Phil Niekro, Spahn to Johnny Sain, Tom Glavine to Greg Maddux and John

Smoltz, all the big names are here, along with former team owner Ted Turner and popular television commentator Skip Caray.

If you're a stat geek, you'll enjoy the "Braves Leader Board," a giant scoreboard that tracks the team's all-time leaders in a variety of statistical categories. Even when games are in progress, the board is constantly updating.

Before and during games, the museum is open to ticket holders at a cost of $2.00. If you're visiting Atlanta on an off day during the season or before a night game, you can access the museum at a cost of $5.00. During the season and off-season the hours of operation vary, so consult the museum website for the latest information.

- -

Across the street from the new Minnesota Vikings' stadium, and just a few blocks from the Twins' beautiful Target Field, you will find an unobtrusive storefront that appears to be little more than one of the ubiquitous souvenir shops you can find outside practically any professional sports stadium. Upon stepping into Dome-Plus Souvenirs, however, you quickly realize you've stumbled upon something special. The Original Baseball Hall of Fame Museum of Minnesota is a free emporium that resides within a separate room in this 3,000-square-foot shop that has been catering to Twins and Vikings fans since back when both teams played at the Hubert H. Humphrey Metrodome. Although the dome was demolished in 2014, Dome-Plus and its quirky little museum are still going strong.

A man by the name of Ray Crump is responsible for creating this slightly off-the-wall assemblage of Twins gear and artifacts. Crump spent parts of four decades working for

99. The Original Baseball Hall of Fame Museum of Minnesota

Dome-Plus Souvenirs
901 South Third Street
Minneapolis, Minnesota 55415
(612) 375-9707
www.domeplus.com/Museum/
index.htm

the Washington Senators and then Minnesota Twins. He began working for the Senators in 1948 as an errand boy, and was eventually promoted to batboy. Before long, he progressed to the position of visiting clubhouse manager at Washington's Griffith Stadium. When the Senators moved to Minneapolis in 1961, Crump tagged along and became the first equipment

Ray Crump can be found at Dome-Plus daily.

manager at Metropolitan Stadium. Crump eventually retired from the game in 1984 and two years later opened Dome-Plus Souvenirs across the street from the Metrodome's Gate A. Immediately, he realized there were some items he just wasn't prepared to sell. And those items form the backbone of the museum that still exists today.

Over the years, Crump was in a unique position to collect extra pieces of baseball equipment, apparel, and player-worn and player-signed memorabilia. As uniforms were replaced with newer designs, he held onto an example or two from each era. As players upgraded to newer

model bats and cast their old ones aside, he scooped up the extras. And when he wanted a player to sign the odd piece of gear he acquired, they were happy to accommodate him. There's an old saying in big-league circles: You take care of the clubhouse guys because they're the guys who take care of you.

Crump's collection presents a unique window—or series of windows—into the evolution of baseball equipment and uniform design . . . with a Twins focus, of course. Remember those baby blue Twins uniforms of the 1980s? If not, pay the Original Baseball Hall of Fame Museum of Minnesota a visit, and the pajama-esque horror will come flooding back to you! A visit to the museum will also introduce you to such oddities as a commemorative 1965 World Series double-sided ashtray shaped like a cut-in-half baseball, and the world's largest bobblehead doll, a 7-footer adorned with the Twin Cities logo for Minneapolis and St. Paul. You'll also find a Kirby Puckett exhibit complete with Wheaties box covers, baseball cards, newspaper clippings, and bats; more than 200 photos of Crump posing with different players from around the American League; old team photos and yearbooks; autographed bats and baseball cards; and other trinkets, like a Minnesota Twins pocketknife from the 1970s and "Domer Hankies," which Crump invented for the 1987 World Series, only to see the *Minneapolis Star Tribune*'s own "Homer Hankies" get all of the press for some reason.

The self-guided museum tour offers chances for you to sit in a stadium seat from Metropolitan Stadium and to walk on a patch of the Metrodome's artificial turf. You also find a wall covered with baseballs autographed by not only players but pop culture icons; it's an eclectic collection that ranges from Harmon Killebrew to Elvis Presley, Casey Stengel to Frank Sinatra. The museum's most fascinating attraction, though, is its benefactor, Mr. Crump, who enjoys sharing his many colorful stories from his years interacting with players, team executives, umpires, sportswriters, and fans of baseball's glorified 1950s decade, rough-and-tumble 1960s, and groovy 1970s.

One story Crump will tell you involves a revolutionary batting helmet he invented for the Twins in 1962. After slugger Earl Battey was twice struck in the face by pitched balls, Crump attached a metal flap to the left side of his helmet to hang down over his cheek. Reassured by the added protection, Battey went on to hit a career-best twenty-six homers in 1963. And the helmet flap Crump created became standard baseball equipment throughout the game.

The store and its free museum are open Monday through Friday from 9:00 a.m. to 4:00 p.m., and Saturday from noon to 3:00 p.m. It is also open whenever the Twins or Vikings have a home game.

• •

In recent years several minor-league teams have incorporated a hall of fame into their ballpark designs so that game-day fans and, in some cases, even fans who arrive on off days, can pay tribute to the local legends that have graced their diamonds through the years. The Wilmington Blue Rocks of the Class-A Carolina League have taken the concept one step further, opening on their grounds a hall of fame that pays tribute to all of the great athletes who have excelled in a wide variety of sports in Delaware.

For baseball fans, the museum's exquisitely detailed "Hallway of the Decades" chronicles the rise and fall of the original Blue Rocks, who played in the Interstate League from 1940 to 1952. The team played at old Wilmington Park, first as a Philadelphia A's affiliate and then as a Philadelphia Phillies farm club, starring future big leaguers like Robin Roberts, Curt Simmons, and Elmer Valo. Later, you find the details of the new Blue Rocks' arrival as a Kansas City Royals affiliate in 1993, and of Frawley Stadium's construction. Frawley debuted that same year. Both the effort to revive the team after a thirty-five-year hiatus and to build the park were led by Matt Minker, a former baseball standout at the University of Delaware, who became part-owner of the team and built the park with his own construction company. Minker was also a proponent of adding the 5,000-square-foot Delaware Sports Museum and Hall of Fame into the first base side of the stadium. Previously, inductees to Delaware's hall had been honored with plaques hung at Wilmington's Grand Opera House, the Bank of Delaware, the Wilmington Senior Center, and in the lobby of a local law firm.

Thanks to the incorporation of the museum into the stadium, former big leaguers like Frank Coveleski, Dallas Green, Dwayne Henry, and Delino DeShields—all "First State" natives—today enjoy a permanent "home" in the Delaware Sports Museum and Hall of Fame's plaque gallery.

But the highlight of the museum is the exhibit dedicated to Negro Leagues star Judy Johnson. Delaware remembers its lone son to earn enshrinement in Cooperstown with a one-of-a-kind display. The Judy Johnson exhibit depicts a life-size Johnson mannequin sitting in a rocking chair and telling his story in his own words. The recording conveys Johnson's passion for the game and rich catalog of baseball

memories he carried with him throughout his life until he passed away in 1989. Also on display is the Hall of Fame plaque that Johnson received from the National Baseball Hall of Fame at the time of his induction in 1975.

Johnson, who is also honored with a statue outside the ballpark officially known as Judy Johnson Field at Daniel S. Frawley Stadium, played in the Negro Leagues from 1921 through 1938. A third baseman who consistently batted better than .300, he starred on the famed Philadelphia Hilldales teams of the 1920s, then later wore the uniforms of the Darby Daisies, the Homestead Grays, and the Pittsburgh Crawfords, playing alongside fellow future Hall of Famers Satchel Paige, Josh Gibson, and Cool Papa Bell. In retirement Johnson returned to Wilmington with his wife, Anita, and served as a baseball scout, first for the A's and then for the Phillies. He was so appreciative of being inducted into the National Baseball Hall of Fame that he broke down in tears during his acceptance speech on induction day. The next year he was voted into the Delaware Sports Hall of Fame.

Johnson is also one of the twelve individuals honored with a statue on the Field of Legends at the Negro Leagues Baseball Museum in Kansas City. And he is honored with a statue in PNC Park's Highmark Legacy Square Negro Leagues tribute in Pittsburgh. **The Wilmington Johnson statue** is unique because rather than depicting him swinging a bat, it portrays him crouched in a fielder's position with his glove and throwing hand resting on his knees.

To keep the memory of Johnson and the Negro Leagues alive, each year the Blue Rocks host an annual Judy Johnson Tribute Game. The event raises money and awareness for the Judy Johnson Memorial Foundation, which was founded by local baseball historian Joe Mitchell, a close friend of Johnson's in his later years. The popular evening begins with a pregame ceremony that recalls the accomplishments of Johnson and of one other Negro Leagues star per year. Then, when it is time for the game, the Blue Rocks and their opponents take the field in throwback uniforms that replicate the jerseys worn by famous Negro Leagues teams. Since they're a Kansas City Royals affiliate, the Blue Rocks wear Kansas City Monarchs uniforms.

The Delaware Sports Museum and Hall of Fame is open April through October, Tuesday through Friday, from noon to 5:00 p.m. Admission costs $4.00 for adults, $3.00 for adults fifty and older, and $2.00 for teens. Children twelve and younger are admitted free of charge.

• •

Shortly after the third incarnation of Busch Stadium opened in 2006, the Cardinals unveiled a plan to turn the abutting 10-acre plot—where Busch Memorial Stadium had stood from 1966 until its demolition in November of 2005—into an innovative entertainment zone that would provide Redbird fans with the ultimate game-day experience. The downturn in the economy slowed down those plans for a while, but finally in 2014 the Cardinals and their development partners opened the first phase of their Ballpark Village.

When it is complete the $650 million project will have turned the seven blocks across the street from Busch Stadium into a fan-paradise that integrates places to eat and drink with a rich array of memorabilia and historic exhibits, and unique ways to watch the games taking place a fly ball away. And you probably thought the proprietors of those rooftop bleachers in Wrigleyville had the market cornered on the just-outside-the-gates ballpark experience!

The first phase of the project features a four-level 34,000-square-foot building called Cardinal Nation, which rises beyond the outfield seats at Busch Stadium. The first two floors comprise a trendy restaurant and bar laden with Redbird memorabilia. Upstairs, in the foyer outside the new Cardinals Museum, a plaque gallery honors

101. St. Louis Ballpark Village

Broadway and Clark Street
St. Louis, Missouri 63102
www.stlballparkvillage.com

members of the **Cardinals Hall of Fame.** Even if you don't want to buy a ticket to the museum, you can still peruse the plaques, which were produced by the same company that makes the ones that hang at the National Baseball Hall of Fame in Cooperstown.

In early 2014, the Cardinals announced their Hall's inaugural class of twenty-two players, including Jim Bottomley, Ken Boyer, Lou Brock, Jack Buck, August A. "Gussie" Busch Jr., Dizzy Dean, Frank Frisch, Bob Gibson, Chick Hafey, Jesse Haines, Whitey Herzog, Rogers Hornsby, Tony La Russa, Joe Medwick, Johnny Mize, Stan Musial, Branch Rickey, Red Schoendienst, Enos Slaughter, Ozzie Smith, Billy Southworth, and Bruce Sutter. Conspicuously absent, of course, was Mark McGwire.

Inside, the 8,000-square-foot **Cardinals Museum** contains many but not all of the items

Cardinals Nation, the first phase of St. Louis Ballpark Village, opened in 2014.

it spent several years displaying a rotating crop of exhibits at Busch Stadium. Now that it has a permanent home, the museum displays models of Sportsman's Park and of the original Busch Stadium, as well as stadium chairs and lockers from the old yards; the Cardinals' world championship trophies from 1967, 1982, and 2006; and many photos and artifacts related to the Cardinals, St. Louis Browns, and Negro Leagues St. Louis Stars.

Upstairs, on the **Cardinal Nation rooftop,** you find 300 ticketed seats overlooking Busch Stadium's left field lawn. This is the Cardinals' answer to those rooftop seats on the North Side of Chicago. The sightlines are clear and management even pipes in audio from the stadium. This is a great place to eat a few brats or some frozen custard while enjoying a bird's-eye view of the game.

Down at ground level, meanwhile, the slightly raised **infield from Busch Stadium** has been transformed into a plaza that hosts concerts and other festivities. A massive LED screen shows batting practice as it takes place inside the park. Once the game begins—whether the Cardinals are home or on the road—the screen shows the game broadcast.

once held at the museum's previous locations. As you may recall, for a time the Cardinals Museum shared a building with the International Bowling Hall of Fame. After the Bowling Museum moved to Texas in November of 2008, the Cardinals Museum closed though, and, while waiting for its new home to open in Ballpark Village,

Once completed, Ballpark Village will contain many more restaurants and retail shops, as well as commercial and even residential spaces. For a diehard Cardinals fan, living at Ballpark Village would be a lot like living at the ballpark, which sounds pretty incredible.

Acknowledgments

As always, the completion of my latest book is an appropriate time to extend my love and thanks to all of my friends and family members who support my writing, especially my wife, Heather, and children, Spencer and Lauren. I thank too my parents and in-laws, who help Heather and me cover the bases around the house when I'm working, and spread the word about my books: my thanks to Richard and Cathy Pahigian, Judy and Ed Gurrie, Butch Razoyk and Lynn Pastor, and to my brother, Jamie. I also wish to acknowledge my highly talented and dedicated literary agent at the Doe Coover Agency, Colleen Mohyde.

For believing in the first edition of this book, I thank Rob Kirkpatrick, who helped turn my idea into a reality. I also sincerely appreciate the contributions of my current editor at Lyons, Keith Wallman, and I'm not just saying that because he's a Red Sox fan!

I would not have been able to complete this new edition of *101 Baseball Places to See Before You Strike Out* without the contributions of the following people who patiently fielded my questions about their baseball places, provided me with reams of information often on short notice, and generously took the time to lead me through their sites. I also couldn't have produced the book without the contributions of my friends across the country who tagged along so I wouldn't have to be a lone wanderer, snapped photos at my side or in my absence, and passed along their local knowledge of various sites so I could incorporate them into the book. These contributors include Lisa Alpert, Lisa Anderson, Vince Baldemor, Danny Barnts, Joe Bird, Jim Bottorff, David Brewer, Terry Cannon, Bill Chapman, Jim Chappell, Maureen Chappell, Tom Cioch, Nate Cloutier, Scott Crawford, Ray Crump, Brent Curry, Ray Doswell, Joe Doud, Joe Edwards, Jimmy Emerson, Patrick Feller, Laura Fontanills, Heather Freitag, Adam Gehrke, Michael Gibbons, George Gratto Jr., Mike Gustafson, Joe Harrington, Kelly Harrington, Rick Heath, Bruce Hellerstein, Sharri Hobbs, Annie Huidekoper, Joanne Hulbert, Janna Jahn, Anne Jewel, Lisa Johnson, Kevin Jenks, David Kaplan, Crissy Terawaki Kawamoto, Rachel Kuiken, Will Liu, Michael Locke, Meryl Loop, Marion Mann, Arlene Marcley, Mike McElwaine, B. J. McFadden, Jim McGonigle, Joe McKiernan, John Melangio, J. P. Meyers, Joe Mitchell, John Newkirk, Kevin O'Connell, Erik Ofgang, Jennifer Pendergraft, Tarra Petras, Evan Petty, Mike Rengel, Julie Ridgway, Bill Rieter, Michael Rusignuolo, Erik Ruiz, Brandon Sawalich, Matthew Schmitz, John Shannahan, Tom Siedler, John Traub, Ken Silliman, Steve Silverman, Chris Siriano, Carol Jean Smetana, Chris Stagno, Mark Susina, Paul Taylor, Laura Verillo, Michael Wade, Hank Waddles, Jason Webber, Tom Whaley, and Brooke Zumas.

Photo Credits

1. pp. 1 and 2 courtesy of the National Baseball Hall of Fame Library, Cooperstown, NY.
2. p. 5 courtesy of the Negro Leagues Baseball Museum, Inc.
3. p. 7 courtesy Brooke Zumas, ZumPhotography.com.
4. pp. 9, 10, and 11 courtesy of Bill Chapman.
5. pp. v (left) and 13 Wikimedia Commons photo by Ruhrfisch.
6. pp. 15 and 16 courtesy of Richard Heath. All rights reserved.
7. pp. v (right) and 19 by Josh Pahigian.
8. pp. vi (right) and 21 courtesy of College World Series of Omaha, Inc; p. 22 Wikimedia Commons photo by Skinzfan23.
9. p. 24 courtesy of Friends of Bohemian National Cemetery of Chicago.
10. pp. 26 and 27 courtesy of the City of Cleveland.
11. p. 29 courtesy of the Durham Convention & Visitors Bureau.
12. pp. 31 and 32 courtesy of Meryl Loop, Wichita Wingnuts.
13. pp. vi (top left) and 34 courtesy of Michael Locke, photographer.
14. p. 36 Wikimedia Commons photo by Anthony22.
15. p. 39 Wikimedia Commons, public domain.
16. p. 41 Wikimedia Commons, public domain.
17. pp. vii (top left), 43, and 44 courtesy of the GUP Collection.
18. pp. 46 and 47 courtesy of the National Ballpark Museum.
19. p. 48 courtesy of Matthew Schmitz.
20. p. 51 Wikimedia Commons, public domain.
21. pp. vi (bottom left), 53, and 54 courtesy of City Kayak.
22. pp. vii (bottom left) and 55 courtesy of the Babe Ruth Museum.
23. p. 58 courtesy of the Saint Paul Saints.
24. pp. 60 and 61 courtesy of the Canadian Baseball Hall of Fame and Museum, St. Marys, Ontario.
25. p. 63 courtesy of Jorge de la Torre.
26. pp. vii (right) 64 courtesy of the Louisville Slugger Museum and Factory.
27. pp. 66, 67, and 68 courtesy of the World Wiffle Ball Championship and the Skokie Park District.
28. p. 70 by Josh Pahigian.
29. p. 72 Wikimedia Commons photo by Delaywaves.
30. p. 74 courtesy of the Tampa Bay Rays/Skip Milos.
31. pp. 75 and 76 courtesy of Chris Stagno.
32. p. 78 courtesy of Heather Freitag.
33. p. 79 courtesy of Jamie Pahigian; p. 80 by Josh Pahigian.
34. pp. viii (left) and 82 Wikimedia Commons, public domain.
35. p. 85 by Josh Pahigian.
36. p. 87 Wikimedia Commons photo by Ian Munroe.
37. p. 89 courtesy of Jim Chappell.
38. pp. 91 and 92 courtesy of Evan Petty.
39. p. 94 by Josh Pahigian.
40. p. 96 courtesy of Baseball Oogie/ Baseballoogie.blogspot.com.
41. p. 99 courtesy of J. P. Myers.
42. p. 101 Wikimedia Commons photo by Jtesla16.
43. p. 103 courtesy of the National Baseball Hall of Fame Library, Cooperstown, NY.
44. p. 105 Wikimedia Commons photo by Peter Bond.
45. p. 107 courtesy of the Ty Cobb Museum.

46. p. 109 (top) courtesy of Maureen Chappell, Archdiocese of Detroit Cemeteries; p. 109 (bottom) courtesy of Tommy Sea.
47. p. 111 by Josh Pahigian.
48. p. 113 courtesy of Crissy Terawaki Kawamoto.
49. p. 116 by Josh Pahigian.
50. pp. 117 and 118 by Josh Pahigian.
51. p. 120 courtesy of the Yogi Berra Museum.
52. pp. 122 and 123 courtesy of Albuquerque Isotopes.
53. p. 124 courtesy of the Shoeless Joe Jackson Museum; p. 125 courtesy of the Greenville, SC, Chamber of Commerce.
54. p. 128 by Josh Pahigian.
55. p. 130 courtesy of Jimmy S. Emerson, DVM.
56. p. 131 courtesy of Will Liu.
57. p. 134 courtesy of Hank Waddles.
58. p. 136 photos courtesy of the Engel Foundation.
59. pp. 138 and 139 by Josh Pahigian.
60. p. 141 by Aaron Morales, courtesy of the Stockton Ports.
61. pp. 142 and 143 courtesy of Christopher Siriano.
62. p. 146 courtesy of the Library of Congress.
63. p. 148 Wikimedia Commons photo by The Silent Wind of Doom; p. 149 by Josh Pahigian.
64. p. 151 courtesy of the Mesa Historical Museum.
65. pp. viii (right) and 153 courtesy of Patrick Feller.
66. p. 155 courtesy of Joe McKiernan.
67. p. 157 courtesy of Adam Gehrke.
68. p. 159 courtesy of the Library of Congress.
69. p. 161 by Josh Pahigian.
70. p. 163 by Hope Edwards, courtesy of the St. Louis Walk of Fame.
71. p. 165 Wikimedia Commons photo by wyliepoon.
72. pp. 167 and 168 courtesy of the Vermont Lake Monsters.

73. p. 170 courtesy of the Bob Feller Museum.
74. p. 172 courtesy of the City of Blue Ash, Ohio.
75. p. 174 courtesy of Suzanne H. Shannahan; p. 175 courtesy of Mudville Baseball Club.
76. p. 177 photos courtesy of the Baseball Reliquary.
77. pp. 179 and 180 by John Mark Newkirk.
78. pp. 181 and 182 by Josh Pahigian.
80. p. 186 Wikimedia Commons, public domain.
81. p. 188 Flickr Creative Commons photo by Bryce Edwards.
82. pp. 189 and 190 courtesy of the College Baseball Foundation.
83. p. 192 courtesy of Erik Ofgang.
84. p. 194 Flickr Creative Commons photo by Ola Christian Gundelsby.
85. pp. 197 and 198 courtesy of the Tampa Baseball Museum at the Al Lopez House.
86. p. 199 by Mike McElwaine, Major League Photos, LLC.
87. p. 201 by Josh Pahigian.
88. p. 203 Wikimedia Commons.
89. p. 205 by Josh Pahigian.
90. pp. 207 and 208 courtesy of Ken Weisenberger, www.strike3photos.com.
91. p. 210 courtesy of the Mississippi Sports Hall of Fame and Museum.
93. pp. 214 and 215 courtesy of the Oklahoma City RedHawks.
95. p. 218 courtesy of the Babe Ruth Museum.
96. p. 220 courtesy of Mike Greenwell.
97. p. 222 and 224 by Josh Pahigian.
98. p. 226 courtesy of the GUP Collection.
99. p. 228 courtesy of Ray Crump Jr.
101. p. 232 courtesy of Michael Rengel, www .flickr.com/photos/echoman.
Author photo on p. 238 courtesy of Josh Pahigian.

Index

About the Author

Josh Pahigian grew up in Central Massachusetts, where he spent his childhood dreaming of one day playing third base for the Boston Red Sox. He fell considerably short of that dream, but has made the game he loves a part of his professional life through his writing. Josh holds a BA in English from the College of the Holy Cross and an MFA in Creative Writing from Emerson College.

Josh's other Lyons titles include *The Ultimate Baseball Road Trip* and *Why I Hate the Yankees*, which he cowrote with his friend Kevin O'Connell, *The Ultimate Minor League Baseball Road Trip*, and *The Seventh Inning Stretch*. He is also the author of a spring training travel guide entitled *Spring Training Handbook*, a Red Sox history book entitled *The Red Sox in the Playoffs*, and a mystery novel entitled *Strangers on the Beach*. In addition to writing books, Josh has written for ESPN.com, *Men's Health*, *Writer's Digest*, *Family Fun Magazine*, the *Portland Press Herald*, the *Worcester Telegram & Gazette*, and other print and web-based periodicals.

In addition to writing, Josh serves as an adjunct faculty member at the University of New England, and as a writing mentor in the Western Connecticut State University low-residency MFA program in Creative and Professional Writing. When he's not teaching, writing, or sitting at a ballpark, Josh enjoys spending time outdoors with his wife, Heather, and children, Spencer and Lauren. Josh has two "home" parks these days, both a half hour's drive from his house in Maine: Hadlock Field, home of the Eastern League's Portland Sea Dogs; and The Ball Park, home of the Futures Collegiate Baseball League's Old Orchard Beach Raging Tide.

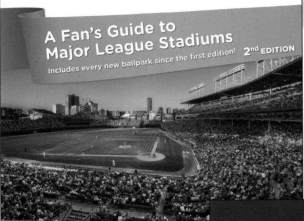

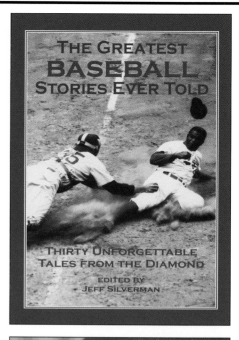

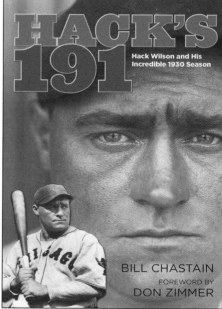

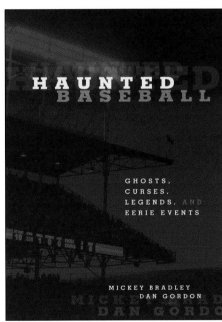
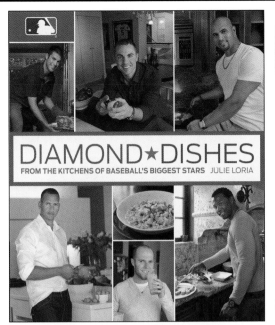
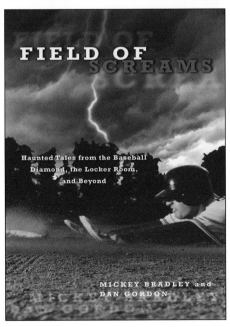

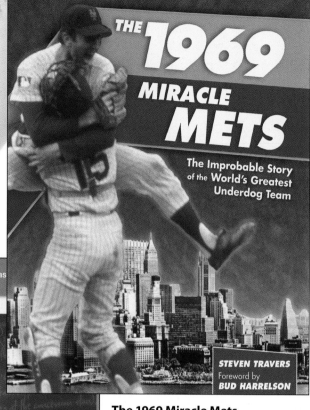

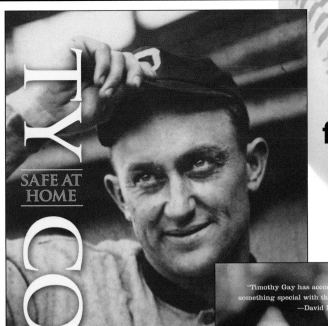
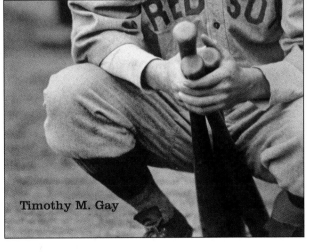

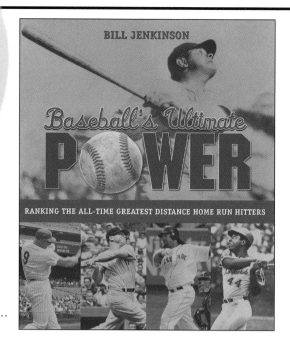
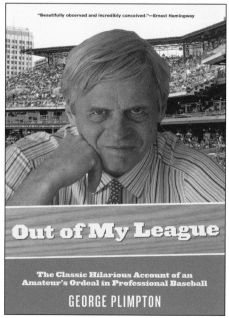
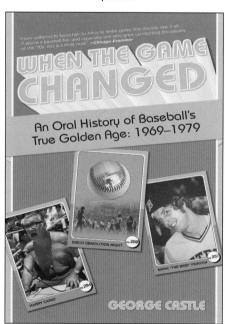